# Life Writing After Empire

A watershed moment of the twentieth century, the end of empire saw upheavals to global power structures and national identities. However, decolonisation profoundly affected individual subjectivities too. *Life Writing After Empire* examines how people around the globe have made sense of the post-imperial condition through the practice of life writing in its multifarious expressions, from auto/biography through travel writing to oral history and photography. Through interdisciplinary approaches that draw on literature and history alike, the contributors explore how we might approach these genres differently in order to understand how individual life writing reflects broader societal changes. From far-flung corners of the former British Empire, people have turned to life writing to manage painful or nostalgic memories, as well as to think about the past and future of the nation anew through the personal experience. In a range of innovative and insightful contributions, some of the foremost scholars of the field challenge the way we think about narrative, memory, and identity after empire. This book was originally published as a special issue of *Life Writing*.

**Astrid Rasch** teaches imperial history and postcolonial literature in the English Department at the University of Copenhagen, Denmark. She recently submitted her PhD thesis, 'Autobiography After Empire: Individual and Collective Memory in Dialogue', which examines the relationship between individual and collective memory after decolonisation in autobiographies from the Caribbean, Australia, and Zimbabwe.

# Life Writing After Empire

*Edited by*
Astrid Rasch

LONDON AND NEW YORK

First published 2017
by Routledge
2 Park Square, Milton Park, Abingdon, Oxon, OX14 4RN, UK

and by Routledge
711 Third Avenue, New York, NY 10017, USA

*Routledge is an imprint of the Taylor & Francis Group, an informa business*

© 2017 Taylor & Francis

All rights reserved. No part of this book may be reprinted or reproduced or utilised in any form or by any electronic, mechanical, or other means, now known or hereafter invented, including photocopying and recording, or in any information storage or retrieval system, without permission in writing from the publishers.

*Trademark notice*: Product or corporate names may be trademarks or registered trademarks, and are used only for identification and explanation without intent to infringe.

*British Library Cataloguing in Publication Data*
A catalogue record for this book is available from the British Library

ISBN 13: 978-1-138-22321-9

Typeset in MinionPro
by diacriTech, Chennai.

**Publisher's Note**
The publisher accepts responsibility for any inconsistencies that may have arisen during the conversion of this book from journal articles to book chapters, namely the possible inclusion of journal terminology.

**Disclaimer**
Every effort has been made to contact copyright holders for their permission to reprint material in this book. The publishers would be grateful to hear from any copyright holder who is not here acknowledged and will undertake to rectify any errors or omissions in future editions of this book.

# Contents

*Citation Information*   vii
*Notes on Contributors*   ix
*Dedication*   xi

Introduction: Life Writing After Empire   1
*Astrid Rasch*

1. Collusions and Imbrications: Life Writing and Colonial Spaces   7
   *Charles Lock*

2. Tears and Garlands: Lim Chin Siong, Coldstore, and the End(s) of Narrative   27
   *Philip Holden*

3. 'National Awakening', Autobiography, and the Invention of Manning Clark   43
   *Mark McKenna*

4. The Relational Imaginary of M. G. Vassanji's *A Place Within*   57
   *Vera Alexander*

5. 'A Nation on the Move': The Indian Constitution, Life Writing and Cosmopolitanism   73
   *Javed Majeed*

6. 'This Union-Jacked Time': Memories of Education as Post-Imperial Positioning   91
   *Astrid Rasch*

**Reflection**

7. Gibraltarian Oral Histories: Walking the Line Between Critical Distance and Subjectivity   109
   *Jennifer Ballantine Perera and Andrew Canessa*

## CONTENTS

**Review**

8. *How Empire Shaped Us*, edited by Antoinette Burton and
   Dane Kennedy　　　　　　　　　　　　　　　　　　　　　　　123
   *Stephen Howe*

   Afterword: The Ends of Empire: *In memory of Bart Moore-Gilbert,
   1952–2015*　　　　　　　　　　　　　　　　　　　　　　　　131
   *Gillian Whitlock*

   *Index*　　　　　　　　　　　　　　　　　　　　　　　　　　141

# Citation Information

The chapters in this book were originally published in *Life Writing*, volume 13, issue 2 (June 2016). When citing this material, please use the original page numbering for each article, as follows:

**Introduction**
*Life Writing After Empire*
Astrid Rasch
*Life Writing*, volume 13, issue 2 (June 2016) pp. 163–170

**Chapter 1**
*Collusions and Imbrications: Life Writing and Colonial Spaces*
Charles Lock
*Life Writing*, volume 13, issue 2 (June 2016) pp. 171–190

**Chapter 2**
*Tears and Garlands: Lim Chin Siong, Coldstore, and the End(s) of Narrative*
Philip Holden
*Life Writing*, volume 13, issue 2 (June 2016) pp. 191–205

**Chapter 3**
*'National Awakening', Autobiography, and the Invention of Manning Clark*
Mark McKenna
*Life Writing*, volume 13, issue 2 (June 2016) pp. 207–220

**Chapter 4**
*The Relational Imaginary of M. G. Vassanji's* A Place Within
Vera Alexander
*Life Writing*, volume 13, issue 2 (June 2016) pp. 221–236

**Chapter 5**
*'A Nation on the Move': The Indian Constitution, Life Writing and Cosmopolitanism*
Javed Majeed
*Life Writing*, volume 13, issue 2 (June 2016) pp. 237–253

# CITATION INFORMATION

**Chapter 6**
'This Union-Jacked Time': Memories of Education as Post-Imperial Positioning
Astrid Rasch
*Life Writing*, volume 13, issue 2 (June 2016) pp. 255–270

**Chapter 7**
Gibraltarian Oral Histories: Walking the Line Between Critical Distance and Subjectivity
Jennifer Ballantine Perera and Andrew Canessa
*Life Writing*, volume 13, issue 2 (June 2016) pp. 273–283

**Chapter 8**
*Review:* How Empire Shaped Us
Stephen Howe
*Life Writing*, volume 13, issue 2 (June 2016) pp. 287–293

**Afterword**
*Afterword: The Ends of Empire:* In memory of Bart Moore-Gilbert, 1952–2015
Gillian Whitlock
*Life Writing*, volume 13, issue 2 (June 2016) pp. 295–303

For any permission-related enquiries please visit:
http://www.tandfonline.com/page/help/permissions

# Notes on Contributors

**Vera Alexander** is a Lecturer in English in the Department of European Languages and Cultures at the University of Groningen, The Netherlands. Her research interests comprise English and Anglophone literatures and cultures, ecocriticism, travel and mobility, life writing, the bildungsroman, children's writing, heterotopia, diaspora, and transculturality.

**Jennifer Ballantine Perera** is the Director of the Gibraltar Garrison Library and is affiliated to the University of Gibraltar as the Director of the Institute for Gibraltar and Mediterranean Studies. Her main area of research is Gibraltar, with focus on social and colonial history, constitutional change, and expressions of self-determination. She is the founder director of Calpe Press, a publishing house dedicated to promoting Gibraltar writings, and is the current editor of the *Gibraltar Heritage Journal*.

**Andrew Canessa** is an anthropologist at the University of Essex, UK. Much of his career has been spent studying indigenous people in Latin America, particularly Aymara people of highland Bolivia. His most recent publications include *Intimate Indigeneities: Exploring Race, Sex and History in the Small Spaces of Andean Life* (2012) and *Género, Complementariedades y Exclusiones en Mesoamerica y los Andes* (with Aida Hernandez, 2012). He is currently working on an oral history project on Gibraltarian identity funded by the UK Economic and Social Research Council.

**Philip Holden** is a Professor of English at the National University of Singapore, where he researches life writing and Southeast Asian writing in English, often with a focus on issues relating to gender and multiculturalism. He is the author of *Autobiography and Decolonization: Modernity, Masculinity, and the Nation-State* (2008) and coauthor of *The Routledge Concise History of Southeast Asian Writing in English* (2009). His present research examines life writing as a social practice.

**Stephen Howe** is a Senior Research Fellow in History at the University of Bristol, UK; coeditor of the *Journal of Imperial and Commonwealth History*; and a Fellow of the Royal Historical Society. His most recent books include *Ireland and Empire: Colonial Legacies in Irish History and Culture* (2000); *Empire: A Very Short Introduction* (2002); and, as editor, *The New Imperial Histories Reader* (2009). He is also the author of the forthcoming *Intellectual Consequences of Decolonisation*.

**Charles Lock** is a Professor of English Literature at the University of Copenhagen, Denmark. He has taught at the University of Karlstad, Sweden, and the University of Toronto, Canada. Among his publications are essays on Patrick White, Derek Walcott, Les Murray, Amos Tutuola, and Ken Saro-Wiwa.

# NOTES ON CONTRIBUTORS

**Javed Majeed** is currently a Professor of English and Comparative Literature at King's College London, UK. His interdisciplinary research combines literary studies with the intellectual and cultural history of colonialism and postcolonialism in the Indian subcontinent. His most recent publications include *Autobiography, Travel and Postnational Identity: Gandhi, Nehru and Iqbal* (2007) and *Muhammad Iqbal: Islam, Aesthetics and Postcolonialism* (2009).

**Mark McKenna** is a Professor of History at Sydney University, Australia, and is one of Australia's leading historians. He has published widely on Aboriginal history, the history and politics of Australian republicanism, and biography. His 2011 biography of an Australian historian, *An Eye for Eternity: The Life of Manning Clark*, won five national awards, including the 2012 Prime Minister's Prize for Non-Fiction.

**Astrid Rasch** teaches imperial history and postcolonial literature in the English Department at the University of Copenhagen, Denmark. She recently submitted her PhD thesis, 'Autobiography After Empire: Individual and Collective Memory in Dialogue', which examines the relationship between individual and collective memory after decolonisation in autobiographies from the Caribbean, Australia, and Zimbabwe.

**Gillian Whitlock** is a Professor in the School of Communication and Arts at the University of Queensland, Australia, and a Fellow of the Academy of the Humanities. Her most recent book is *Postcolonial Life Narrative: Testimonial Transactions* (2015), and she is currently working on asylum seeker artefacts in the archives for a book, *The Testimony of Things*.

# Dedication

As this special issue on 'Life Writing After Empire' was in production, we learned of the untimely death of one of the scholars, authors, and teachers who has helped define this field: Professor Bart Moore-Gilbert. He was, necessarily, included in this project until his illness intervened. Bart's book, *Postcolonial Life-Writing: Culture, Politics and Self-Representation* (2009), and numerous articles that extended this project are a key reference point for our work. More recently, his memoir *The Setting Sun* (2014) introduces his own autobiography into our thinking on empire and aftermath.

Both this book, and the special issue on which it is based, are dedicated to Bart, and mark his enduring influence on postcolonial life narrative.

INTRODUCTION

# Life Writing After Empire

For centuries, the imperial expansion of Europe affected not only global power structures, but also individual subject positions of colonisers and colonised alike. With the changed world order of decolonisation came significant shifts in cultural assumptions and individual identities. Just as many new nations embarked upon rewriting their collective national histories, so too did individuals. The upheavals of decolonisation challenged people to make sense of their past from the perspective of the present, sometimes struggling to impose coherence upon disparate experiences and identities. While the end of empire has often been studied at the level of politics, economics and cultural movements, we have perhaps neglected to consider how individuals have responded to and navigated within a changing world order. Life writing provides us with a lens through which to consider the end of empire anew and in the process learn more about what life writing is and does in a post-imperial world.

This special issue is the result of a workshop in May 2015 at the University of Copenhagen. The ambition of the workshop was to bring together people from both history and literary studies to discuss our common interest in the manifold expressions of life writing after empire. While postcolonial studies has developed a critical apparatus for the engagement with literature from the imperial and post-imperial era, the field has occasionally been accused of being too detached from the actual historical context which has produced the texts (Ashcroft, Griffiths and Tiffin 2; Boehmer *Colonial* 6–7; Gikandi 182–3; Moore-Gilbert, Stanton and Maley 58–9). Historians working on the end of the British Empire have, for their part, traditionally drawn on public records and the archives of politicians, leaving literature to the literary critics. But in recent years, historians and literary scholars working on the end of empire have increasingly recognised the usefulness of their respective fields. As this special issue sets out to demonstrate, life writing may be a productive venue for the meeting of historical and literary approaches to the end of empire. The fact that life writing is at once aesthetic and referential makes it an interesting entry point for examinations of the cultural effects and articulations of historical change.

Breaking down the title into its constituent parts will show some of the themes and approaches that reappear in the essays. To begin with the genre 'life writing', the workshop aimed to include a diversity of text types as well as different disciplines and methodological approaches. Life writing comprises many sources for understanding the relationship between individuals and collectives at the end of empire. Thus, the essays draw on biography and autobiography, travel writing and memoir, letter, blog, diary and oral history as well as texts that challenge the limits of genre like the autobiographical novel, poetry and photography. Several of the contributors demonstrate the synergies that arise when reading different kinds of life writing by the same author together or when similar texts from different contexts are compared. This multitude of sources adds to our understanding of how the end of empire has been interpreted and articulated by individuals.

# LIFE WRITING AFTER EMPIRE

To examine 'life writing' is also to consider how these different texts might be approached. The study of life writing has often been carried out in the separate spheres of literature and history. The aim of this workshop was to bring people from both disciplines with a special interest in empire and its legacies into the same room for a conversation about our approaches to life writing and to encourage cross-fertilisation of the fields. The result is truly interdisciplinary: Javed Majeed reads a text normally studied by historians and political scientists, the Indian Constitution, alongside anti-colonial life-writing to see what new insights we might gain from reconsidering the Constitution in a different textual landscape. By reading the Constitution as an aesthetic work, Majeed is able to draw out its peculiar tone and texture and show its dialogue with other texts and how it, like anti-colonial life writing, dramatizes self-rule. Mark McKenna draws on his experience as the biographer of Australian historian Manning Clark to trace the autobiographical vein that runs throughout Clark's works, irrespective of whether they were labelled 'history' or 'autobiography'. Clark saw himself as the great chronicler of Australia's past at the moment when the country was casting about for a new identity, and McKenna shows how he tended to conflate his own life with that of the nation. The mix of disciplines within and across the essays makes this volume of interest to scholars of life writing and postcolonial literature as well as (post-)imperial history.

Just as feminist scholars have revolutionised the field of life writing studies, so too, in recent years, have postcolonial critics expanded and challenged the way we think about life writing. Alongside the important works of scholars like Elleke Boehmer, Bart Moore-Gilbert and David Huddart, several of the writers from this volume have contributed to that movement, notably Philip Holden, Javed Majeed and Gillian Whitlock (Boehmer *Stories*; Holden; Huddart; Majeed; Moore-Gilbert; Whitlock *Intimate*; Whitlock *Postcolonial*). Like the interventions from feminism and other fields like disability studies, postcolonial critics have not only broadened the field of relevant texts but have also asked us to take a step back and consider the assumptions we bring to the texts and the tools we use to understand them. This special issue seeks to add to that development, and several of the contributors suggest new methods that challenge our conventional way of reading life narrative. Thus, Philip Holden argues that the prominence of biographies in the narration of Singapore's decolonisation history has meant a binary understanding of the past and proposes instead that we study poetry and images as a way to overcome the constrictions of narrative. Vera Alexander suggests that the concept of relationality, which has become so central in life writing studies, ought perhaps to be applied to non-human relations too, like places and books. In this expansion of the relational, she demonstrates how the diasporic subject of M. G. Vassanji's travel self-narrative is constituted through an emotional and imaginary attachment to India and how he manages that attachment through recourse to his literary forebears.

To turn to the 'after empire' part of the title, this invokes questions of when and where. The 'after' may signal both the time the texts were written and our postcolonial reading perspective. It can be a chronological marker or signal interest in the decolonising moment, but it can also describe our own position and how the questions we ask of texts are formed by postcolonial concerns or it can describe the perspective of the writers we study. The 'after empire' can signify the moment in which the object of study was produced or the moment in which we take up the study; it may refer to the empirical material or to the methodology. We may consider the very consequences of this 'afterness', how the end of empire affects or is portrayed in life writing. The postcolonial innovations referred to above reflect such a recalibration of approaches to texts, whether they are written before or after formal decolonisation. But the historical study of decolonisation has also undergone substantial changes, with the old settler colonies now also studied under that rubric, and with a greater attention to cultural production and the relationship between political change and popular attitudes (Hopkins; Howe; Ward).

When trying to fix the date of the end of the British Empire, we enter inherently nebulous terrain. Some point to India's independence in 1947 as the turning point, while others trace the dissolution of the Empire back in time, seeing the Second World War as an emblem of decolonisation or invoking the Treaty of Versailles and the so-called 'Wilsonian moment' as seminal (Boyce; Darwin; Manela). Most historians, however, have reached a consensus that the process we now refer to as 'decolonisation' concerns a 'twenty year crisis' following 1945, at the end of which the global map had been fundamentally reshaped (Shipway). In addition to this difficulty of periodisation, a common objection is that the effects of colonialism continue to manifest themselves to such an extent that we cannot yet speak of decolonisation in the past tense. In spite of these challenges, this volume maintains that 'life writing after empire' can fruitfully function as a rubric of study, to demonstrate both the diversity of that field and the commonalities that occur across the board. Thus, the exact date of the end of empire is less important than the sense that there is an 'after empire' in which one has to navigate, an afterness which affects texts and scholars alike.

While Holden, McKenna and Majeed focus on the time immediately after the break with Britain, other authors demonstrate that decolonisation was not a one-off process of the second half of the twentieth century. Using life writing in a broad sense as an entry point, Charles Lock reminds us of those places and moments which tend to escape analysis as postcolonial. He traces life writing after empire all the way back to the American Revolution to include Benjamin Franklin's *Autobiography*. This early instance of decolonisation is, like the later case of Ireland, not often considered within the purview of the end of empire, but examining them may draw out interesting parallels to later iterations of postcolonial life writing.

Jennifer Ballantine Perera takes us up to the present day to alert us to a context which is not necessarily to be thought of as 'after empire', even in 2016. She discusses the ambiguous position of Gibraltar as a colony in a decolonised world and considers how individual life stories negotiate within a field of hegemonic narratives about the relationship to Britain and Spain. This relates to a concern of other essays, namely how the colonial past is told in a postcolonial present. My own contribution considers how individuals position themselves in a postcolonial age and how the changes to dominant narratives brought about by decolonisation affect the way they narrate their personal past. And Stephen Howe shows how the practice of imperial history seems to lend itself to autobiographical reflection, in ways that mirror and underscore the myriad ideological legacies of the imperial past.

The British Empire, famously colouring a quarter of the world red, can hardly be contained within a single volume. However, the contributions here do take us to most corners of the globe: to India, Ireland, Kenya, Singapore, the Caribbean, Australia, Nigeria, Gibraltar, Britain, South Africa and the US. Many of the essays reflect the necessity of a transnational lens if we are to make sense of the border-crossing trajectories of individual lives, imperial influences and post-imperial narratives. Some study people whose lives were transnational: M. G. Vassanji of Alexander's essay is a Kenyan of Indian background now settled in Canada and writes a travel memoir of his journey to an India he has never seen before, describing the mixed experience of familiarity and strangeness of that encounter. And Gillian Whitlock follows Bart Moore-Gilbert's memories of his African childhood as well as his journey from Britain to India to learn more about his father. Others, like Lock and myself, compare texts from dispersed contexts to study interesting commonalities as well as important differences. And some concentrate on one national context but show how that must be read in relation to the world around it, like Ballantine Perera's reflections on Gibraltar's complex relationships to both Britain and to Spain, or Majeed's interpretation of India's Constitution as a text engaged in a cosmopolitan dialogue with other constitutions around the world. Furthermore, Lock and Alexander both demonstrate the importance of places and spaces as more than a mere background for the text. Instead they argue for the constitutive role of place in the formation of individual subjectivity as well as in the production and reception of a piece of life writing. While the essays in this volume all discuss areas of the former British Empire, we hope that students of other post-imperial contexts will find the approaches and insights useful.

Reading these contributions together, we learn about the entanglement of the collective and the individual in life writing after empire: we see people who cast themselves as embodying the nation (McKenna), people whose personal reflections about the new nation feed into that country's founding text (Majeed) and people whose lives are used to tell the national story in terms of friends and foes (Holden). There are people for whom a return to an ancestral country is a personal journey of inward discovery (Alexander) and people whose life narratives negotiate places of writing and places of reception (Lock). There are those for whom the personal memories of empire are disturbing as well as nostalgic (Whitlock) and those whose memories jar with prevailing narratives and who doubt the value of their own experience (Ballantine Perera). And we have people who use their memories to position themselves in a postcolonial society (Rasch) or to take stock of the development of the academic field of imperial history (Howe). All of these essays demonstrate the interaction between societal changes and individual experience and expression. This indicates that studying life writing after empire can give scholars of life narratives a better grasp of the formative context of writing and give students of the end of empire access to a more intimate level of analysis of historical phenomena.

One cannot examine life writing after empire without considering the tremendous contribution to that field by Bart Moore-Gilbert. He was scheduled to participate in the workshop that resulted in this special issue, where he would present on the experience of being at once a critic of postcolonial life writing and a writer of an end of empire memoir. Tragically, Moore-Gilbert was forced to cancel his participation by the cancer that would end his life too early in December 2015. In her afterword to this special issue, Gillian Whitlock pays tribute to Bart Moore-Gilbert and his work by considering precisely his memoir and his critical engagement with life writing after empire. Reading his memoir alongside his *Postcolonial Life-Writing* and his blog 'oftherightkidney', she studies *The Setting Sun* in the tradition of the patriography and considers how that genre negotiates painful memories at the end of empire.

I would like to thank the funding agencies that made this workshop and the subsequent publication possible, the Velux Foundation and the Centre for European Studies at the University of Copenhagen. Also, a word of gratitude to Stuart Ward for his invaluable help in organising the workshop as well as his generous advice on all stages of the process and to Maureen Perkins for her continued assistance and patience and her enthusiasm about the issue. Finally, of course, my heartfelt thanks to all the contributors to this special issue who have taken seriously the challenge of thinking about life writing after empire and provided their individual and original takes on the theme.

## *References*

Ashcroft, Bill, Gareth Griffiths, and Helen Tiffin. "General Introduction." *Post-Colonial Studies Reader*. Ed. Bill Ashcroft, Gareth Griffiths, and Helen Tiffin. 2nd ed. Oxford: Routledge, 2006. 1–4. Print.
Boehmer, Elleke. *Colonial and Postcolonial Literature: Migrant Metaphors*. 2nd ed. Oxford: Oxford UP, 2005. Print.
Boehmer, Elleke. *Stories of Women : Gender and Narrative in the Postcolonial Nation*. Manchester: Manchester UP, 2005. Print.
Boyce, D. George. *Decolonisation and the British Empire, 1775–1997*. London: Palgrave, 1999. Print.
Darwin, John. *The Empire Project, the Rise and Fall of the British World-System, 1830–1970*. New York: Cambridge UP, 2009. Print.

Gikandi, Simon. "Back to the Future: Lamming and Decolonization." *The Locations of George Lamming*. Ed. Bill Schwarz. Oxford: Macmillan Caribbean, 2007. Print.

Holden, Philip. *Autobiography and Decolonization, Modernity, Masculinity, and the Nation-State*. Madison: U of Wisconsin P, 2008. Print.

Hopkins, A. G. 'Rethinking Decolonization.' *Past & Present* 200.1 (2008): 211–247.

Howe, Stephen. 'Crosswinds and Countercurrents: Macmillan's Africa in the "Long View" of Decolonization.' *The Wind of Change: Harold Macmillan and British Decolonization*. Ed. by Larry Butler and Sarah Stockwell. Houndmills: Palgrave Macmillan, 2013. 116–139.

Huddart, David. *Postcolonial Theory and Autobiography*. London: Routledge, 2008.

Majeed, Javed. *Autobiography, Travel and Postnational Identity: Gandhi, Nehru and Iqbal*. Basingstoke and New York: Palgrave Macmillan, 2007.

Manela, Erez. *The Wilsonian Moment: Self-Determination and the International Origins of Anticolonial Nationalism*. New York: Oxford University Press, 2007.

Moore-Gilbert, Bart. *Postcolonial Life-Writing: Culture, Politics and Self-Representation*. London: Routledge, 2009.

Moore-Gilbert, Bart, Gareth Stanton, and Willy Maley, eds. *Postcolonial Criticism*. London; New York: Longman, 1997.

Shipway, Martin. *Decolonization and Its Impact: A Comparative Approach to the End of the Colonial Empires*. Malden, MA: Blackwell Pub., 2008.

Ward, Stuart, ed. *British Culture and the End of Empire*. Manchester, UK: Manchester University Press, 2001.

Whitlock, Gillian. *Postcolonial Life Narrative: Testimonial Transactions*. Oxford: Oxford University Press, 2015.

Whitlock, Gillian. *The Intimate Empire, Reading Women's Autobiography*. London and New York: Cassell, 2000.

Astrid Rasch
*University of Copenhagen*

# Collusions and Imbrications: Life Writing and Colonial Spaces

Charles Lock

Department of English, Germanic and Romance Studies, University of Copenhagen, Copenhagen, Denmark

**ABSTRACT**
This essay offers an investigation into the characteristics or distinctive features of life writing in colonial and postcolonial spaces. Among the examples of life writing here considered are George Lamming's *In The Castle of My Skin* and C. L. R. James's *Beyond a Boundary*, and, less often treated in this context, works by Benjamin Franklin and James Joyce; stress is placed on the importance of American literature for early articulations of the problems and dilemmas of postcolonial life writing. Further emphasis is laid on place, and on the need for bibliographical research into the place of publication of works written in or concerned with colonial spaces.

## Vita, biography, life writing

The term 'life writing' usefully elides the sharp distinction made by and constitutive of the more familiar terms 'biography' and 'autobiography'. A distinction often too sharp, for one who writes a biography has invested much of her or his own life in the writing: Boswell's *Life of Johnson* is also Boswell's life, as it would occupy years thereof, and not only in the writing but in the sharing and keeping of the Doctor's company.[1] And Samuel Johnson's *Lives of the Poets* are also Johnsonian lives, reflections on what a poet's life might be, and should be. Every autobiography obviously tells of more lives than the writer's alone; no less plainly, unlike a biography, it cannot aim to tell the whole life. Biography is often conditioned, not only for legal reasons, by the deed of closure represented in 'last words'.

'Life' may be either the object or the subject of 'writing'. The term 'life writing' delicately plays with life, as the object written or as the subject writing: the life as a text written by its author, or the life lived by the one who writes. Most valuably, whether taken in the gerundial or in the participial form, the term draws our attention to the activity, the process, the ways and means of transmuting life into written, printed and published words.

'Life writing' can be traced in English to Francis Atterbury in 1687, just a few years after the first recorded use of 'biography' as an English word, by Dryden in 1683, with reference to Plutarch's *Lives*; this term is drawn from the French *biographie* attested in 1583. The classical and medieval worlds knew only *vitae*, the text thus indistinguishable from what it represents, in an ambivalence that will be preserved and echoed in Johnson's title, *The Lives of the Poets*.[2] Through the middle ages the lives of saints are *vitae*, without modification to indicate holiness; 'hagiography', as we shall see, emerges much later, among Protestants who conspicuously spurn the genre.

A further emancipatory effect of the term 'life writing'—as it has developed and distinguished itself from the *vita*—is that it dispenses with any notion of completeness or totality, with the idea that a life is bounded; just as, according to Solon, one should call no man happy until he is dead, so no life should be judged until it is over, and even then posterity reserves the right to overturn the verdict. The writer of an autobiography will have made her case, but there can be many a slip between publication and the grave. By contrast, life writing need not be beholden to teleology: episode, anecdote, adventure, affair, voyage, exploit, a post or a posting, each of these can be comprehended within the genre, and each of these alone might suffice to make and shape a work.

## Colonial spaces

Life writing in the colonies raises questions of particular interest. These may be arranged under three headings, of the space and place of writing, the place of publication, and the readership addressed. Each presents a complication not normally to be found in the circumstances of life writing outside of colonial spaces. Rhetoric and thematics are not enough to encompass such a difference, for colonial and postcolonial life writing is deeply inflected by the material circumstances and locations of its composition and publication, and indeed by the places and conditions in which it is read, reviewed and circulated.

Numerous texts might come to mind as instances of life writing in or about colonial spaces, or emerging from them. Some are loosely framed as novels—here 'life writing' risks becoming too capacious a term—of which a celebrated instance, from the position of the colonial administration, is George Orwell's *Burmese Days* (1935). George Lamming's novel of growing up in Barbados, *In the Castle of My Skin* (1953) endures as a classic of childhood and the sensitivity and awareness particular to the colonial condition. In this it is indebted to James Joyce's *Portrait of the Artist as a Young Man* (1916), a work of such stature that its colonial spaces are not always given their due.

*Beyond a Boundary* is now a classic, though it remains hard to classify; C. L. R. James was an intellectual whose historical and political writings exercised an incalculable influence on independence movements, even beyond the boundaries of the British Empire. Yet his most enduring work is the writing of a life in which cricket is as central as the title would indicate, though the boundary is of course the periphery of the pitch; there is much poetry and wit in his deployment of cricketing terms. Published in 1963, the book has seldom been out of print. *Beyond a Boundary* was recently reissued on its fiftieth anniversary by Duke University Press, with a reverence—even a scholarly apparatus—similar to what is due to a canonical work of literature: the introduction is by a sports journalist, the foreword by a specialist in Caribbean studies. Of course, when such a book is issued in the United States there must be some explanation, for few readers there can be expected to know the rules and idioms of cricket. *Beyond a Boundary* exemplifies, even in its title, the problems of space and location; its theme indicates something of the complicity between radicals and the Establishment, between the periphery and the metropolis.

C. L. R. James (1901–1989) was a Trotskyite who as early as the 1930s was advocating independence for the West Indies, preferably as a single federated state of all the islands that had been British possessions. After independence this vision was lost, though James did salvage a cricket team representing the West Indies; the other institution to survive is the University of the West Indies. James remains honoured and celebrated by audiences and readers quite extreme in their diversity: revolutionaries (including in the 1960s leading figures in the Black Power movement), historians of empire and resistance—notably for the pioneering and now classic work, *The Black Jacobins: Toussaint L'Ouverture and the San Domingo Revolution* (1938)—and lovers of cricket. He had no trouble publishing his historical works and political analyses, nor in placing reports of cricket matches in British newspapers. But when he tried to publish his work of life writing, with cricket at its core, he encountered many difficulties. James turned for help to his friend George Lamming who recommended it to Hutchinson's, in London, along the way providing the title, 'Beyond the Boundary'; 'the' was changed to 'a' at the publisher's insistence, for no obvious reason. (S. James)

When a 'non-colonial' engages in life writing there need be no particular tension between living and writing, nor between writing and publishing.[3] When a colonial does so there is almost always a dependence, in and as the very condition of the possibility of publication, on those from whom the writer is seeking independence. In the making of the books of colonial life writing we usually find some complicity of the centre with the periphery. There is no boundary to colonial spaces, nowhere within which they can be contained, for they are always imbricated, overladen with the space of the elsewhere to which they continue to owe their constitutional identity, even after independence. In this respect, the 'postcolonial' is more than usually hard to distinguish from the 'colonial'. C. L. R. James shows no inhibitions in confessing the two spaces that he occupied, as a most precocious child in Trinidad: 'A British intellectual long before I was ten, already an alien in my own environment among my own people, even my own family' (C. James 18); 'Intellectually I lived abroad, chiefly in England' (C. James 65).

Colonial spaces have material consequences for literature, and especially for life writing. While in postcolonial studies many narratives of growing up are valued as witnesses to colonialism and its aftermath, this does not exhaust their interest. There are particular pressures in colonial circumstance that give new shape and significance to the genre, not just in thematic or rhetorical terms but in the very act of writing, and of reading (Moore-Gilbert). There, writing (beyond the clerical) is an activity seldom without political implication, each text its own sign and flag of independence. Many instances of such life writing describe a childhood and an education—the learning to read and write—that are synchronised with the colony's reaching for independence. There is thus a strong likeness to the *Bildungsroman*, which specifies, for the German case (most genres are 'loan-genres' from Aristotle's Greek; this one is conspicuously German), a particularly abbreviated form of life writing, one that closes with the reaching of maturity. Yet while a *Bildungsroman* tends to trace the growth of the protagonist out of the community and away from the family, especially in the subgenre of the *Künstlerroman*, there is a recursion in the telling of the young colonial life, whereby the emancipated individual becomes a representative of the postcolonial nation. This may be 'biographical fact' as much as literary device: such are the pressures of historical and social circumstance on the developments and diversifications of genres. The narrative of emancipation and escape turns on itself so that the protagonist becomes the hero not only of his own tale but also a participant in the colony's destined emergence into nationhood (Holden; Boehmer).

## Colonial authors, London publishers, British readers

In colonial life writing a great deal depends on the selecting of a readership, and therefore on the place of publication. Is the story being told—insofar as a work of literature might have an overt political purpose—by way of admonition to the colonial power, or by way of encouragement to fellow colonial subjects? An exemplary case of the first is *Burmese Days*, a colonial officer's report, in the guise of fiction, on what he has witnessed. Orwell's presentation of British colonial rule was a shocking exposure, certain to be met with hostility among the governing class. For this reason, the book was first published in New York, in 1934, and only a year later in London. The intent was to test a less sensitive readership, far away, so as to dilute the force of controversy in the British Establishment. Fear of libel might well have been the chief motive for Orwell choosing to shape his experiences in the guise of fiction.

At this very time, in the mid-1930s, four Indian writers—considered now the founders of Indian writing in English—each had his first novel published, in every case in London: R. K. Narayan's *Swami and Friends*, Mulk Raj Anand's *Untouchable* (both 1935), Raja Rao's *Kanthapura* (1938), and Ahmed Ali's *Twilight in Delhi* (1940) (Khozan and Lock). Each of these novels was, by virtue of the place of publication, aimed at readers in Britain who took an interest in India, some of whom might have had influence over imperial policy and colonial affairs. The readership of those novels in India itself is hard to determine. It was certainly an achievement for these writers to find publishers in London, but one wonders what publisher in India might have been interested. What sort of readership might have been addressed in India, and would these novels not have been rather different had the novelists aimed to please an Indian publisher and Indian readers?

The potential readership is widely dispersed though not in any respect provincial. One wonders how easy it was then to obtain in India a book written by an Indian and published in London. The writer's dilemma is not only a matter of trying to address two very divergent readerships. The place of publication will determine how the book is reviewed and how its reception will be shaped. It will also determine how easily readers around the 'Anglophone periphery' might obtain such books.[4]

The peripheral should not be confused with the provincial. In England a work of life writing might be deemed of insufficient interest for a London publisher, though of considerable interest to readers who can be reached by a publisher in one of the (English) provinces. But there is nothing provincial about those readers in Lagos—or Accra, or Nairobi, or Trinidad—who would want to read Achebe *and* Naipaul *and* Lamming: how would a reader in Kenya get hold of a book published in Lagos, or in Barbados? The problem is still with us. Such a 'peripheral' readership may circumvent the publishing centre but it need leave no boundary uncovered. By contrast, the provincial is singular, and is unconcerned with any province other than its own. Here the examples of C. L. R. James and George Lamming are important, and representative: the former was involved in Ghana's struggle for independence, while Lamming's first book became part of the Black Power movement. The question is whether their books could travel as freely as the authors, not just as 'titles', finding publishers on one continent and then another, but as single copies, reaching a readership other than the usual purchasers and borrowers of books issued by large publishers in London and New York.

Lamming's *In the Castle of my Skin* was published in London in 1953.[5] It appeared in New York in 1954, carrying a foreword by Richard Wright whose *Native Son* had been published in 1940; 1954 was the year in which Wright coined, or made famous, the phrase *Black Power* as the title of his report on the struggle for independence in the Gold Coast, soon to be known as Ghana (Wright's friend C. L. R. James was also active there). In his foreword Wright performs the work of introduction, explanation and advocacy that had been undertaken for the novels of those London-published Indian writers by such figures as E. M. Forster, Graham Greene and George Orwell. Yet where these were of the Establishment, albeit of progressive views, Wright, the first Afro-American novelist to reach a wide audience, was a controversial figure in American life; it was as such that he was chosen to introduce the work of another person of African descent whom it would be erroneous to describe as Afro-American, and whose conflicts and disaffections were quite different. This is a typical instance of a divided readership: for British readers *In the Castle of My Skin* was a colonial text, a fictionalised account of growing up in Barbados, within a context already supplied by writers from India, including George Orwell and, of course, Rudyard Kipling. In the United States there was no such recent tradition of colonial writing, whether by those governing or by those subjected; the position of the oppressed was taken by the Afro-American and thus George Lamming was conscripted within a political movement in which his book could hardly be expected to resonate.[6]

## Contextual deficits

Language and literacy are questions that pose challenges to both the centre and the boundary. English is the language of writing in the former British colonies of the Caribbean as of sub-Saharan Africa. It is only one of a number of written languages in India. And who, anywhere, can read this language? The educated middle classes in India and throughout the colonies, and anyone in the English-speaking world: that is the obvious answer. But who would be interested in this sort of writing? By no means all of those who can read English, for 'native' as one might be as a speaker, most readers tend to be locally indued to their own element and habitation. English literature is predominantly set—thematically, circumstantially—in England, and the training of readers in English is a training not only in literary genres but also in the themes and locations and social circumstances of the canonical texts. Readers in the colonies like to speak of a 'deficit', on the reader's account, of cathedrals, pubs and village greens, and of everything else that makes up English life, not as it is lived but as it has been characterised and typified in English literature.

This phenomenon in the history of literature first emerged in the United States. The 'colonial deficit'—the disjunction between language (English) and context (not English)—was most forcefully expressed by Henry James in his book on Nathaniel Hawthorne of 1879:

> The negative side of the spectacle on which Hawthorne looked out, in his contemplative saunterings and reveries, might, indeed, with a little ingenuity, be made almost ludicrous;

one might enumerate the items of high civilization, as it exists in other countries, which are absent from the texture of American life, until it should becomea wonder to know what was left. No State, in the European sense of the word, and indeed barely a specific national name. No sovereign, no court, no personal loyalty, no aristocracy, no church, no clergy, no army, no diplomatic service, no country gentlemen, no palaces, no castles, nor manors, norold country houses, nor parsonages, nor thatched cottages nor ivied ruins; no cathedrals, nor abbeys, nor little Norman churches; no great Universities nor public schools—no Oxford, nor Eton, nor Harrow; no literature, no novels, no museums, no pictures, no political society, no sporting class—no Epsom nor Ascot! Some such list as that might be drawn up of the absent things in American life—especially in the American life of forty years ago, the effect of which, upon an English or a French imagination, would probably as a general thing be appalling. (H. James 34–35)

Henry James had been commissioned by Macmillan in London to write the volume on Hawthorne for the series 'English Men of Letters'. Celebrated as one great writer's tribute to another, James's *Hawthorne* ought also to be given consideration for the colonial spaces that it invokes. Nobody before Henry James had felt the need to apologise in either direction; that is, for English books being 'too English' in theme or context for readers outside of England, or for books from elsewhere being too alien for readers in England. What Henry James articulates is a rate of exchange of writing worlds, and of worlds written, a reaching for balance between two distinct communities of writers and readers who have one language between them. The United States was the first 'postcolonial' nation whose readership was of sufficient size and importance to register the *thematic* obstacles to the reading of literature, even in one's own language when there were no philological difficulties. We note that James allows that what is lacking in England has its counterparts in France, whose lack would be no less strongly felt in America; but at this date only the English language had a significant readership outside its 'motherland'.[7]

Indeed, this may be an unprecedented event in the entire history of literature, one that could emerge only under two conditions: when the mode of literature is 'realism', and when the language is spoken beyond the boundaries of the reality represented. The term 'American literature' is recorded in the 1780s; it was in 1837 that Emerson's lecture 'The American Scholar' advocated a distinct cultural entity, to be realised when the first course entitled 'American Literature' was taught, at the University of Michigan, in 1875 (Giles 255; Graff 211; Lock 'Words'). For all the interest in the United States in tracing the origin of the term, it seems to have escaped notice that this was the first time, ever, that any body of literature had been modified not by its language but by its nation.

The postcolonial condition, of which the United States is the founding instance in modernity, thus makes an accommodation between its inheritance and its disinheritance: 'One language, two literatures'. Reciprocally, the rest of English literature came to be known in the US (and then elsewhere) as 'British Literature' in a colonial riposte of such boldness as to deprive the English of their own tongue.

Readers in Britain had enjoyed the novels of Fenimore Cooper, for there was no deficit in the Leatherstocking Tales that could not be made good by recourse to Scott's Waverley Novels. Hawthorne's tales are very different, and *The Scarlet Letter* (1848) was manifestly unlike any book in English literature even though it was written in English. What followed —to name only *Moby-Dick* and *Leaves of Grass*—created a literature that would challenge readers as never before: native (English) readers, alien themes. In 1879 Henry James could acknowledge the deficit that any American felt in reading an English novel, and he cited that deficit to plead the oddity of Hawthorne's imagination as it might appear to English readers.

The distinctiveness of American literature has provided the first and most instructively enduring model of a postcolonial literature; it is regrettable that the thirteen colonies and their successor states should have been so seldom considered in the light of postcolonial studies. In the colonial aspiration for independence there are, as we have mentioned, two quite distinct sorts of readership: people whose circumstances resemble those of the writer, living in a colonial space, who might draw inspiration from what is written and be encouraged towards independence; and those in Britain, who would learn about the ways of colonial life, and might have some influence on imperial policy. Initially the works of 'colonials' were published in London and New York, as we have seen in the case of Indian and Caribbean writers.

Printing presses in the colonies were mostly controlled by the governing class, and had far more important uses than the printing of literature: there was hardly a shortage of government business, information and instruction to be circulated. The first book printed in the American colonies was the 'Bay Psalm Book', in 1640, and there would have to be many presses and much cheap paper before the printing of literature could be tolerated on practical grounds, to say nothing of the sorts of ideological objections to fiction and fancy—the reading of which is a particularly diabolical form of idleness—vividly presented by Hawthorne in 'The Custom-House', through which one must pass to reach the 'romance' of *The Scarlet Letter*.

Life writing in the colonies and in post-colonial states is bound up with education, literacy, the deed of writing, as both condition and theme; more than that, it involves the very making of books, their printing and marketing. In the United States, from the mid-nineteenth century, literature was to be marketed not only in terms of class and education; there was a topographical division between 'American literature' and the English or British kind, setting boundaries for the reader in what we might call 'thematic competence'. At some point in the decolonising process an aspiring author in India or Nigeria or the West Indies, or Australia or Canada, must have looked first to a local printer and publisher, not out of a lack of ambition but rather in defiance. The publishers in late colonial conditions would be keen to solicit works from writers already successful in London, as well as from those as yet unpublished. At what point did writers who were engaged by a local publisher abandon any accommodation to the needs and expectations of readers in Britain? These things are hard to gauge, apart from explicit declarations of independence; in *Decolonising the Mind* (1986) Ngũgĩ wa Thiong'o expresses his sense of relief at the new freedom to address his own people without consideration for the expectations and conventions of readers elsewhere.

Readers of the colonial writer's own kind and 'habitus' may share all sorts of references and idioms that would baffle readers in England, but there might not be a sufficient number of such readers with a literary competence (distinct from the thematic) to constitute (commercially) a readership. The first published novel in English by a West African was Amos Tutuola's *The Palm-Wine Drinkard*, so irregular in its phrasings as to put off most readers except for those in London who in 1952 arranged for its publication, notably T. S. Eliot; its enthusiastic reviewers included Dylan Thomas. Here was written English to be admired by those who had read *Ulysses* and *Finnegans Wake*, though Tutuola had no notion of them, nor of the literary modernism into which he had been conscripted. In 1953

*The Palm-Wine Drinkard* was published in New York by the Grove Press, who would the following year publish the first edition (in English) of Samuel Beckett's *Waiting for Godot*. There can hardly be a more stark disjunction between 'thematic competence' and literary sophistication. Indeed, its first edition, issued by Faber, includes a facsimile of one page of the manuscript of *The Palm-Wine Drinkard* as submitted, presumably as a voucher for the absence of editorial interference (Lock, 'Amos').

## Life writing and place writing

Life writing in colonial spaces has a complex relationship to place, as exemplified by the title *Beyond a Boundary*. Life writing includes many instances of place writing, especially through an episode of a sojourn or retreat, such as Thoreau's *Walden* (1854). The 'deficit' of English attributes in colonial spaces has had a dislocating effect. 'Walden' is a fictional name, and the pond itself is natural in an oddly universal way, such at least as to present no problems for those unfamiliar with the New England landscape, of which the most unfamiliar aspect, to readers in Britain, might well be the place-names. *Walden* marks a reduction in local specificity, almost an 'achieved deficit'; this is very different from the topographical and toponymical precision of much place writing in England of which an early and typical instance is Wordsworth's *Guide to the Lakes* of 1810. There is for Wordsworth, as for Richard Jefferies, W. H. Hudson and all those in the tradition of English 'life and place writing', a confidence in the reader's understanding; and there is little thought of accommodating such texts, by comparison and analogy, to the understanding of those who know little of the particularities of English topography.

By contrast, colonial life writing of place has depended on another readership than that which is in possession of local knowledge. The description of exotic spaces when aimed at readers in England relies on analogy and on the making of comparisons between the exotic and the familiar. Yet because England is familiar in outline through the canon of English literature, the colonial life writer has some precise analogies available, where the writer who knows only England would reach for stereotypes by way of comparison. In the colonial text, the sense of imbrication in colonial space—layered by both history and analogy—can unfold itself into a narrative trajectory, from here to there, from periphery to centre.

Colonial life writing leads us on many journeys, figured often as escape, flight, emancipation; it is seldom characterised by the pleasures of staying put or the adequacy of here, such as we find voiced by Wordsworth or Hardy. Romanticism insists on the value of place, and on the privilege of the place of birth, even (or especially) if one is native to a heath or some form of rustic retreat. Colonial writing in general is not at ease with this aspect of Romanticism, presumably because its spaces are not regarded as sites of origin nor of value sufficient in themselves, as places in England can often appear in English life writing in the nineteenth century and beyond.[8]

This conflict between colonial spaces and Romanticism's valuation of places in England is the subject of *The Enigma of Arrival* (1979), V. S. Naipaul's novel or memoir. Its four hundred pages include the 'life' of his deceased brother Shiva. Biography as an 'embedded genre', the completed life framed by the frustrations and unfulfilments of the biographer's own, makes for a most intricately layered instance of postcolonial life writing. The defiantly metropolitan author commemorates his younger brother who unlike him had not spurned Trinidad and the world shared in childhood. Elsewhere in the *Enigma* we are in deepest Wiltshire, meditating on the English landscape and all but explicitly negotiating and playing with degrees and disjunctions of 'thematic competence': on Salisbury Plain a Trinidadian writer of Indian descent finds no 'Cathedral deficit'.

Thematic incompetence can be a most enticing challenge, especially when the literary genres are being shaped anew, shaped, that is, by the pressure of postcolonial spaces. There is no disjunction but rather a conjunction of thematic incompetence—received as a challenge—with a high degree of literary sophistication. The tension endures in postcolonial studies between sympathy for the peripheral and the oppressed and an acknowledgment of how much has depended and still depends on the admiration and advocacy of those—publishers, editors, readers—neither peripheral nor oppressed. Naipaul is not inhibited in expressing his debt to London publishers; the nuance and wonder is in his deep unease at being in any place.

The dilemma over address and readership involves a complicity in the very making of books, as we have seen with the Indian novels of the 1930s: a complicity between London publishers and reviewers and their life writing subjects, whose rhetoric of subjugation and struggle is not always willing to acknowledge the help and encouragement received. Many writers in colonial spaces have written the life that moves, takes wing to the centre, that centre being the enabling condition for the book that we are reading. Might there be a colonial narrative of stasis, topographically speaking, of a narrator content to stay put and celebrate one place? One postcolonial location has been celebrated, in Botswana. Yet even in Serowe the complicity with the centre is quite as thorough as in R. K. Narayan's Malgudi, the village in which most of his stories are set.

Bessie Head's *Serowe: Village of the Rain Wind* was published in 1981, by Heinemann in London (paperback) and by David Philip in Cape Town (hardback). Having only one of these editions I am unable to undertake the sort of textual investigation that is usually accorded to canonical works of literature; such attention seems conspicuously absent from the postcolonial, yet it is in this literature very far from contingent. For annotation and paratextual matter can be introduced by way of an exchange mechanism, mediating between those readers who are familiar with the context and those who are not. Postcolonial critics may prefer not to acknowledge that Bessie Head's *Serowe* carries a foreword by Ronald Blythe whose once celebrated study of an English village, *Akenfield* (1969), had inspired Bessie Head to interview the inhabitants of a town in Botswana. Thus a firmly located place in southern Africa is celebrated in literature as a mirror of *Akenfield*.[9] No disencumbering of imbrication there, we must conclude; and yet (or of course) *Serowe* remains an exceptional work of colonial space and life writing. There is a further irony in that David Philip, a South African educated at Oxford, had hugely admired his tutor who had then encouraged him to set up as a publisher: the tutor was C. S. Lewis. As well as archives we are also, in the case of the postcolonial, especially in need of life writing by publishers and editors, for anecdotes are not here to be banished to the periphery of scholarship.[10]

## Colonial and postcolonial archives

Editors, publishers, reviewers, critics, all play their part, and all have lives that might be written. One person can hold many roles. Amos Tutuola has been largely neglected in the story of West African literature, where primacy has been granted to Chinua

Achebe's *Things Fall Apart*, published by Heinemann in 1958. Heinemann's African Writers Series was founded in 1962, with Achebe as its editor, and *Things Fall Apart* was the inaugurating volume. Faber held on to Tutuola, and loyally published each of his books in subsequent decades, though they never took on other African writers, nor released any of Tutuola's works for an appropriate series. From the 1960s Heinemann and Longman between them 're-colonised' the literature of the Commonwealth and kept its centre firmly in London. The story has been told in part, over recent years, though not in sufficient detail, for though we possess some of the archives of the major London houses, we seldom have, or have access to, the archives of those small operations in Lagos or Mombasa or Kampala or Barbados where some of the 'classics' of postcolonial literature were first published (Davis; Low; Huggan). How many editorial adjustments, provisions of glossaries or annotations, were made between the 'indigenous edition' and the London re-printing? It seems that glossaries were often supplied for London editions, though it has seldom been disclosed who supplied the notes, definitions, explanations.

We should also note with respect those London publishers who deliberately chose not to take on African writers. According to his editor, Diana Athill, André Deutsch reckoned that 'instead of providing Nigeria and Kenya with books made in Britain … Britain should help them develop publishing industries of their own'(Athill 104). Deutsch invested in two such enterprises, and refrained from giving any advice on editorial matters; regrettably, neither seems to have flourished.

In colonial and postcolonial writing it would be valuable to trace the shifts in readership (measured by sales figures and library records), and those in modes of compositional address (measured by analysis of texts and paratexts). Clearly they have altered drastically since the 1930s, but this remains a question that could probably be solved only by material in archives. Yet nowhere is there a library that holds all the editions of these works, often so significantly different in each of their variants; place of publication becomes itself a significant variant. Archives are indispensable if we are to take the gerund of 'life writing' in the measure of its coming into being, as a process.

*Books that Matter* (2014) is an example of life writing by a publisher (and a publisher's widow), Marie Philip, that honours the house that played an important role in the fight against apartheid and in the promotion of African literature. Happily, the David Philip archive has been donated to the National English Literary Museum (NELM), in Grahamstown (South Africa) (Philip 111, 127). The NELM, dedicated to South African writing in English, was founded in 1972 by the poet and scholar Guy Butler; in 2016 the collection moves into an exceptional architectural space. One could dream that such an institution might either widen its scope to encompass colonial and postcolonial writing in English, or set an example to other nations that have emerged from colonial rule.

The Library of Congress, though not founded until 1800, was first proposed in 1783, almost as soon as hostilities ceased. The Commonwealth Institute was intended to provide a repository for books published around the Commonwealth. Founded in 1882 as the Imperial Institute in South Kensington and renamed the Commonwealth Institute in 1958, a special building was dedicated in 1962, where was amassed a collection of some twenty or thirty thousand volumes (perhaps more: records are hard to find); at any rate this was by far the largest such collection in the world. In 2000 the library was closed for repairs, and in 2002, with far too little protest, the entire collection was disbanded, many of the volumes being returned to the appropriate commonwealth nation, while the remainder—some 12,000—were deposited in the new British Empire and Commonwealth Museum in Bristol. In an appalling tale of curatorial dereliction, it was found that items had been sold off illegally. The Museum, founded in 2002 as of considerable importance for understanding British history, and the background of a large segment of the British population, was closed down in 2008, without any explanation adequate to the event. Whatever survived of the largest collection of colonial and postcolonial literature in the world was then deposited in the Bristol City Museum. For students of postcolonial literature the consequences are not easily to be measured.

In the absence of a single archive gathering the publishers of literary works in the British Empire and Commonwealth, we are unable to determine with any certainty the first work of postcolonial literature to be published, in its first edition, outside of London (or New York).[11] The two here proposed may be tentative in their claims to precedence but must be exemplary in their literary significance: Derek Walcott's first and second books of poetry, *25 Poems* (1948) and *Epitaph for the Young: A Poem in XII Cantos* (1949). The author, aged 17, had arranged for their publication in Bridgetown, Barbados, by the Advocate Company, whose name suggests that its main line of business was either missionary or legal. Might the correspondence of that firm still survive? Walcott's mother had paid the printing expenses but this should not be considered vanity publishing; in that case, precedence could hardly be established, and we would have to include Patrick White's *Thirteen Poems* (1929 or 1930), privately printed in Sydney by White's mother without his knowledge or consent, and to his lifelong embarrassment. Where White's booklet remains a mere curiosity, Walcott's was to shape the literature of the West Indies, and indeed literature in English.

Among the young Walcott's readers was a slightly older Barbadian, George Lamming, who adjusted a line from a poem in *Epitaph*, 'in the castle of your skin' and in 1953 (as we have seen) used it as the title of one of the outstanding works of postcolonial life writing. It was first published in London by Michael Joseph, not through mere contingency but because Michael Joseph had a particular interest that the following year led him to publish the first British edition of James Baldwin's *Go Tell it on the Mountain*. Hence the foreword to Lamming's book in its US edition in 1954 by Richard Wright, and its co-opting in the emerging Civil Rights movement. Yet thirty years later *In the Castle of My Skin* would be re-issued in the 'Longman Caribbean Writers' series, as though that were its proper place. Lamming had reservations about the manner of his book's American publication, but the distinguished part it played in the politics of Britain and the US in the 1950s and 1960s seems now to be forgotten. In the words of David Williams in the introduction to the 1986 edition, Lamming's is (merely) 'a portrait of the artist as a young colonial'.

That phrasing should alert us to the other large absence from the postcolonial purview, apart from the US: Ireland. The exclusion of the literature of these two nations from postcolonial studies is perplexing. These are however the only nations to have achieved independence from Britain without having assumed (or, in Ireland's case, accepted) membership in the Commonwealth; it may be that these two had been properly (if pedantically) excluded under the older rubric of 'Commonwealth Literature', and that they have quite improperly remained so under the rubric of the postcolonial.

The point needs to be stressed, for one of the greatest of all works of life writing is not only in political and biographical terms a colonial work; it explicitly protests against the colonial circumstances of its writing, though it refuses to reject the English language or to regard it as in any way a constraint. James Joyce would have learnt already from the Americans that the English language was far too good for the English to be granted a monopoly on its literary use. David Williams's paraphrase of Joyce's title rather pales when one realszes that one of the most cosmopolitan of modern writers had himself once been just that, a young colonial. Further, his exemplary *Künstlerroman* displays that turn, mid-flight, that we have identified with the postcolonial: in escaping his circumstances —to 'fly by those nets' of nationality, language and religion—Stephen Dedalus will (in the book's penultimate sentence) speak for all: 'to forge in the smithy of my soul the uncreated conscience of my race' (Joyce 299).

Lamming had of course read Joyce as well as Walcott, not only as the model for any ambitious young writer, but also as a colonial precursor: *In the Castle of My Skin* holds many echoes of *A Portrait of the Artist as a Young Man* (whose first edition was, by no means incidentally, published in New York, not in London). Among the most vivid passages is that where the boys discuss the portrait of the king on the penny:

> It was a real face, and the face they had seen in other pictures. Some said it was really a photograph of the king ... This face on the penny was very fascinating. Could you have a penny without a face? ... You couldn't involve a king in all that nonsense of melting down copper and making a drawing. And how would he find time to sit till all those pennies were done? ... One penny, that is the first penny ever made, was the real penny, and all the others were made by a kind of stamp ... That meant, someone asked, that you couldn't spend the first penny. (Lamming, *Castle* 44–7)

Barbados was once widely known as 'Little England', and all its schoolchildren would have been taught that even between 1649 and 1660 its monarch was Charles II, for in Barbados, alone, there was no interregnum: Barbados never betrayed its king to Cromwell, and it was all of England over which the King reigned. This scene of the pennies provides a parodic hyperbole of loyal fascination; yet it owes much to the *Portrait of the Artist*, the use of childish ignorance to create the effect of defamiliarisation, as championed by the Russian formalists at around the time that *Portrait* was published. Yet unlike Lamming's schoolboys, Stephen Dedalus thinks about England only in oppressive terms. His is in almost all respects the exemplary narrative of colonial life writing, from childhood and school, to the sense of separateness, of the outcast, then the visionary moment, the epiphany, and the determination to escape—though not to London. Ireland was the only British possession whose population was predominantly Roman Catholic, and London never had the symbolic and magnetic attraction that it exercised over every other part of Britain's empire.

Detailing the bibliographical trajectories and the transposings of texts and editions is of the essence for understanding the tensions and predicaments of colonial and postcolonial life writing. We have traced the regrettable limiting of Lamming's work, since 1986, within the Caribbean boundary; bibliographical enquiry can also follow a writing career that does not begin in London but, like its author, arrives there. Launched by a small press in Georgetown, Barbados, Walcott would soon be taken up in London by Jonathan Cape, and then in New York by Farrar, Strauss and, in succession to Cape in London, by Faber. Taken up, not as an exotic colonial but as a major English poet, which is to say a poet writing in English who, in this most eminent case, by means of myth and history—and an astonishing command of analogy—negotiates those local realities (never to be abandoned) which might test the thematic competence of readers outside the Caribbean.

## Benjamin Franklin and colonial autobiography

If *A Portrait of the Artist* has flown by the net of 'postcolonial life writing', so also has an even more famous work. For surely by far the most celebrated and widely read of all colonial autobiographies must be Benjamin Franklin's. Published posthumously, it was composed in two sections, in 1771 and 1784, thus spanning the first war of independence of any British colony; adjustments were made to the text up to Franklin's death in 1790. The book seems to be little read among students of the history and literature of colonial societies (the US excepted), and indeed its readership seems to have become ever more exclusively American. Despite its status as a founding text of the new nation, Franklin's celebration of the freedoms available in Philadelphia and throughout the North American colonies is not predicated on independence; Franklin would have been happy with some sort of autonomous government of the thirteen colonies united (devolved, as we might now say) within the British empire, not unlike the West Indies Federation from 1958 to 1962. It is forgotten, in the teleological schema that has made the book required reading for all American schoolchildren, how ambivalent Franklin was about independence. He enjoyed life in England, where he had close friends; it was while staying with the Shipleys near Winchester—'Twyford, at the Bishop of St Asaph's 1771'—that he began to write his memoirs.

That ambivalence seems to characterise colonial and postcolonial life writing: to dislike the English but to be devoted to the language; to seek independence and yet to maintain relations with publishers in London; to write for one's own people while seeking to find and impress a larger readership. Franklin's offers us, for once, no moral instance in the matter of publication, for it was intended, or so the opening would have its readers believe, merely as a record for his son William. William was by then Governor of New Jersey; after 1776 he remained a Loyalist, and from 1784 lived as a pensioner in London. The irony of Franklin's son may serve as a fable, of the complications and complicities entailed by independence when the two parties, or nations, or states, have lived so long together, and cannot help but share a language.

Yet the first publication of the text was not in Franklin's English but in a translator's French. This appeared in Paris in 1791, just after Franklin's death, as *Mémoires de la vie privée de Benjamin Franklin*. A version was published in London in 1793, though this was not Franklin's English either, but a further translation made from the French. Parts of the English text were published in 1818, but it was not until John Bigelow acquired and assembled Franklin's various manuscripts, now widely scattered, that Franklin's full text was eventually published, in 1868. This was almost a hundred years after Franklin had begun to write, and its belated publication gave it the status of an archaeological find, or even a relic. Here is the life written and revised almost to the point of the writer's death: its posthumous publication made the book seem less Franklin's defence or apology than posterity's own verdict

Such a long delay meant that the book could now be entitled not *Memoirs* but *Autobiography*—a word that had not been coined until the early nineteenth century. First recorded in the German form in 1793, 'autobiography' is attested in English in 1809, attributed to the Poet Laureate, Robert Southey. Southey was also responsible, in 1821, for the word 'hagiography', to be used in tones of protestant disapproval. Thus Southey is responsible for two important coinages in English, and one invention not to be ascribed to 'the great inventor' is the word by which Franklin's book would become known; it is likely that Southey's coinage 'autobiography' entered into currency through the title of Franklin's book.[12]

The parts of the *Autobiography* that all American schoolchildren are supposed to have read are those recounting events that occurred on the North American continent. This is what legitimates the book as the founding text of a nation. But the larger part of the book is concerned with England, where much of it was composed. That the book is little known in Britain is evident from the fact that Franklin, one of the most significant figures in the history of printing, offers the most detailed account we have of daily routines and working practices in the London printing industry. Yet in all the histories of printing in London that I have consulted, Franklin's *Autobiography* is not mentioned. Here we can see how colonial and national canon-formation has divided books from their proper readers, and this not at all on grounds of 'thematic competence' but simply by the author's association with the United States; for all but the last six of his 84 years he was a British subject. There is no difficulty at all, thematically, for the British reader of Franklin's memoirs. Rather, it seems that the book has become so canonically American (increasingly so since 1945) that the rest of the world has assumed that only Americans need to read it.

It seems in order, however anecdotal, to confess that I read Franklin's *Autobiography* for the first time less than ten years ago, and then for reasons of local (English) topography; often as I had heard it mentioned, I cannot recall the book ever being recommended for my reading. Franklin tells us that he owed much to Bunyan's *Pilgrim's Progress*, a copy of which almost miraculously manifests itself to him from under the water. All subsequent life writers in English (notably those of autobiographies) have owed a great deal to Franklin, and it is striking that Franklin should pay his deep respects to Bunyan while failing to mention either of the two 'autobiographies', both entitled 'Confessions', that are central to the western tradition: those of St. Augustine and Jean-Jacques Rousseau. Franklin's is not just, with the possible exception of *A Portrait,* the greatest of all colonial autobiographies; it may have shaped life writing in English more than any other book composed in English.

## Conclusion: old home, new nation, imbricated spaces

Taking the United States as the normative former colony, we can observe that the mother country was already for Franklin an object of humorous toleration, a comfortable myth later to be exemplified by Hawthorne's *Our Old Home* of 1863, before becoming the object of Henry James's veneration in *English Hours* (1905), and T. S. Eliot's in *Four Quartets*. But, in comparison with the postcolonial memoirs of the past century, what is striking about American autobiography, from Franklin onwards, is how little England matters symbolically, no matter how much it figures. *The Education of Henry Adams* (1918)—among the least appeased or appeasing of all autobiographies, and intended for posthumous publication—tells us plenty about England, much of it deprecating if not contemptuous, but there is nothing symbolic about it. A long section of George Santayana's *Last Puritan: A Memoir in the Form of a Novel* (1936)—another remarkable example of life writing—takes place in and around the most charming parts of Oxford, but with very little reverence or sense of deficit. Here is T. S. Eliot's cousin, the eminent historian Samuel Eliot Morison, in *One Boy's Boston 1897–1901* (1962) challenging prevailing assumptions:

> Another favourite cliché of latter-day gossip columnists is that Boston society was fanatically pro-British ... My recollections are all to the contrary ... It was only after growing up that I began to entertain feelings of kindness and admiration toward our mother country. (Morison 66–7)

Of those two former colonies that are not members of the Commonwealth (the only ones) it must be said that Britain did very little to endear itself to either. The Irish as Roman Catholics felt excluded from an Empire made ideologically cohesive by Protestantism; nor could the Irish look to England as a place of cultural or ethnic origin. By contrast, America was Protestant, and New Englanders certainly looked to Old England as the point of origin and departure, a place where continuities and lineages could be traced. Yet there is not in American life writing any sense of London as the centre, symbolically or culturally: independence came early, and by the mid nineteenth century, when Britain's imperial symbolism became most potent, the Americans had moved on, beyond the post- of the post-colonial. Yet in all the other colonies—those now part of the Commonwealth—whatever the political force and economic exploitation, at the symbolic level Britain had been rather successful in creating loyalty throughout much of the empire in the late nineteenth and early twentieth centuries. Even those writing their lives against the Empire could not dispense with English as a language, nor could they renounce many of the attributes of Englishness as represented in the colonies. This attitude seldom survived the passage to England in the 1950s and 1960s, where the lack of welcome came as a shock precisely because West Indians and others had been brought up to think of England as home. That disappointment is registered in *The Lonely Londoners* and other novels of Sam Selvon; disillusionment find its expression in Selvon's successors.

Even in the US in the mid nineteenth century Hawthorne gives voice again to Franklin's lament that the American colonists had had no great wish for independence, but that the behaviour of George III and his ministries had made it inevitable. Describing the English roots still entangled with American heart-strings, Hawthorne, in a book not ironically entitled *Our Old Home*, wonders at the inability of England to maintain the loyalty of its American colonists:

> It has required nothing less than the boorishness, the stolidity, the self-sufficiency, the contemptuous jealousy, the half-sagacity, invariably blind of one eye and often distorted of the other, that characterize this strange people, to compel us to be a great nation in our own right, instead of continuing virtually, if not in name, a province of their small island. What pains did they take to shake us off, and have ever since taken to keep us wide apart from them! (Hawthorne 16)

This is very different in tone and sentiment from almost anything we find in the literature of what is now the Commonwealth over the past hundred years or so. Those works of life writing from the British colonies that achieved independence some two centuries after the thirteen show a sort of fascination with England, or at least a deep collusion with its symbolic repertory, hardly able to avoid mention of the flag, the sovereign, the coinage; the vast machinery of imperial representation seems inescapable even to the most disaffected recollection. One of the forces of Empire seems to lie in dislocating the imagination of those who would envisage a colonial space as home.

It is not easy to make sense or order of these diverse instances of life writing from the colonies over the past 250 years. It might be hazarded that the particular qualities of colonial and postcolonial life writing are to be found in the tensions made clear by the idea of independence: the writing lives in the power of the attachment that must be overcome, and in the force of the language that uproots even as it celebrates.[13]

Throughout these works we can detect complicity and the need to address deeply divergent readerships in economic and technological circumstances over most of which the imperial power has kept control even to this day. Derek Walcott is among the writers of colonial spaces who has most openly recognised the conflicts at work—the conflicts without which writing will not work—famously in the dilemma voiced in the early poem 'A Far Cry from Africa' (Walcott 1962): 'how choose / Between this Africa and the English tongue I love?' Walcott's 'Eulogy to W. H. Auden' (1983) is one master's tribute to another, and a meditation on space as colony, including outer space. The particularity of place and horizon—the evocation of childhood's own topographics—is registered in the force of the word 'there'. Here Walcott acknowledges collusion, and negotiates imbrication, at the pitch of the sublime:

> Once, past a wooden vestry,
> down still colonial streets,
> the hoisted chords of Wesley
> were strong as miners' throats;
>
> in treachery and in union,
> despite your Empire's wrong,
> I made my first communion
> there, with the English tongue.
>
> It was such dispossession
> that made possession joy,
> when, strict as Psalm or Lesson,
> I learnt your poetry.[14]

## Notes

1. For fictional reflection on these matters one can recommend the novel by Bernard Malamud, *Dubin's Lives* (1979), whose title plays between lives led and biographies written.
2. *Lives of the Poets* is not Johnson's title but one of convenience, behind which lies a tangle of authorial intentions and bibliographical adjustments.
3. There may be books written by colonial subjects that are entirely in support of colonial governance, but these are seldom read; Kipling, John Buchan and others provide plenty of examples of books by members of the governing class in support of their own status, yet there is nuance in these, and some of them—such as the novels by Joyce Cary set in Nigeria—deserve renewed attention, not least in terms of life writing.

4. The term 'Anglophone periphery' may be thought anglocentric; there is no reason to deny the centrality of Britain in regard to publishing.
5. Though the most celebrated of early works by Caribbean writers, *In the Castle of My Skin* was not the first. Caribbean literature in English seems to have been inaugurated by Edgar Mittelholzer's *Corentyne Thunder*, published by Eyre and Spottiswoode in 1941; Mittelholzer's second, *A Morning at the Office*, was published by Leonard Woolf at the Hogarth Press in 1950, and by Doubleday, in the same year, under a contrastingly exotic title: *A Morning in Trinidad*.
6. In *Pleasures of Exile* (1960) Lamming discusses the way his first book had been presented and marketed in the US; for a detailed account see Lowe.
7. The claim is implicitly limited to European languages; it would be interesting to learn when Spanish and Portuguese readers and writers outside the Iberian Peninsula first articulated such anxieties.
8. The tendency is movingly anatomised by Raymond Williams in *The Country and the City*, and is exemplified by Thomas Hood's 'I remember, I remember / The house where I was born ... ' from 1827.
9. *Akenfield* is atypical of the tradition of English place writing in that this is a fictional name to conceal and protect (for legal reasons) the identity of the place and its residents. Just as Walden is an indifferently located pond, so Akenfield is a 'generic village', and perhaps it was this that appealed to Bessie Head.
10. Those interested in Jean Rhys—a salient and brilliant exemplar of life writing within and around colonial spaces—must turn to the anecdotal memoirs of Diana Athill, Rhys's editor at André Deutsch, herself a most engaging exponent of life writing in old age.
11. There are of course many books by Indians in English that were published in India in the nineteenth century, and even before; the concern here is with writing since the 1930s, during and beyond the struggle for independence.
12. In this flurry of coinages concerning discourses of the self and the emerging subject, recording and recorded, it should be noted that the word *Bildungsroman* is remarkably synchronic with 'autobiography' both in its coinage and in its first widespread usage: 'autobiography' was coined by Southey in 1809 and was made famous as the title of Franklin's memoirs when they were published in 1868; *Bildungsroman* was coined by Karl Morgenstern in 1819 and put into circulation by Dilthey in the 1870s.
13. I know of two writers, Ngũgĩ wa Thiong'o (formerly James Ngugi) and Chinweizu, who have renounced the use of English; there may well be others. Chinweizu announced his intention in a letter to the *Times Literary Supplement*, c. 1987.
14. "Eulogy to W. H. Auden (Read at the Cathedral of St. John the Divine, New York, October 17, 1983)", *The Arkansas Testament*, 63–64.

## Disclosure statement

No potential conflict of interest was reported by the author.

## References

(Where appropriate for tracing the trajectories and intersections of texts and publishers more than one edition of each work is cited: usually the first American and British editions, and sometimes others as well.)

Adams, Henry. *The Education of Henry Adams: An Autobiography.* Boston: Houghton Mifflin, 1918; London: Constable, 1918. Print.

Ali, Ahmed. *Twilight in Delhi.* London: Hogarth, 1940. Print.

Anand, Mulk Raj. *Untouchable.* London: Wishart, 1935. Print.

Athill, Diana. *Stet: An Editor's Life.* London: Granta, 2000. Print.

Baldwin, James. *Go Tell it on the Mountain.* New York: Knopf, 1953; London: Michael Joseph, 1954. Print.

Blythe, Ronald. *Akenfield: Portrait of an English Village.* London: Allen Lane, 1969. Print.

Boehmer, Elleke. *Stories of Women: Gender and Narrative in the Postcolonial Nation.* Manchester: Manchester UP, 2009. Print.

Davis, Caroline. *Creating Postcolonial Literature: African Writers and British Publishers.* Basingstoke: Palgrave, 2013. Print.

Franklin, Benjamin. *Benjamin Franklin's Autobiography.* Ed. Joyce E. Chaplin. New York: Norton, 2012. Print.

Giles, Paul. *The Global Remapping of American Literature.* Princeton: Princeton UP, 2011. Print.

Graff, Gerald. *Professing Literature: An Institutional History.* Chicago: U of Chicago P, 1987. Print.

Hawthorne, Nathaniel. *Our Old Home: a Series of English Sketches.* Boston: Ticknor & Fields, 1863; Edinburgh: William Paterson, 1884. Print.

Head, Bessie. *Serowe: Village of the Rain Wind.* London: Heinemann, 1981; Cape Town: David Philip, 1981. Print.

Holden, Philip. *Autobiography and Decolonization: Modernity, Masculinity, and the Nation-State.* Madison: U of Wisconsin P, 2008. Print.

Huggan, Graham. *The Postcolonial Exotic: Marketing the Margins.* London: Routledge, 2001. Print.

James, C. L. R. *Beyond a Boundary.* London: Hutchinson, 1963; Durham, NC: Duke University Press (introduction by Robert Lipsyte, foreword by Paget Henry), 2013. Print.

James, Henry. *Hawthorne.* London: Macmillan, 1879; New York: Harper, 1880; Ithaca: Cornell UP, 1997. Print.

James, Selma. "How *Beyond a Boundary* broke down the barriers of race, class and empire". *Guardian* 2 Apr. 2015. Print.

Joyce, James. *A Portrait of the Artist as a Young Man.* New York: B. W. Huebsch, 1916. Print.

Khozan, Maryam and Charles Lock. 'Touching the *Untouchable*: on the Reception of Indian Fiction in Britain in the 1930s". *Unhinging Hinglish: The Languages and Politics of Fiction in English from the Indian Subcontinent.* Eds. Nanette Hale and Tabish Khair. Copenhagen: Museum Tusculanum, 2001. 23–39. Print.

Lamming, George. *In The Castle of My Skin.* London: Michael Joseph, 1953; New York: McGraw-Hill, with an introduction by Richard Wright, 1954; London: Longman, Caribbean Writers Series, with an introduction by David Williams, 1986. Print.

Lamming, George. *The Pleasures of Exile.* London: Michael Joseph, 1960. Print.

Lock, Charles. "Amos Tutuola and Ken Saro-Wiwa: a Heritage of Rotten English". *Kiabàrà: Journal of Humanities* 8.1 (2002): 1–10. Print.

Lock, Charles. "Words, War and Play". *Literary Research/Recherche Littéraire* 19.37–8 (2003): 292–303. Print.

Low, Gail. *Publishing the Postcolonial: Anglophone West African and Caribbean Writing in the UK 1948–1968.* London: Routledge, 2011. Print.

Lowe, John. "Richard Wright and the CircumCaribbean". *Richard Wright: New Readings in the 21st Century.* Ed. Alice Mikal Craven. Basingstoke: Palgrave, 2011. 249–66. Print.

Moore-Gilbert, Bart. *Postcolonial Life-Writing: Culture, Politics, and Self-Representation.* London: Routledge, 2009. Print.

Morison, Samuel Eliot. *One Boy's Boston 1897–1901.* Boston: Houghton Mifflin, 1962. Print.

Naipaul, V. S. *The Enigma of Arrival.* London: Viking, 1987; New York, Knopf, 1987. Print.

Narayan, R. K. *Swami and Friends.* London: Hamish Hamilton, 1935. Print.

Ngũgĩ wa Thiong'o. *Decolonising the Mind: The Politics of Language in African Literature.* London: James Currey/Heinemann, 1986. Print.

Orwell, George. *Burmese Days.* New York: Harper, 1934; London: Gollancz, 1935. Print.

Philip, Marie. *Books that Matter: David Philip Publishers during the apartheid years*. Cape Town: Philip, 2014. Print.

Rao, Raja. *Kanthapura*. London: George Allen & Unwin, 1938; New York: New Directions, 1963. Print.

Santayana, George. *The Last Puritan: A Memoir in the Form of a Novel*. London: Constable, 1935; New York: Scribners, 1936. Print.

Selvon, Sam. *The Lonely Londoners*. London: Longman, 1956; New York: St. Martin's, 1956. Print.

Thoreau, Henry David. *Walden: or, Life in the Woods*. Boston: Ticknor & Fields, 1854; London: Scott, 1886. Print.

Tutuola, Amos. *The Palm-Wine Drinkard*. London: Faber, 1952; New York: Grove, 1953. Print.

Walcott, Derek. *25 Poems*. Bridgetown, Barbados: Advocate, 1948. Print.

Walcott, Derek. *Epitaph for the Young: A Poem in XII Cantos*. Bridgetown, Barbados: Advocate, 1949. Print.

Walcott, Derek. *In a Green Night: Poems 1948–1960*. London: Jonathan Cape, 1962. Print.

Walcott, Derek. *The Arkansas Testament*. New York: Farrar, 1987; London: Faber, 1988. Print.

Williams, Raymond. *The Country and the City*. London: Chatto & Windus, 1973. Print.

Wright, Richard. *Black Power: A Record of Reaction in a Land of Pathos*. New York: Harper, 1954; London: Dobson, 1956. Print.

# Tears and Garlands: Lim Chin Siong, Coldstore, and the End(s) of Narrative

Philip Holden

Department of English Language and Literature, National University of Singapore, Singapore

**ABSTRACT**
This paper considers the role of biography in contemporary remembrance of the moment of decolonisation in Singapore. To challenge a hegemonic developmental narrative told through the biography of Singapore's first Prime Minister, Lee Kuan Yew, many popular and academic historians have focused on the lives of political figures previously written out of history. Most notable among these is the opposition leader Lim Chin Siong, who was detained in 1963 in Operation Coldstore, one of several waves of detentions by the security forces during Singapore's transition from internal self government in 1959, through membership of the Malaysian Federation in 1963, to independent nationhood in 1965. Such acts of storytelling, however, while having an important status as testimony, often simply invert the dominant narrative, trapping their protagonists in a new series of historical binarisms. In contrast, life writing in media less closely wedded to narrative, such as poetry and photography, has perhaps a more radical ability to ask questions of history, through a focus not on storytelling but on images extracted from contexts, on the moment before narrative starts.

In Singapore, as in many postcolonies, biography and the question of national narratives are always closely intertwined. I began writing this essay in late March 2015, in my Housing and Development Board flat in Bukit Batok, Singapore, one of many modernist public housing estates that ring Singapore's city centre, and yet in the public imagination constitute its heartland. It was a day like any other. The estate, in the late morning, was empty of people apart from the very young and the very old: even the mass rapid transit trains were empty, full not of people but of sunlight. And yet it was a day different from any other: Lee Kuan Yew, Singapore's first Prime Minister was in intensive care in Singapore General Hospital, with a terse series of announcements confirming his worsening condition. I am finishing it in September, after a General Election marked by the fading echoes of the unprecedented public expression of mourning and catharsis at his passing. As a Singapore permanent resident who has spent an overwhelming proportion of my adult life in the city-state I, with richly ambivalent feelings, queued in the long lines for the lying-in-state at Parliament House, and waited in the crowds on Clementi Road for the funeral procession.

One Facebook friend described the event as Singapore's 'Diana moment', but the event, in terms of historical and political significance, was surely far more important than the public mourning that accompanied the passing of Diana, Princess of Wales, in 1997.

In earlier research, I took Lee's autobiography, *The Singapore Story*, as a touchstone for thinking about a genre I called national autobiography: autobiographies and memoirs produced by and indeed producing 'national fathers', national leaders superintending the process of decolonisation. These autobiographies, I argued, were less about the production of imagined communities than imagined individuals: the nation-state was written into existence as a masculine subject, with statist disciplines of development applied to an unruly national body (Holden). Lee's memoirs, indeed, were something of a latecomer to a genre that reached its height of popularity through Jawaharlal Nehru and Kwame Nkrumah, and which might plausibly, and paradoxically, be traced back to colonial autobiography. Yet the late arrival of Lee's memoirs also signified something unusual: Singapore's 50-year history as postcolonial developmental state that delivered the economic growth on which its ruling elite's legitimacy was founded. Nkrumah's Convention People's Party and Nehru's Indian National Congress had long ceded their hold on power. In contrast, Lee's People's Action Party (PAP) had delivered economic development in an avowedly illiberal democracy, and been elected with strong majorities in regular, secret ballot elections, long after Lee himself had relinquished the premiership in November 1990.

The response to Lee's death indicated both the ongoing purchase of such a developmental narrative, but also the limits of its utility in thinking of new possibilities for the future. In the first two days after his demise, there seemed to be a genuine possibility of a space in which a series of responses that would acknowledge the complexity of his legacy might be expressed. Such responses might acknowledge the very real achievements of his premiership, yet also extend to embrace the views of the large minority of Singaporeans who do not support the People's Action Party, as well as a smaller group, made up of figures such as former political detainees, whose lives have been adversely affected by the Party's actions in government. The memorialisation that saturated the mass media under conditions of 'networked hegemony' (George 202) during the week of national mourning from 23 to 29 of March, however, tended to reiterate the same dominant story of a national Romance with Lee as an idealised protagonist. Many Singaporeans found themselves identifying with it, and with a newly remembered idealism of the early years of the developmental state contrasted with an apparent loss of ideals in a neoliberal present; others remained stubbornly disengaged.

Such identification, as with the national mourning in the United Kingdom on the death of Diana, Princess of Wales, has a series of public and private meanings that cannot simply be dismissed as false consciousness. Yet in Singapore, its expression also led to the drowning out of voices that expressed alternative views. Low Thia Khiang, leader of the Opposition Workers' Party, gave an inflected speech in which he praised many of Lee's achievements, but noted that he was also a 'controversial figure': his criticisms were amplified and criticised in a report in *Today*, one of Singapore's English-language dailies, which later apologised, claiming that in the process of translation from Mandarin to English the paper had 'misunderstood Mr Low' ('Workers' Party Secretary-General Low Thia Khiang … '). Singapore's English-language daily of record, the *Straits Times*, published an article summarising some more critical responses made by members of the arts community to Lee's passing in social media. While the journalist involved did withdraw many of the quotations after the writers protested, this only served to make the playwright Alfian Sa'at, whose comments were not removed, more vulnerable to online attacks (Nanda). At the end of the period of public mourning, a further social panic occurred regarding a YouTube video made by the teenager Amos Yee which attacked Lee's legacy and made some incidental criticism of Christianity. Yee was the subject of over 20 police reports, imprisoned on remand, and eventually convicted of wounding religious feelings and distributing obscene material ("Amos Yee"). Each act of criticism was in itself biographised in the public sphere, and online responses often attacked the character of the commentator, contrasting putatively self-serving criticism to the sacrifice that Lee himself made to the nation.

This paper takes the occasion of Lee's passing as a touchstone to consider the role of biography in renewed discussions of the place of decolonisation in Singapore's national narrative. To replace the dominant developmental narrative with which Lee is associated, many historians, both popular and academic, have argued for a proliferation of narratives, of competing Singapore stories, rather than a Singapore story. Yet such acts of storytelling, if they are unreflexive, may simply replace the dominant story with a counter-narrative that changes terms, but remains identical in its construction. Close examination of a contested moment in Singapore's history suggests an alternative strategy, one to move beyond the binarisms of dominant and alternative narratives: a focus on the image, to focus on the moment before narrative starts.

## Contested history: Coldstore and its aftermaths

On September 18, 1963, Singapore joined Malaya and the territories of North Borneo and Sarawak to form Malaysia; in doing so, it finally severed colonial bonds with the United Kingdom that had already been loosened with the granting of full internal self-government in 1959. This historical moment and its associated period might initially seem very remote, and yet in recent years in Singapore, it has received a great deal of public attention in traditional, alternative and social media. In particular, public debate has focused on an incident that took place earlier in 1963, in a time of waiting after the plebiscite in Singapore in September 1962 in which Singaporeans had, faced with a narrow choice of possibilities, endorsed merger, and yet before the formal founding of Malaysia. The nature of this event, commencing early in the morning of 2 September, is perhaps best captured through memoir and fiction. Here is the Malaysian writer Lee Kok Liang, describing this, or perhaps a later, congruent moment:

> When he switched on their bedside lamp, his wife turned over in their bed, her hair brushing against his throat. The glare of the light revealed a soft brown face, puffy with sleep. As he got up, she blinked rapidly, raising herself on her elbows. Their child was asleep in the cot, embracing a dutch-wife, and the dummy still clung to the tiny parted lips. 'Where are you going?' she had asked in a slurred voice. He noted the look of surprise on her face. 'Someone is knocking on the door. Don't know who.' She started to yawn bringing her hand to her mouth. He leant over and kissed her, pressing his nose into the warm mound of her cheek. She then scratched her breasts beneath her blouse, scraping off the remnants of sleep as she got up. It was only when he stood before the door that he became frightened. He heard voices in whispers on the other side. No, it could not happen to him. Of course he had rattled off something pretty hard on the platform, about the Government not doing this

or that. But surely that was not sufficient. Anyway he would look ridiculous if he had said something else. (7)

Lee's protagonist opens the door only to find that his fears are confirmed. In the morning of 2 February, Police and Special Branch Offices throughout Singapore conducted raids in which they arrested over a hundred opposition party members, trade unionists, and social activists, including 24 key members of Singapore's main opposition party, the Barisan Socialis.

At the time, the operation, code-named Coldstore, was presented by the government and in a largely compliant media as a necessary security operation. The detainees, it was argued at the time, were part of a Communist United Front, ready to 'depart from constitutional methods' and 'mount violence or disorder in the closing stages of the establishment of the Federation of Malaysia' (United Kingdom 'Colonial Office'). This construction of Coldstore has persisted as part of a larger dominant nationalist historiography. Such narrativisation sees the People's Action Party from its formation in 1954 as 'riding the tiger' of Communist popular mobilisation in order to win power in 1959, and then, having established public safety through a purging of a potential communist threat, superintending an as-yet-unfinished process of development. As this developmental narrative has evolved after independence in 1965, an early focus on democratic socialism has gradually been supplanted by a stress on neoliberal self-fashioning and the production of entrepreneurial but apolitical citizen-subjects. Yet these histories are founded on Coldstore as a political necessity. Dennis Bloodworth's *The Tiger and the Trojan Horse*, for instance, completely identifies with the security apparatus, noting gleefully that by 4 February 1963, 'the pigeons were back in the cage' (277), while in Lee Kuan Yew's autobiography, *The Singapore Story*, individuals identified as 'pro-communists' before Coldstore are described with certainty as 'communists' in its aftermath (472). Yet even such conventional developmental historiography, in retrospect, has its flaws and fissures. John Drysdale, whose *Singapore: Struggle for Success* is normally thought of as sympathetic to the PAP, notes that in press accounts at the time 'the political grounds for the mass arrests, as distinct from the security grounds, were given the wrong emphasis' (320). While Drysdale attempts to argue that such media emphasis on politics was misplaced, he also notes that post-Coldstore interrogations of the detainees were not 'illuminating', producing no new evidence of 'connections with the Communist underground movement', thus inadvertently supporting a reading of the operation as politically motivated (320). Mary Turnbull, attempting an ideologically neutral account of Singapore's history that is inevitably still discursively influenced by dominant paradigms, also hints at political expedience in her comment regarding Coldstore that 'the PAP's rivals had been removed at a dangerous time in circumstances in which the responsibility could be laid at the doors of others, this time the British and Malayans' (282).

In the late 1990s, these fissures opened further. British scholars S. J. Ball and Matthew Jones, making use of Colonial Office files and Cabinet Papers released over the previous decade, both argued that the process of decolonisation leading up to the formation of Malaysia was much less tidy than had been previously proposed. British, Malayan, and Singaporean representatives on the Internal Security Council jockeyed for political advantage, faced with a fractured and fractious political opposition in Singapore. Ball focused on the reservations of local British officials, in particular George Selkirk, UK Commissioner for Singapore and Commissioner-General for Southeast Asia, regarding the Coldstore arrests. Selkirk's correspondence, Ball's essay demonstrates, indicates a growing suspicion that Lee Kuan Yew's insistence on the raids was driven by political rather than security matters, by a desire to eliminate a democratically elected opposition while blaming the British for the arrests. Jones reached a wider conclusion that several local British officers acquiesced to the Coldstore arrests 'with great reluctance' in order to accommodate the 'needs and demands of nationalist elites' in Singapore and Malaysia (86).

While both Ball's and Jones's work is rich and detailed in its use of archival sources, it might plausibly be critiqued as having its own unconscious ideological imperative: a favourable revisioning of the role of British officials at the end of empire in which figures such as Selkirk are redeemed as honourable men who had to make unpalatable choices faced with the inevitability of decolonisation. In Singapore, concerns have been less with the end of empire than the founding of a nation-state. The archive has expanded further, with additional material becoming available from UK and Australian sources, and through the declassification of the Foreign and Commonwealth Office Migrated Archives over the last few years. This has been supplemented with a new kind of resource: the published autobiographical and biographical writings and oral history interviews of former detainees, eager to give their side of the story. The new material is complex, at times contradictory, and is driven by rhetorical and ideological imperatives of its own, but in sum it tends to support a reading that Coldstore was motivated by more than simply security concerns.

Over the last decade and a half, the new material has resulted in Coldstore becoming a touchstone for many historians of Singapore writing from a variety of different perspectives, but each attempting to evolve new ways of imagining Singapore's historical narrative. This re-imagining is not simply academic: it responds to what we might call a contemporary structure of feeling in the city-state that the dominant narrative of the developmental state has lost explanatory force in the present. Voter support for the People's Action Party has ebbed and flowed, with the growth of a more visible and vocal political opposition and civil society. This is only part of the picture. There has also been an erosion of confidence in state institutions such as the Central Provident Fund, Singapore's contributory retirement scheme, and the Housing and Development Board, the statutory board that builds and manages the vast majority of housing in the city-state. The outpouring of public grief on Lee's death, indeed, might be read as a part of this. While Lee's passing was marked by a powerful effort by state institutions and the mainstream media to reiterate the dominant narrative, one marked feature of it on the ground was a nostalgia for the earlier post-independence years when the developmental narrative had explanatory force, allied to a desire for transcendence of the mundane in a present in which the state has less power to protect its citizens from the forces of the market.

Indeed, in the period 2000–2012, it seemed momentarily as though a richer public historical narrative of those early years might be developed, one that would acknowledge the contributions of those written out of history (Poh, Tan, and Hong 11–2), and thus that would have utility in rethinking the social challenges posed by a globalised present. Yet a revised view of the events concerning Coldstore might ultimately problematise even such a modified narrative, because it questions the origins of an imagined social compact between the ruling People's Action Party and its citizens, in which citizens freely acquiesce, through the ballot box, to a form of illiberal democracy in exchange for security and economic growth. What if this compact began not with an honest, informed choice, but with deception, with what Lysa Hong has termed 'the Party's original sin'? ('They do').

The return of Coldstore to the popular imaginary was completed by a public commemoration by former detainees and sympathisers of its fiftieth anniversary at Hong Lim Park in Singapore February 2013, and the publication of a collection of essays by scholars and former detainees in both English and Chinese. Concern with Coldstore moved increasingly into the public sphere, with articles on independent news websites such as the *Independent* and the *Online Citizen*. In late 2014, the government responded, and a series of articles in the mainstream media questioned 'revisionist history', Lee Kuan Yew's series of anti-Communist talks from 1961, *Battle For Merger*, were reprinted, and an exhibition of the same title was held at the National Library, depicting 'a battle with the Communists for the hearts and minds of the people of Singapore' and conspicuously not referring to the new scholarship on the early 1960s (National Library Board). This response was supplemented by other initiatives. In December 2014, Burhan Gafoor, Singapore's High Commissioner to Australia, made a detailed response to an article on Coldstore by Poh Soo Kai, one of the original detainees, in the online Australian journal the *New Mandala*, criticising him 'and other revisionists' for selective quotation of archival documents. Finally, in April 2015, Kumar Ramakrishna, a scholar in policy studies at Nanyang Technological University, published *Original Sin? Revising the Revisionist Critique of the 1963 Operation Coldstore in Singapore,* which again conflated most of the scholarship of the previous decade as the product of 'revisionists', and which made use of privileged, although highly selective, access to Singapore Internal Security Department archives. Media attention granted to the slim volume, which contained far less documentation than the 'revisionist' historical work it criticised as selective and partial, was disproportionate to its scholarly weight. A summative article in the *Straits Times* in April, for instance, gave far more emphasis to Ramakrishna and an older generation of scholars whose major work was produced in an earlier period when less documentation was available, than to contemporary scholars who had been active in the debate ('Revisiting Operation Coldstore').

## Biographising Coldstore: the case of Lim Chin Siong

Popular history is often told through dramatic narratives involving actors: in essence, through biographies. Just as a dominant developmental narrative has often been expressed through Lee's life, so contentions regarding Coldstore have often condensed into questions of biography surrounding the most prominent of the detainees, Barisan Sosialis secretary-general Lim Chin Siong. Lim was one of the founders of the People's Action Party in 1954, and was elected, along with Lee Kuan Yew, to the Legislative Assembly in 1955. 10 years younger than Lee, a powerful orator and fully at home—as Lee was not—in a Chinese-speaking world, Lim was a key figure on the left of the party. In 1961, he had joined many assemblymen and the majority of the PAP party branch committees in quitting the party and forming the Barisan Sosialis. After his detention under Coldstore, he effectively vanished from political history, imprisoned until 1969, when, suffering from depression, he was permitted to leave Singapore to go to London. He returned to the city-state in 1979, to live quietly at home until his early death in 1996.

The re-evaluation of Lim's role in Singapore history began in the same year as his death, when he was included in Melanie Chew's *Leaders of Singapore*, a series of detailed interviews with politicians and other prominent social actors. In 1999, Wee Wan-ling published an account of Lim's career as part of Kevin Tan and Lam Peng Er's collection of essays *Lee's Lieutenants: Singapore's Old Guard*, which attempted to widen discussion of Singapore's late colonial and post-independence history by examining the contribution of a number of first generation of People's Action Party leaders. Wee was cautious in his re-evaluation of Lim, but raised the possibility that his life offered contemporary Singaporeans the chance to 'reflect on Singapore's national narrative of arrival', and to then develop a more nuanced history (190). Two years later, Wee's essay was followed by the first book-length study of Lim, the essay collection *Comet in Our Sky: Lim Chin Siong in History* (2001), edited by K. S. Jomo and Tan Jing Quee, the latter one of Lim's Barisan colleagues and a fellow detainee. The collection contains both personal reminiscences but also important essays by Tan, M. K. Rajakumar, and historians Tim Harper and Greg Poulgrain that attempt to place Lim within an expanded history of Singapore.

Such writings do not simply restore Lim to a historical narrative, but attempt to break the narrative mould into which his life story has been forced by dominant historiography. In accounts from Lee's own *Battle For Merger* onwards, Lim has been figured as a subversive, forming alliances of convenience with Singapore's future founding fathers on the right of the PAP when expedient, yet always working subversively against a future national interest. A particular focus has been brought to bear on Lim's alleged membership of the Communist Party of Malaya: Lim always denied membership, and even Ramakrishna's book, the most hostile account to make extensive use of archival evidence, is at best inconclusive.[1] Yet the story continues to be repeated. In Prime Minister Lee Hsien Loong's Facebook posting regarding revisionist history in December 2014, Lee repeated, with no new evidence, that 'Lim Chin Siong was a Communist, and the Barisan Sosialis was Communist controlled', and made the surprising assertion, contradicting all available evidence, that recently declassified British documents left no 'doubt that the Barisan was formed at the instigation of the CPM [Communist Party of Malaya], and that Lim Chin Siong was a Communist cadre.' The impulse here seems to be very much similar to the accusations of Communist Party membership thrown at Nelson Mandela and Kwame Nkrumah during the Cold War: if one is a Communist, one serves another master, and cannot be a genuine patriot. As Chua Beng Huat noted, this results in the paradox that Singapore is now one of the very few countries where Communism is still alive: it continues to receive obsessive attention, since it has a constitutive role in a national narrative.

To counteract this narrative, one natural tendency has been to write alternative histories in which Lim becomes the hero, and Lee the villain. Some of the narratives in *Comet in Our Sky* perform this function, putting Lim forward as a figure who 'flashed brilliantly across the Singapore sky like a meteor, bringing hope … to a people coming out of the intellectual darkness of colonialism' (Rajakumar 112), or as a hero whose example might counterbalance the 'current credo' of 'youthful cynicism' and 'political apathy' in Singapore (Tan 'Lim Chin' 91). Such new biographies are important as testimony to different histories, and yet they parallel the dominant narrative in the way that they smooth out the wrinkles of history. Indeed, the most interesting accounts of Lim are often not those that actively seek to restore him to his place in history, but those in which he is an incidental figure, seen from an oblique angle. Tan Jing Quee's 'Lim Chin Siong—A Political Life' presents Lim in a heroic mode, yet Tan's more reflective account of his own political awakening and detention, published a decade later, reveals a much more human side of

Lim, seeing facets of his life such as his mental illness as something more than simply a disintegration of self under intolerable pressure ('I Won Them' 295, 303–04).

Registering Lim as a complex historical figure removes him from the binarisms in which his life has been trapped. Indeed, in Lee's own narrative of self-discovery in *The Singapore Story*, Lim occupies an ambiguous position, serving both as other and a secret, subterranean self. Archival evidence suggests that Lee saw his relationship with Lim in uniquely personalised terms. Selkirk records himself warning Lee against his obsession with Lim, and Lee offered Lim, uniquely of all the detainees, the chance to leave Singapore with 'passage to any country' rather than be detained: Lim, predictably, refused (United Kingdom 'Telegram'). In Lee's autobiography, indeed, there's a revealing moment about Lim. Lee describes Lim accompanying him to the constitutional talks in London in 1956, and being impressed by his 'modest, humble' demeanour. In a sudden switch of focalisation, Lee sees himself though Lim's eyes: 'He probably did not know what to make of me. I was a golf-playing, beer-swilling bourgeois, but he must also have sensed that I was not without a serious purpose' (*Singapore Story* 233). Lee's imagined relationship to Lim is, then, the moment when the personal condenses into the political. In Lee's writing and his speeches of the 1960s, English-educated Chinese Singaporeans are often castigated as effete, mentally colonised, decorative 'angelfish, ... black mollies, ... [and] red carps' in a domestic aquarium in contrast to disciplined, self-assured Chinese-educated citizens, described as 'tigerfish, piranhas—man-eating type of fish' ('University Autonomy' 589). Lim's imagined approving glance at Lee cuts through the accoutrements of a body debilitated by colonialism to a 'serious' self, just as Lee himself would later attempt to discipline a society through a rejection of the trappings of the West, and through a life-long struggle to learn Mandarin, to make his own personal reconnection to what he identified as cultural roots.

How might we move beyond seeing these two figures in opposition to each other, and instead use Lim's life, and the question of Coldstore, as a basis for other forms of reflection? One answer is given by a series of literary texts written in Singapore that have attempted to make use of the figure of Lim, and yet have also abstracted him from a narrative context. A recent example was *Public Enemy*, a version of Henrik Ibsen's *An Enemy of the People* adapted by David Harrower, directed by Glen Goei, and staged by Singaporean company WILD R!CE in April 2015, after Lee's death and before the upcoming SG50 Celebrations in August. A few changes in the script relocated the play to Singapore, with Dr Thomas Stockmann renamed Dr Thomas Chee, a transparent reference to opposition leader Dr Chee Soon Juan. Yet the play did not simply celebrate an individual bearing witness to truth in opposition to a hostile and censorious state. Through illustrating Thomas Chee's own flawed character, his self-dramatising vanguardism and need for public approval, it also asked the audience to reflect on the way in which publics alternately condemn and then celebrate those who stand in opposition to power. The programme that accompanied the play featured a two-page spread that foregrounded other 'public enemies', including Salman Rushdie, Julian Assange, and Singapore blogger Roy Ngerng. Prominent among the list of individuals whose ideas had 'earned them widespread scorn and reprobation—sometimes for good reason' was Lim Chin Siong.

The reference to Lim thus invited the audience to stand outside their own received narratives, whether celebratory or condemnatory. Such a gesture is made more strongly in other forms of art where narrative is temporarily suspended, or stops. Consider, for example, the poem 'On History' by Teng Qian Xi, one of an important new generation of Singapore poets who emerged in the early years of this century:

> A radiant young man opens his hands and releases a dove. Someone has draped a garland round his neck; the weight is reassuring, like a comrade's arm. The bird is a little flustered by its freedom, swooping in unsteady arches before it soars into the sky and alights onto a branch. The young man doesn't have the time to contemplate its flight .... Things are happening so fast in his country that they drown out the white thrashing of wings. This only resurfaces years later, after more pain and prison pushes him off his country and the flashing political days end for good. In his London exile .... he thinks of another man, the long-faced one with a Cambridge accent and tiny eyes. The one they called visionary because he spent his whole life forcing gold gloves on the 'digits' he ruled so they would not clench into fists. Now he hears that the government has decided to put public money into bird-feed, giving them so much to eat that they no longer sing at twilight or move their fattened wings. (17)

The moment celebrated here is on 4 June 1959 when Lim and other political prisoners were released from Changi jail, after the PAP won the first election under the provisions of full internal self-government. Lee is referenced here as the 'long-faced' man 'with a Cambridge accent and tiny eyes'; Lim's 'radiant' example contrasts to a future Singapore in which all poetry and idealism has been submerged under the comforting dullness of capital. And yet the poem does not simply oppose Lee and Lim. In that moment of release, it focuses not so much on Lim himself, but on the dove, and the 'white thrashing of wings' of a bird that is the symbol of, but not an agent in, a wider narrative.

Teng's poem thus asks us to think more deeply about the iconography that surrounds Lim. Lim represents two things for a younger generation of Singaporeans that Lee does not. The first is youth. Lim lived on, of course, for more than 30 years after Coldstore, but he did so in obscurity. In collective memory, he is always young. Lee, in contrast, visibly aged, and most Singaporeans remember him primarily as he was in his later years. The second is the moments with which both men are irrevocably associated. With Lim, it is that moment of arrival: 1959, self-rule, when the prison doors opened, the moment that Teng celebrates in her poem. Lee is inseparably attached to the moment of anguish, and his tears during a press conference held when Singapore achieved independence through its reluctant and unforeseen exit from Malaysia in 1965. The image of youth and the moment of arrival do not so much provide the basis for a new Singapore story, but they pull us back from a habitual way of seeing the world. They remind us of the complexity of the developmental narrative in which Lim and Lee both participated, and, above all, of elements of utopianism now submerged under a pragmatic acceptance of the common sense of neoliberalism.

Teng's poem also reminds us of the power of the image, of how frequently accounts of Lim condense into the unforgettable image the moment of release: of a young man, garlanded, supremely happy (Figure 1). In thinking of what the iconography surrounding Lim represents, then, we might turn away from the proposal to write new histories and new Singapore stories to something else. Teng's poem, indeed, reprises something in common with many representations of Lim, including those in Sonny Liew's recent celebrated graphic novel, *The Art of Charlie Chan Hock Chye*: a focus on an image, temporarily extracted from the historical narrative of which it is part. And this, in turn, might lead us to reflect more intensely on the relationship of the documentary photograph to history.[2]

**Figure 1.** Lim Chin Siong garlanded on his release from Changi Prison, 4 June 1959. Source: Private Collection. Photographer Unknown.[3]

Over the past half-century or more, scholars in cultural studies have addressed a paradox of photography. Photographs are referential: they stand for their subject, which in turn is enmeshed within a system of cultural codes. At the same time, the act of taking a photograph abstracts the subject from the narrative of progression of time, producing an estrangement from its context. André Bazin writes of photographs in family albums, in contrast to earlier portraiture, as 'no longer traditional family portraits but rather the disturbing presence of lives halted at a set moment in their duration, freed from their destiny' (8). If every photographic image appears to simply represent an object, Bazin notes, every object that the camera's shutter opens and then closes to becomes an image abstracted from a narrative and cultural context that gives it meaning. Thus, paradoxically, each act of photographing 'produces an image that is a reality of nature, namely, an hallucination that is also a fact' (9). Bazin's paradox of a material hallucination is taken up in Roland Barthes' famous distinction between the *studium* and the *punctum*, between the 'field of cultural interest' (94) in which the photograph is embedded, and a 'detail' that resists coding, that disturbs because its significance cannot be precisely named (51). In subsequent discussion, Barthes remarks on a particular *punctum* possessed by documentary photographs: their 'defeat of Time', as exemplified in an Alexander Gardner photograph of a criminal waiting to be hanged in his cell. The young man in the photograph is alive, Barthes notes, and yet of course historically already dead: in the photograph viewers thus experience a 'vertigo of time defeated' (97) even as they apprehend the *studium,* the historical significance of the scene itself. Jacques Rancière, a generation later, is dismissive of the manner in which Barthes celebrates the *punctum* as a form of presence that poststructuralism should properly reject. For Rancière, Barthes' apparent escape from signifying systems through the presence of the *punctum* is an attempt 'to expiate the sin of the former mythologist' who had in his earlier work made the world into 'a great web of symptoms and a seedy exchange of signs' (10). Yet despite their philosophical differences Rancière, in his own analysis, also turns to the duality of the photographic image. It is, he writes, in a formulation that echoes both Bazin and Barthes, 'simultaneously or separately, two things: the legible testimony of history written on faces or objects and pure blocs of visibility, impervious to any narrativization, any intersection of meaning' (11).

Rancière's phrase 'simultaneously or separately' gives us an insight into how to approach the iconography that surrounds Lim. The use of photographic plates in political biography in Singapore and elsewhere emphasises the *studium,* or Rancière's 'legible testimony of history'. Photographs corroborate and illustrate a historical narrative elaborated in the accompanying text: readers experience pleasure in recognising in images moments from a narrative that they already know or are coming to know. Such images add to the narrative's verisimilitude, not only by illustrating actors in the story, but also in the plenitude of incidental detail they offer: clothing, faces in crowds, or the facades of familiar buildings. Lee himself uses such a technique in *The Singapore Story*, in which photographs are scattered throughout the text. And this use of images extends beyond biographical texts into public acts of commemoration. When others and I queued at Parliament House to pay our respects to Lee in the early hours of the morning after his lying-in-state was announced, we found that large screens had been placed by the security checkpoint area we all had to pass through. Lee's speeches were played, but the audio was lost in the hubbub: what remained were the images on the screens, images that took us chronologically through the life. These abstracted moments from the life served, Virginia Woolf once wrote of the realist novel, as 'a series of gig lamps symmetrically arranged', illuminating the nation's past and then stretching ahead in a linear fashion into the darkness of the future (189). And to return to the text of Lee's autobiography, what we notice is a conscious attempt to catch up Lim in the same national developmental narrative, to place photographs of him within the *studium*.

Consider, for instance, the photograph in Figure 2, taken in June 1959, just after the PAP's election victory and Lim's release from prison. In Lee's autobiography, it is captioned as 'Lim Chin Siong (seated) and Fong Swee Suan at PAP headquarters, releasing their declaration to the press soon after they were freed on 4 June 1959, (Figure 2). The declaration referred to was a document that the detainees had drafted committing themselves to 'a united, independent, democratic and non-communist and socialist Malaya'

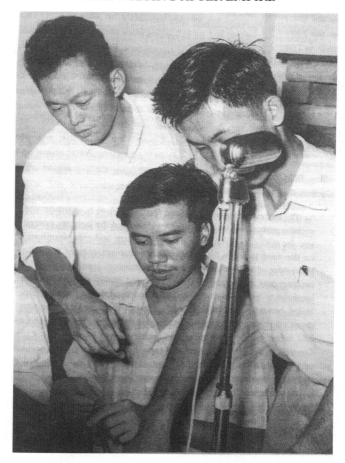

**Figure 2.** Lee Kuan Yew, Lim Chin Siong (seated), and Fong Swee Suan at PAP headquarters, 4 June 1959.
Source: *The Straits Times* © Singapore Press Holdings Limited. Permission required for reproduction.

(Lee, *The Singapore Story* 310). Lim and Lee agree in their recollections that the declaration was devised by fellow detainee C. Devan Nair on Lee's prompting, and that Lim was reluctant to sign (Lee, *The Singapore Story* 290–1; Lim qtd. in Chew 118; Nair qtd. in Chew 107–8). They differ in the reasons for Lim's reluctance: Lee sees it as a calculated move lacking in sincerity (291, 312), while Lim maintains he was reluctant on a matter of principle, his impression being that all 'political detainees had to sign a statement pledging support to the PAP leadership' as a condition of release (118). The captioning of the photograph confirms Lee as superintending a historical narrative. Yet when the photograph was originally published, in the *Straits Times* on 5 June 1959, the caption was very different: 'The Prime Minister-designate Mr. Lee Kuan Yew and a party member held Mr. Lim Chin Siong (seated) to untangle the wires of a microphone at PAP headquarters in South Bridge Road yesterday' ('At PAP HQ'). Here the caption is less retrospective: it explains the physical arrangement of the figures, but not their larger motives in a narrative.

What literary and visual texts that abstract images from narrative can do, perhaps, is to focus on a *punctum*, and to place the *studium* temporarily in abeyance. What is interesting about Teng's poem is its persistent focus on the moment. It gives a history of consequences, of what happened afterwards, but in its concluding metaphor it infects the present with a memory, transforms the quotidian of the present into a negative of the image from the past. The images that we know of Lee are inescapably embedded in a historical narrative: we will always remember that moment of anguish. And yet Lee's own narrative of the Singapore Story, as the popular response to his passing indicates, also possesses a redemptive quality: a possibility, however briefly glimpsed, of a life beyond an individual surrender to neoliberalism's market. Lim's image offers more: a moment of arrival to which we can endlessly return, and a continual means of critique of the present.

If there is a wider significance in this remembrance of a particular moment of decolonisation beyond Singapore, it is perhaps found in the *punctum* of Lim's image. If the time of decolonisation has now receded, it echoes in a more mundane activity: the periodic elections held under the aegis of democracy worldwide, with their concomitant, if always circumscribed, hopes for change. It is difficult now to construct alternative narratives of what the world might be, and too easy, and too unreflexive, to indulge in Fanonian fantasies of what might have been. Lim himself, like Lee, grew old. But Lim's backward glance at that moment provides the possibility of an interruption of storytelling, a defamiliarisation of the common sense of the present, and with it the possibility of imagining other futures.

## Notes

1. Ramakrishna ultimately rests his case on a statement that Lim 'had finally admitted his CPM ties' in a 1982 Internal Security Department interview (120). Yet 'ties' are not membership, and the excerpts of Lim's testimony from this and subsequent interviews that Ramakrishna quotes fail to show a persistent direct connection between Lim and the CPM.
2. Liew's graphic novel came to public attention in Singapore in May 2015, when its Arts Council publishing grant was withdrawn for alleged sensitive political content. The novel is a fictional biography of a Singapore comic artist, but two of is central characters are Lee Kuan Yew and Lim Chin Siong: it is the visual elements of the text that perhaps enable the most radical historiographic questioning.
3. We have made every effort to locate the copyright holder of the photograph. Anyone with such information is encouraged to contact the author.

## References

"Amos Yee charged with 3 offences against Mr Lee Kuan Yew and Christianity." *Asia One* 31 Mar. 2015. Web. 15 Apr. 2015.

"At PAP HQ: Mr. Lee meets Mr. Lim." *Straits Times* 5 June 1959: 4. Print.

Barthes, Roland. *Camera Lucida*. Trans. Richard Howard. New York: Hill, 1981. Print.

Ball, S. J. "Selkirk in Singapore." *Twentieth Century British History* 10.2 (1999): 162–91. Web. 11 Mar. 2015.

Bazin, André. "The Ontology of the Photographic Image." *Film Quarterly* 13.4 (1960): 4–9. JSTOR. Web. 19 Apr. 2015.

Bloodworth, Dennis. *The Tiger and the Trojan Horse*. Singapore: Times, 1986. Print.

Chew, Melanie. *Leaders of Singapore*. Singapore: Resource, 1996. Print.

Chua, Beng Huat. "The Banning of a Film." *Living With Myths VII: Discipline and Proscribe*. Muse House, 22 Marshall Road, Singapore. 14 Feb. 2015. Panel Presentation.

Drysdale, John. *Singapore: Struggle for Success*. Singapore: Times, 1984. Print.

Gafoor, Burham. "Response to Poh Soo Kai's Allegations." *New Mandala*. Australian National U, 18 Dec. 2014. Web. 18 Apr. 2015.

George, Cherian. *Freedom from the Press: Journalism and State Power in Singapore*. Singapore: NUS P, 2012. Print.

Holden, Philip. *Autobiography and Decolonization: Modernity, Masculinity, and the Nation-State*. Madison: U of Wisconsin P, 2008. Print.

Hong, Lysa. "They do say the darnest things: What a to-do about Operation Coldstore." *mini myna: on knowing the past in Singapore*. 29 Sep. 2014. Web. 18 Jan. 2016.

Jones, Matthew. "Creating Malaysia: Singapore Security, the Borneo Territories, and the Contours of British Policy, 1961–63." *The Journal of Imperial and Commonwealth History* 28:2 (2000): 85–109. Web. 8 Mar. 2015.

Lee Hsien Loong. "I Visited the Battle for Merger Exhibition in October ... " *Facebook.com*. 20 Dec. 2015. Web. 6 Feb. 2016. <https://www.facebook.com/leehsienloong/photos/a.344710778924968.83425.125845680811480/823863401009701/>

Lee, Kok Liang. "It"s All in a Dream." *Tumasek* 2 (1964): 6–17. Print.

Lee, Kuan Yew. "University Autonomy, Academic Freedom and Social Responsibility." Address at the Historical Society, University of Singapore, 24 Nov. 1966. *The Papers of Lee Kuan Yew: Speeches, Interviews and Dialogues*. Vol. 3: 1965–1966. Singapore: Gale Asia, 2012. 555–582. *Gale Virtual Reference Library*. Web. 21 Apr. 2015.

Lee, Kuan Yew. *The Singapore Story: Memoirs of Lee Kuan Yew*. Singapore: Times, 1998. Print.

Liew, Sonny. *The Art of Charlie Chan Hock Chye*. Singapore: Epigram, 2015. Print.

Nanda, Akshita. "Playwright Alfian Sa'at questions LKY Legacy." *Straits Times* 27 Mar. 2015: n. pag. Web. 28 Apr. 2015.

National Library Board, Singapore. "The Battle for Merger Exhibition." *GoLibrary*. n.d. Web. 19 Apr. 2015.

Poh, Soo Kai, Tan Kok Fang and Hong Lysa, eds. *The 1963 Operation Coldstore in Singapore: Commemorating 50 Years*. Petaling Jaya: Strategic Information and Research Development Centre, 2013. Print.

Ramakrishna, Kumar. *"Original Sin"? Revising the Revisionist Critique of the 1963 Operation Coldstore in Singapore*. Singapore: ISEAS, 2015. Print.

Rajakumar, M. K. "Lim Chin Siong's Place in History." *Comet in Our Sky: Lim Chin Siong in History*. Ed. Tan Jing Quee and Jomo K. S. Petaling Jaya: Insan, 2001. 98–113. Print.

Rancière, Jacques. *The Future of the Image*. Trans. Gregory Elliott. London: Verso, 2007. Print.

"Revisiting Operation Coldstore." *Straits Times* 11 Apr. 2015: n. pag. *Factiva*. Web. 20 Apr. 2015.

Tan, Jing Quee. "'I Won then Back One by One.'" *The 1963 Operation Coldstore in Singapore: Commemorating 50 Years*. Eds. Poh Soo Kai, Tan Kok Fang, and Hong Lysa. Singapore: ISEAS, 2015. 267–310. Print.

Tan, Jing Quee. "Lim Chin Siong: A Political Life." *Comet in Our Sky: Lim Chin Siong in History*. Ed. Tan Jing Quee and Jomo K. S. Petaling Jaya: Insan, 2001. 56–97. Print.

Turnbull, C. M. *A History of Modern Singapore, 1819–2005*. Singapore: NUS P, 2009. Print

Teng, Qian Xi. *They Hear Salt Crystallising*. Singapore: firstfruits, 2010. Print

United Kingdom. Colonial Office Information Department. *Internal Security Measures in Singapore*. 2 Feb. 1963. TS. The National Archives of the UK (TNA): CO 1030/1573, no. 5.

United Kingdom. *Telegram Singapore (Selkirk) to Secretary of State (Sandys)*. 1 Feb. 1963. TS. The National Archives of the UK (TNA): CO 1030/1577, no. 96.

Wee, Wan-ling, C. J. "The Vanquished: Lim Chin Siong and a Progressivist National Narrative." *Lee's Lieutenants: Singapore's Old Guard*. Ed. Lam Peng Er and Kevin Y. L. Tan. St Leonards: Allen, 1999. 169–190. Print.

Woolf, Virginia. *The Common Reader*. London: Hogarth, 1951. Print.

"Workers' Party Secretary-General Low Thia Khiang ... " *Facebook.com*. 26 Mar. 2015. Web. Apr. 28, 2015. <https://www.facebook.com/todayonline/photos/a.10150128555382572.286750.147858757571/10152826185637572/>

Zakir, Hussein. "Operation Coldstore: the Evidence is Clear, Says P.M." *Straits Times* 21 Dec. 2014: n. pag. *Factiva*. Web. 20 Apr. 2015.

# 'National Awakening', Autobiography, and the Invention of Manning Clark

Mark McKenna

Department of History, Sydney University, Sydney, Australia

**ABSTRACT**
In the late twentieth century, Australian historian Manning Clark (1915–1991) was the nation's leading historian and public intellectual. Clark published a six-volume history of Australia (1962–1987) and was one of a vanguard of intellectuals striving to articulate a new Australian nationalism in the wake of the British Empire's decline. His best-known volumes of autobiography were published in quick succession. *Puzzles of Childhood* (1989), which tells the story of his parents' lives and the 'nightmares and terrors' of his childhood, and *Quest for Grace* (1990), which begins from his days as a student at Melbourne and Oxford universities in the 1930s and ends just as the first volume of *A History of Australia* is published in 1962. In addition to these two volumes, Clark's autobiographical writings extended to reflections on historical writing, essays, speeches and interviews. This paper argues that all of Clark's writing (including his histories) can be seen as inherently autobiographical. As Clark remarked, 'everything one writes is a fragment in a gigantic confession of life'. Clark's autobiographical writings point not only to the notorious unreliability of autobiography but also to much larger questions, such as the relationship between autobiographical truth and his invention as a national figure, and the author's right to own their life story. Finally, perhaps more than any other Australian intellectual of his generation, Clark's autobiographies narrate his life story as an allegory of national awakening.

*Perhaps this is the worst deceiver of all—we make up our pasts.*

Doris Lessing

By any measure, Manning Clark (1915–1991) is Australia's most well-known and controversial historian. Born only seven weeks before Australian soldiers landed at Anzac Cove on 25 April 1915, Clark's intellectual life was framed by the great ideological struggle of the twentieth century, which began with the Russian Revolution in 1917 and ended with the fall of the Berlin Wall in 1989. By the time of his death on 23 May 1991, he had also witnessed the slow yet inexorable decline of the British connection in Australia.

As Professor of Australian History at the Australian National University (ANU) in Canberra, Clark produced an exceptional volume of work over a period of 40 years; three volumes of historical documents (the bedrock of university courses in Australian history for more than two decades), *A Short History of Australia* (which was translated into several European and Asian languages and sold widely overseas), an extremely controversial short book on his visit to the Soviet Union in the late 50s—*Meeting Soviet Man*—another on the writer Henry Lawson, the ABC Boyer Lectures in 1976, a collection of essays, two volumes of short stories, hundreds of articles, reviews, newspaper op-eds and two volumes of autobiography. Five further volumes of speeches, letters, history and autobiographical writings were published posthumously. From 1938, the time of his scholarship to Oxford at age 23 until his death in 1991, Clark also kept personal diaries, documenting his inner life often with fierce and uncompromising honesty, as well as tracking the personal lives of many of his friends and colleagues in sometimes brutal fashion, all of it in his barely-legible ink scrawl, a script once compared to 'micro barbed-wire'. In addition, he kept copious notebooks over the same period mapping his reading and the conceptual development of his work. Taken together, this output, most of it completed while he was still teaching, easily exceeded that of many of his contemporaries. And yet remarkably the above list of publications excludes the work for which he is best known, his six-volume *A History of Australia*, published between 1962 and 1987. Clark's six volumes comprised well over one million words and their extraordinary popularity kept Melbourne University Press afloat for over two decades (selling an average of 40,000 copies per volume).

In media interviews, Clark's personal story of the creation of the six volumes became part of his success, as if the nation were waiting for the next instalment in the story of its own creation. In the 1970s and 1980s, he was interviewed both after each volume was published and when he had completed successive drafts. Clark's ability to dramatise the writing process usually involved a disarming cocktail of self-deprecation and special pleading, particularly in the 1980s ('I haven't done everyone justice and I regret that I did not have more ability [ ... ] I know I've made a lot of mistakes [ ... ] I don't want to sound too pompous. I've got a reputation for being a bit of a bullshit artist') (Brass). Clark created the illusion that his readers were buying both *A History of Australia* and a latter-day version of Rousseau's *The Confessions*, a deeply personal impression of the past and life itself. He frequently referred to his historical writing as the 'child of his heart.' For Clark, there was no distance between the historian and the past he inhabited.

In the public eye, from his retirement in the early 1970s until his death in 1991, Clark wore his trademark dress—the slightly tattered, black three-piece suit, the watch chain dangling from the fob pocket, the long, thin legs anchored in paddock-bashing boots and the grave, goatee-bearded face of the old man crowned by a crumpled, weather-beaten Akubra. Across Australia, he was renowned as a historical oracle. At the height of his fame in the 1970s and 1980s, he was awarded a Companion of the Order of Australia (1975), named Australian of the Year (1981) and won almost every major Australian literary award. In 1988, the year of Australia's Bicentenary, Clark (and his hat) seemed to be everywhere. He was the frequent subject of cartoonists' caricatures; he penned major critical essays interpreting the historical significance of the Bicentenary for magazines such as *The Bulletin* and *Time Australia* and was easily the nation's most prominent public intellectual. In his last years, after his retirement from teaching, Clark addressed Australia Day events and citizenship ceremonies, launched books, opened art exhibitions, fêtes, music festivals, opera and theatre productions, endorsed rock bands, spoke at school speech nights, ALP campaign rallies and church services.

## LIFE WRITING AFTER EMPIRE

To understand the many causes he fought for from the 1960s to the 1990s is to understand how instrumental his public life was in changing the face of Australia in the twentieth century. Almost two decades before the White Australia policy was dismantled, Clark called for an end to the prejudice and inhumanity inherent in racial discrimination. He opposed the Vietnam War, condemned the proliferation of nuclear weapons, supported the land rights and treaty demands of Indigenous Australians, championed the arts and the importance of teaching Australian history in schools and universities, campaigned to save the Great Barrier Reef, Fraser Island and the Franklin River, spoke against the logging of old-growth forests, lent his name to numerous petitions to save significant historical sites, backed heritage legislation, protested against the Soviet Union's incarceration of Alexander Solzhenitsyn and the repression of the Solidarity movement in Poland, enthusiastically embraced multi-cultural Australia, personally encouraged generations of writers and artists, and worked to challenge long-standing stereotypes of Australia abroad, especially in the United Kingdom. In the last two decades of his life, Clark appeared in every possible media site, including midday television, house and garden programmes, and even managed a cameo role as the preacher in the 1985 film production of the Peter Carey novel, *Bliss*. In all of these appearances and writings, Clark deftly cast his public interventions through the lens of his personal experience. The public telling of autobiographical stories—the modus operandi of the public intellectual—became the means through which Clark established a popular audience and created himself as a national prophet.

In the seven years I spent working on Clark's biography between 2004 and 2011, I never doubted the importance of what I was doing (McKenna). To be sure, I experienced many moments of exasperation and exhaustion. To come close to Clark, to know him intimately, and at the same time to keep my distance was always a struggle. This is the biographer's dilemma: to resolve the tension between closeness and distance, to know and reveal the subject without becoming the subject's ventriloquist. Gradually, I realised that there was something that transcended even the weight of Clark's scholarship and the substantial impact of his public life. On a human level alone—as child, adolescent, lover, friend and father—his life was lived and remembered with such an acute theatrical sensibility that it spoke to readers regardless of their gender, cultural background or nationality. Clark's life contained contradictions numerous and large enough for all of us to recognise shards of our own experience. It was both Australian and universal. But it was also a life given over to public examination in a way that few of us would dare contemplate, one burdened by extreme self-consciousness and a pathological desire to be remembered as a great man. Much of Clark's archival legacy—his anguished diaries, his voluminous correspondence with others (including more than 50 years of letters to his wife Dymphna), his eulogies for departed friends and his irrepressible ministering of others at times of personal crisis—was, as Ken Inglis shrewdly remarked in 1991, more about 'self than subject' (Inglis). Nearly everything Clark wrote and said was self-referential. Narrating the lives of others became a way of seeding the autobiography of C. M. H. Clark in the Australian imagination.

One of the greatest challenges I encountered in writing Clark's biography was not only the question of how to deal with the work of previous biographers such as Brian Matthews and Stephen Holt, but also the far more pressing problem of how to deal with Clark's *autobiographical* writings (Holt, *Manning Clark and Australian History* and *A Short History*;

Matthews). My intention was to write Clark's life as it was *lived*, not as he remembered it. Yet this proved tremendously difficult because he had stamped so much of his own memory on the public image of his life. To write Clark's biography, I had to somehow wrest control of the life from the extremely controlling voice of my subject. Perhaps the most graphic example of this was Clark's tendency to leave directional notes to his biographers throughout his papers. But the sheer volume of his autobiographical writings exacerbated the struggle for biographical distance. To avoid paraphrasing Clark's various accounts of his life and merely accepting his version of events, I had to disarm his autobiographical voice and test his interpretations and recollections against the perspectives of others.

Clark's best-known volumes of autobiography were published in quick succession in 1989 and 1990. First, *The Puzzles of Childhood*, which tells the story of his parents' lives and the 'nightmares and terrors' of his childhood, and then *The Quest for Grace*, which picks up the story from his days as a student at Melbourne University and Oxford in the 1930s and ends just before the first volume of *A History of Australia* is published in 1962. In addition to these two volumes, Clark's autobiographical writings extended to reflections on historical writing (*A Historian's Apprenticeship*), essays, speeches and interviews. In fact, it's perfectly reasonable to include Clark's histories in the same category. For as Clark remarked: 'everything one writes is a fragment in a gigantic confession of life' (*Speaking Out of Turn* 79). He saw all of his writing as inherently autobiographical.

Both as historian and public intellectual, Clark helped to destroy the belief that Australian history was merely a dull, insignificant appendage to British imperial history. Leading much of the post-sixties' public debate around 'new nationalism', he transformed popular understandings of Australian history, an achievement that will undoubtedly prove to be his most lasting contribution. The origins of Clark's *A History of Australia* can be found in the profound schism between the established pastoral background of his pious, Protestant mother (a direct descendant of the Reverend Samuel Marsden) and the working class larrikinism of his Anglo-Catholic father of part-Irish descent, a division which Clark dramatized at every opportunity, portraying the religious and class divisions of Australia as those of his family writ large. More than any other writer of his generation, Clark succeeded in aligning the trajectory of his own life with a larger narrative of national awakening.

His histories were *autobiographical* not only because he infused the past with his own experience but also because he often invented the thoughts and emotions of historical characters. As they rise from their graves and perform their soliloquies, they appear as thinly veiled shadows of their author's alter ego: they are 'tormented' by doubt and guilt, led on by some 'madness of the heart,' and inevitably brought down by their 'fatal flaw.' Women appear in *A History of Australia* in much the same vein as Dymphna Clark appears in the pages of his diary. They are either the temptress or the punisher, more often the latter; women with a sharp, vindictive streak who undermine men's idealism and fail to understand the enormity of their husband's creative genius. In the pages of Clark's history, potted autobiographies rain down one after another, almost as if Clark were conducting an oratorio. In this light, it seems entirely appropriate that *A History of Australia* was made into a musical in 1988 (*Manning Clark's History of Australia: the Musical*). Clark's grand narrative—with its now familiar but at the time quite revolutionary schema of seeing Australia's past through the prism of three great belief systems—Protestantism, Catholicism, and the Enlightenment, lurches from the inspired to the droll, finding tragedy, pathos and existential crisis on every stump and street corner. Part Gibbon, part Macaulay, part Carlyle, and steeped in the language of the Old Testament, it is entirely character driven, mostly a succession of flawed, tormented males, who walk on stage at the allotted time to play out the drama of their biographical roles. At regular intervals, the ghosts of Dostoevsky, Tolstoy, Chekhov and Henry James emerge from behind the arras to provide a guiding aphorism or two. Both in everyday speech, and in the persona of the writer, Clark spoke through the voices of the canon, peppering his language with literary and biblical quotations; Dostoyevsky, Tolstoy and the Book of Ecclesiastes were among his favourite sources of inspiration.

Clark was probably the first historian in Australia to write at length about the inner life of his characters (sketches which frequently mirrored his emotional state at the time of writing). Much of the emotion in his work is grounded in an acute religiosity, the parson's son ministering the souls of Australia's flawed men—Wentworth, Lawson, Burke and Wills, John Curtin and Manning Clark. His feeling was not only for his characters, it was also for place. Until Clark's six volumes, historical melancholy was something Australians imagined resided only in the layered, built environment of Europe. Like Sidney Nolan, Patrick White and Arthur Boyd, Clark found this melancholy in the land itself, a melancholy not only of exile but one born of an awareness of the continent's antiquity and the horror of the violent dispossession of indigenous people, a dispossession which is not so much documented in his work, but rather recurs as an underlying tragic refrain. *A History of Australia* succeeded in attracting a large popular readership because of its narrative flair and Clark's mercurial ability to convince his audience that the story of his own life was a unique window onto Australian history.

A handful of critics and reviewers noted the autobiographical dimension of Clark's history. John Rickard was particularly astute on the way in which Clark increasingly relied on personal experience as the volumes progressed: 'the project which began as history,' Rickard observed, 'has become autobiography' (Rickard). Ken Inglis thought fellow-historians Bede Nairn and Allan Martin were both concerned that Clark had moved from history to fiction and autobiography, with each volume hanging on an encounter between an Anglophile villain (prime ministers Alfred Deakin and Robert Menzies) and an Australian tragic hero (writer Henry Lawson and prime minister John Curtin) (Inglis). Richard White was another who observed that in the last volumes 'history and memory had come too close' (White). Reviewing Volume V in 1981, Edmund Campion noted that the woman seen crying out at the railway station at the end of the book was actually Clark's mother. He drew attention to the way in which Clark introduced his personal memories of Anzac Day in the 1920s and 30s into the history, just as he did with his memories of songs, radio advertisements and the Bodyline cricket series. 'This personal note is something new in our historians,' reflected Campion. 'Indeed, it is so noticeable in Manning Clark that when I first read Volume Six I thought of suggesting to Melbourne University Press that they reject it as his autobiography' (Campion).

Perhaps the first question regarding Manning Clark's volumes of autobiography (and all autobiography for that matter) is why he decided to write? To defend oneself *against* biographers (as Doris Lessing described her motive for writing autobiography); to claim one's life *before* the 'ferrets' (as Kate Grenville described biographers when donating her papers to the National Library of Australia) usurp and misrepresent it, to 'set the record straight', as so many politicians claim is the starting point for their memoirs, or as former Labor minister Barry Jones reflected when writing his autobiography *A Thinking Reed*, 'to explain my life to myself' (1), to subject oneself to gruelling self-examination and at the same time give an existing audience a more personal insight into the object of their admiration. The very term autobiography suggests that the decision to write is self-generated. I am a significant someone, therefore I am an autobiographer. Few autobiographers find themselves at their writing desk because they want to test or reconstitute the boundaries of the genre itself. Historical context, celebrity marketing and the vagaries of the publishing industry are usually far more important determinants in the shaping and publishing of autobiography.

Clark's autobiographies, written towards the end of his life when he was already a well-known figure, were prompted initially not by the urgent need for self-examination about which he spoke so frequently in public, but much more practically by the suggestion of former Labor Senator Susan Ryan, who in the late 1980s worked as an editor for Penguin after leaving politics. Ryan wrote to Clark and asked him if he would consider writing his autobiography (Rutherford). Both volumes of Clark's autobiography were therefore the direct result of his publisher's initiative. Clark received $5000 advance from Penguin to write *Puzzles of Childhood*. Ryan, who had witnessed Clark's enormous public impact first-hand during her time in parliament recognised a commercial opportunity when she saw one. Within months of publication, her decision was vindicated. *Puzzles of Childhood* won national literary awards, climbed to number one in the list of best-selling non-fiction, while Qantas Airways purchased 500 copies to distribute to their passengers on long-haul flights. Although Clark claimed to fellow historian Humphrey McQueen that he was 'upset' by Penguin's marketing campaign for the book—'books should make their own mark without aids from P.R. promoters who probably have not read the book. Penguin makes me feel what I have to say is a commodity'—he appeared to revel in the opportunity to 'confess' his life story to the media (Clark qtd. in McQueen 7 July 1989).

The particular cultural and political context in which Clark's autobiographies were written did much to shape their voice and narrative. They were completed in the shadow of his failing health and the death of many of his closest friends ('my contemporaries, or more accurately, my near contemporaries all seem to be dying') (Clark qtd. in McQueen, 15 Aug. 1988). These were the years that followed the constitutional crisis that had divided Australian society so deeply in 1975, when Governor-General Sir John Kerr dismissed Labor PM Gough Whitlam from office. As one of the leading intellectuals of the Labor Left, Clark was at the forefront of the campaign that condemned Kerr and the conservative parties and demanded a republican constitution. These were also the years of growing consumerism, increasing affluence and economic growth and rampant mining development. The tide of often vague, ill-directed nationalism that accompanied the demise of British Australia, which Clark had ridden so successfully, had helped to push Australian authors, artists and celebrities to the fore remarkably quickly. In Gough Whitlam's Australia, intellectuals were accorded a public platform and authority they had never claimed before. Publishers were keen to capitalise on this cultural awakening and the booming genre of autobiography was no exception. The emotive style of Clark's autobiographies proved an exception to James Walter's identification of 'the dominance in

Australian biography of an empiricist, positivist tradition—strictly chronological, favouring the public life over the private, description over analysis and the preservation of emotional distance—at least up until [the early 1980s]' (James Walter qtd. in Bennett 255). But in other respects his work was typical of broader literary and cultural trends. As Bruce Bennett noted as early as 1998, so many Australian autobiographies published in the late twentieth-century, particularly those by authors such as Patrick White, Donald Horne and Geoffrey Dutton, sought to trace a life as 'part of a national allegory' (Bennett 255; James Walter qtd. in Bennett 255). Clark's autobiographies were probably the prime example.

In *The Puzzles of Childhood*, Clark casts his first years in the harsh light of his latter-day celebrity status. Thus, from the moment of his birth, he is destined to become a national prophet. Early in the book we read his mother's words to the infant Manning: 'one day [you] will be a famous man' (*Puzzles* 48). Clark's mother's observation seems remarkably perceptive given that at this stage her son had not even begun to walk or talk. Other examples of remembering past experience through the imperatives of Clark's latter day status as a national prophet abound. In *Quest for Grace*, Clark continuously complains of the English condescension towards Australians that he experienced in Oxford. 'It made me very conscious of myself as an Australian.' Playing cricket for Oxford, he claimed that the English 'treated [him] as an outsider [ ... ] they didn't accept me as an ordinary human being and I've never forgotten it' (*Australian Playboy*). Yet in his diary during these years, there is very little if any evidence of these sentiments. He certainly remarks on his experience of English superiority, but the young Clark is painfully aware of what he perceives to be the far more cultured existence in England. He yearns to be accepted. In fact, his depiction of his experience in England in the late 1930s in *Quest for Grace* demonstrates how he has retrospectively coloured his memories through the prism of post-Dismissal Australia. A similar rewriting of the past can be observed in Clark's history.

The last three volumes of *A History of Australia*, all written in the wake of the Dismissal, give greater stress to Australian nationalism. The earlier schema of the grand contest between Catholicism, Protestantism and the Enlightenment falls away. In its place is the simplistic polarity of the Old Dead Tree (Britain) and the Young Tree Green (Australia). Clark's depiction of the Anglo-Australian relationship becomes increasingly crude. 'Colonials don't make their own history' he proclaims, 'decisions are made for them in London' (Mitchell 74–5). The Dismissal sharpened Clark's anti-British sentiments. As public intellectual, historian and autobiographer, he wrote both his life story and the nation's history in the image of late twentieth century nationalism. The purpose of Clark's life, as he told it, was to hammer the last nail in the coffin of British Australia. He appears to be born to oversee the end of Empire.

The opening page of *The Puzzles of Childhood* contains a story he first told in 1979. It is December 1919 and Clark is four years old. He is sitting in the backyard lawn of his home in the Sydney suburb Burwood. Looking up in the sky, he sees a mechanical bird soaring above. Curious, he asks his mother what it might be. She explains that the bird is the plane piloted by Keith and Ross Smith; they are on the last leg of their flight from London to Sydney. It is one of Clark's first memories; but like so many of his memories, the facts do not quite match the power of the story. In December 1919, Sir Keith and Ross Smith landed not in Sydney but in Darwin. Due to mechanical problems, their plane did not arrive in Sydney until three months later, on 14 February 1920. As the *Sydney Morning Herald* reported, it was not the first plane that Sydney-siders had set eyes on but 'the thrill came when one thought, as he gazed, this plane had come from England!'. Thousands of people stood on rooftops to catch a glimpse of the plane, which was escorted by three others as it approached the city from the south. The flight-path *did not* take the planes over Clark's home in Burwood, but over the city's northern suburbs. Even if Clark had the date wrong, he would have needed to be on his roof at Burwood, a four-year old boy with sure feet and a telescope, in order to see the Smiths' plane. Fund raising flights also took place in the weeks after the historic occasion— perhaps Clark had mistakenly remembered one of these flights. It is certainly possible that he did see a plane in the sky from his backyard in Burwood in February 1920, but the story as Clark tells it, this powerful opening image of his autobiography, is not about the young Clark, it is about the old Clark.

His apocryphal tale of an innocent child gazing up to the sky to see the arrival of the first flight from England to Australia is a memory tailor made for the grand man of history. His first memory is of a historically significant event. The giant bird in the sky —the portent of war waged from the air, of the coming age of technology and globalisation—brings with it the historical forces of modernity which will shape twentieth century Australia. Memory obediently serves the titanic public figure, lining up family stories and national history until they seem to be one and the same journey. Like so many of Clark's stories, their telling allowed him to be present in the past. He became the witness, already the historian at only four years of age. The final effect was to make the path he chose to follow appear as his inevitable destiny.

Twenty-five years after Clark's death, it is also possible to see that Clark's autobiographies rest on a pillar of falsehoods and half-truths. Perhaps it is commonplace to observe that autobiographies tell more lies than fiction. The late Günter Grass, no stranger to autobiographical fiction himself, reflected that in autobiography, 'the conventions of literary reminiscence and historical recollection are flawed.' Autobiographical truth, Grass insisted, 'all too easily gives way to the old literary lies. The past is elusive, memory plays tricks, the self of narrative is a stranger to the self who writes' (Brunskill). The fictive quality of autobiography has long been established, but Clark's autobiographical writings point not only to the notorious unreliability of autobiography, resting as it does on the paper-thin house of memory, but to much larger questions such as the relationship between autobiographical truth and celebrity status and the autobiographer's right to 'own' their life story. There is a wonderfully revealing moment in an ABC radio interview conducted after the publication of *The Puzzles of Childhood* in 1989. Interviewing Clark, ABC journalist Terry Lane was perplexed by his uncanny ability in the book to know precisely what his father and mother were thinking and feeling at any given point in time, not to mention his astonishing recall of the thoughts and emotions of his childhood self. 'But how can you possibly know these things?', Lane asked Clark incredulously. Slightly unnerved, Manning replied: 'Well Terry, it's my view of my life and my view can't be wrong.' Clark's deadpan response put a swift end to Lane's line of questioning (Lane). Yet it also raised a crucial question for biographers and readers: to what extent can the autobiographer's interpretation and recollection of his life be challenged? Can the biographer know his subject's life better than the subject knows himself? 'There is your life as you know it and also as others know it,' wrote James Salter in his memoir

*Burning the Days*, '[and] it is difficult to realise that you are observed from a number of points and that the sum of them has validity' (4). It was precisely this perspective that Clark rejected. He claimed sole authority to interpret his life. But the autobiographer's recollection of his life can indeed be shown to be wrong. Because so much of Clark's life was lived on the public record, and because he archived his diaries and correspondence so meticulously, it is possible to test many of the claims that he makes in his autobiographies. In fact, the issue of autobiographical truth is crucial in understanding Clark's role in late twentieth century Australia. As Salter further reflected when explaining his methods of recollection in his memoir,

> What I have done is to write about people and events that were important to me, and to be truthful though relying, in one place or another, on mere memory. *Your language is your country* Leautaud said, but memory is also, as well as being a measure, in its imprint, of the value of things. I suppose it could be just as convincingly argued that the opposite is true, that what one chooses to forget is equally revealing. (xi)

Clark concurred with Salter in so far as he relied on what Virginia Woolf described as 'moments of being'—recollections that were deeply inscribed in his memory precisely because of their self-revelatory nature (Woolf qtd. in Lee title page). He did not want to write an autobiography that resembled his impression of Kaplan's biography of Dickens, 'one of those American academic biographies which tells you what he had for breakfast but not what you want to know' (Clark qtd. in McQueen 30 Apr. 1989). If memory was to be employed then it was not an instrument of reference so much as an instrument of self-discovery (Beckett 29). Yet Clark also conspicuously failed to take account of the possibility that what he had misremembered, invented, exaggerated or repressed was potentially more revealing than all of the words set down in his autobiographies. 'What I was trying to do,' Clark explained, 'was to draw a picture of memory [ … ] a portrait of the inside of my head' (Craven). However, his claim to have relied mostly on memory in writing his autobiography is only partially true. Indeed the evidence in Clark's papers shows that he wrote his autobiographies in the same way that he wrote his history, as a series of character sketches interspersed with personal recollections, a performer improvising from primary sources and a mystic led through life by a series of epiphanies. Far from relying on memory alone, Clark carried out extensive research, especially for *The Puzzles of Childhood*. He wrote to various churches and historical societies seeking information on his parents' lives. He copied documents relating to his ancestors such as Samuel Marsden. He sourced newspaper articles and local histories to provide historical context. And he made an attempt to read reflections on autobiography by writers such as Michael Holroyd. Nor was he the only researcher. Dymphna carried out most of his research. The archives are full of copious notes in her handwriting. She corrected grammar and punctuation, she suggested rephrasing and she corrected dates, places and memories. As Clark's editor, some of her marginal comments are telling: 'did you or did you not know where you stood'? 'Was it at Port Jackson (not Botany Bay) that the Aborigines told the British to go away?' 'She needs to be identified—wife or flame?' 'she has been doing it off and on for 140 pages!' 'Do you think it tactful to talk about [your brother's] generosity to "those more gifted" [like yourself]? What about "to those with gifts different from his own" [ … ] Poor you, trapped in this terrible heart-dimming straitening institution, for all these years, pitiful, come on now!' After 50 years of marriage, Dymphna was clearly exasperated by the self-serving nature of Clark's recollections. For her, the lack of truthfulness in Clark's autobiographies undermined their claims to authenticity and their pretensions to literary greatness. For Clark, although he seemed to remain blissfully unaware of his tendency to self-aggrandise, he was nonetheless painfully conscious of his tendency to omit certain details and events in telling the story of his life (Clark Papers Box 173).

As he wrote both volumes of autobiography throughout the late 1980s, Clark frequently exhorted himself to tell the truth about his life. 'How to be truthful without exposing one's own swinishness', he wrote searchingly, and 'how to be honest without offending someone?' (Clark Papers Box 173). Despite his many promises to friends such as Humphrey McQueen that he would not recoil from writing an unvarnished account of his life ('Is the non-truth worth the paper on which it is written? I believe passionately we should all face the truth about ourselves'), the pages of his diary reveal his guilt and self-loathing because of his failure to do so (Clark qtd. in McQueen 28 July 1988). On 11th March 1988, as he was beginning to write *Puzzles of Childhood*, he wallowed in self-pity and disillusionment.

> Last night in bed had an attack of angina. I know my travelling and lecturing are killing me, but, maybe, that is what I want, the pain of living is now so intense. My wife is still taking revenge on me for my past iniquities. My closest friend, the one in whom I placed complete trust, has deserted me in my hour of need, the attacks on my work and character continue and will probably go on for a while after I am dead. I have lost faith in the autobiography. (Clark Diary 11 Mar. 1988)

By the time both volumes of autobiography were published in 1990, Clark was firmly convinced that he had failed the task of self-examination that he had set for himself.

> The two volumes of the autobiography suffer from my failure to address myself to three subjects which have caused me much pain and made me the instrument of pain to other people. They are—First—my infidelities to Dymphna, infidelities of the heart more than the body, and my failure to examine when and why they began. I remember in the beginning my fear of whether I could keep her individual love, or whether she ever loved me. Second, my corruption of other people [ ... ] my [name deleted] who became a drunk just as I was wiping the filth of the gutter off my body. I made a drunkard seem attractive to him [ ... ] Third, those volumes do not confess to another fatal flaw [ ... ] inwardly I go to pieces when criticised, can never speak again to the character sketchers or critics who list the errors in my work. I never forget and never forgive. I do not retaliate, I punish them with silence and do not speak to them again [ ... ] a curt nod, a blank face, a horrible face [ ... ] cutting them, avoiding them. I have not really tried to change, but I doubt whether I could change, that rush of blood to the head floods the rational me. I shake inwardly [ ... ] there has been no improvement except in surface courtesy. (Clark Diary 13 Mar. 1990)

These reflections scribbled hastily in Clark's diary appear far closer to the truth. They demonstrate a capacity for self-criticism that his autobiographies conspicuously lack. As did one particularly frank note that Clark left for his biographer in his papers. In a folder marked 'Illustrations' for *Quest for Grace*, there is a handwritten list in ink of the photographs and the order they appeared in the book. They are numbered with the captions from 1 to 10. Then, a line is drawn at the bottom of the list, in what appears to be fresher ink than the list above, almost certainly added at a later time, most probably as Clark pored over his papers in the last months of his life leaving comments for those he knew would come to his papers after his death. Underneath the line drawn earlier he wrote in fresh ink: 'The photographs, like the book, say nothing—the book is a lie, as it says nothing of what I lived through' (Clark Papers Box 175). Clark sets up a conversation with the biographer whom he knows will come sniffing like a bloodhound to the archive he has constructed. He plays with his own truth, giving prominence to earnest descriptions of his virtues on the one hand, while at the same time suggesting that the whole edifice of his self-invention is nothing but a charade, as if he does not know the truth himself.

Combing through Clark's autobiographies and finding examples of factual errors or misremembered encounters is a pastime one could indulge in for many years. In the pages of *Puzzles of Childhood* and *Quest for Grace*, things happen that never took place. People are born before their time. They die six years too early or four years too late. They stand for Labor Party pre-selection when they never did and they are remembered for doing all manner of things that never occurred. Consistent with Ken Inglis's observation that Clark's recollections of others were often more about 'self than subject', his portrayal of many characters serves merely as a vehicle for dispensing praise to himself. And of course, Clark's memories of his parents differ from those of his siblings, both of whom stated after the publication of *Puzzles for Childhood* that they could not recognise their parents' marriage in his agonised portrayal, just as his accounts of events and friendships differ from the memories of others, some of whom wrote forcefully to tell him how disappointed they were in his recollections. These differences of memory and perspectives are not unusual. And catching Clark out is not my purpose. But a handful of Clark's untruths and fabrications go the heart of his credibility as an historian.

The most notorious example that I discovered of Clark's misremembering—his claim to have been present in Bonn the morning after *Kristallnacht* in November 1938, one repeated frequently in public during the last years of his life—still unsettles me because so much of the circumstantial evidence suggests that he knowingly lied. It was Dymphna who was in Bonn the morning after *Kristallnacht*. She wrote to Clark, who was then in Oxford and would not arrive in Bonn until three weeks later. It was her memories of *Kristallnacht* that Clark largely appropriated in order to claim a greater role for himself in one of European history's darkest moments. Clark had actually omitted the story of his presence that November morning in Bonn from all the drafts of *Quest for Grace* that Dymphna edited before the book's publication. Not until the final typescript draft, when he finally decided on the title and Dymphna's editing was complete, did he decide to insert the claim that he was present in Bonn and that he had indeed seen the smashed glass from the Jewish shop windows on the streets and watched as the smoke from the burning synagogues filled the sky. It was not until the book was published that Dymphna read Clark's last-minute insertion, although she had certainly heard him make the claim previously on radio and television. It is possible that Clark chose to wait until the final draft to insert the claim of his presence the morning after *Kristallnacht* so as to avoid her marking up his claim as false. As she acknowledged after Clark's death in a private interview, '[Manning] says he arrived the morning after *Kristallnacht*. That's not true' (McKenna 638).

Writing about their peers, mentors and influences, let alone their achievements, historians are adept at making the activities of their own kind appear momentous. Nonetheless, Clark's autobiographies do so to a far greater extent than those of most of his peers. He saw himself as the leader of an intellectual vanguard whose self-appointed responsibility was to lead Australia out of its Anglocentric torpor towards an independent, republican, multicultural and more Indigenous-centred future, a completely new vision of the nation. However, this is not to suggest that many of his pronouncements were not prescient. In 1981, when he was asked to name Australia's national day, Clark argued that the country had yet to agree on one. He pointed out that Indigenous Australians were absent from the national anthem and invisible in the national flag and constitution. 'Our national day in the future', he said, 'will be that day in which we made the great step forward on the Aborigines and on the non-British descendants and on [the] question of what sort of society are we going to have in Australia' (Tate).

Janet Malcolm has written that:

> If an autobiography is to be even minimally readable, the autobiographer must step in and subdue what you could call memory's autism, its passion for the tedious. He must not be afraid to invent. Above all he must invent himself. (297–8)

Manning Clark heeded Malcolm's advice. His autobiographies were an attempt to adapt his life story to the needs of Australia at Empire's end. His recollections are always pointing to the future, his authorial voice always pleading for entrance to Valhalla. Clark's autobiographies provided the great man's origin story and they further invented him as a national prophet, the man who would lead Australia out of the wilderness of what he called 'British philistinism' towards a largely unknown and ill-defined but somehow more enlightened Australian future. Towards the end of his life, he sensed that the way in which he had framed this quest—the old dead tree versus the young tree green—was quickly becoming irrelevant. 'The problems of my generation, or the way I formulated them have passed away—maybe are [already] rotting in history's ample rubbish bin' (Clark qtd. in McQueen 24 Apr. 1989). Like so many of his intellectual contemporaries, Clark was also alienated from the nation he sought to advance. He told McQueen that he had grown tired of living in 'a country inhabited by a people who display a vast indifference to what matters in life—and an unwillingness to listen to what you have to say' (Clark qtd. in McQueen 12 Mar. 1990). This seems a strange comment coming from someone who was listened to more than any other intellectual in late twentieth-century Australia. No matter how much of a national figure Clark became, he still craved to be showered in even greater public acclaim. As he wrote to Humphrey McQueen in 1984, 'On Tuesday 22 January at 4pm a BRONZE BUST of me will be unveiled in the Chifley Library. My LITERARY SLANDERERS will not be there. My friends will be. Please come if you can' (Clark qtd. in McQueen 19 Jan. 1984).

In the last weeks of Clark's life, it was rumoured that he was writing a third volume of autobiography. A rough draft clearly existed, as his diaries appear to indicate. Ian Hancock, Clark's former colleague at the ANU, recalled that the departmental secretary was 'shocked' as she typed up the first pages of the manuscript. 'She was shaking when she told me about it. It was full of scandalous revelations. But I think Dymphna put her foot down and refused to allow its publication' (Hancock). Perhaps Clark had finally decided to abide by his many exhortations to bare all. But no such manuscript has survived in his papers.

In early 1990, convinced that his death was now 'only a year or so away', Clark looked again to posterity when he penned the final line of his last letter to Humphrey McQueen before McQueen left Japan for Australia:

[I] have tried, but alas failed to recreate the experience in [*The Quest for Grace*] of the confessions of a great sinner, & a failed human being [ ... ] This ends the Clark part of the Clark-McQueen correspondence. I enjoyed it. You have always been very good to me. My love to you, Ever, Manning. (Clark qtd. in McQueen 12 Mar. 1990)

In the months ahead Clark read the reviews of *Quest* in the literary pages of the broadsheet press, which, as with most of his later work, shifted dramatically from almost foolish adulation to snarling condemnation. Friend and fellow-historian Noel McLachlan claimed that Clark had produced 'the first Australian intellectual biography,' one 'as revelatory as Rousseau's but better,' in which 'astonishingly little seems to be held back' (McLachlan), while Andrew Riemer politely referred to Clark's 'parochialism' in which Clark presents 'the world seen from Melbourne,' riding forth 'like a latter-day Quixote, tilting at windmills perhaps, but keeping alive the noble flame of his idealism' (Riemer). Richard White, however, had come closest to revealing Clark's literary conceit: 'Manning Clark's Australia is Manning Clark himself' (White).

Clark's autobiographies—clearly unreliable, undeniably self-indulgent and yet somehow strangely compelling despite their countless literary flaws—stand not only as allegories of national awakening but also as the final expression of Clark's fictive historical style. For Manning Clark, it was not the facts of history that shaped us but the impression —emotional, intellectual and spiritual—that the telling of history and one's life story left behind. As he told *Playboy* magazine in 1989: 'I remember very vividly that one of my boyhood roles at school, both the state school and at Melbourne Grammar, was the telling of stories. I don't mean fibs of course, but I was a storyteller' (*Australian Playboy*).

## Disclosure statement

No potential conflict of interest was reported by the author.

## References

*Australian Playboy*. Interview with Manning Clark. July 1981. 31–4. Print.
Beckett, Samuel. *Proust and Three Dialogues*. 1965. London: Calder, 1999. Print.
Bennett, Bruce. "Literary Culture since Vietnam." *Oxford Literary History of Australia*. Melbourne: Oxford UP, 1988. 239–64. Print.
Brunskill, Ian. "Gunter Grass." *Times Literary Supplement* 29 Sept. 2006. Web. www.the-tls.co.uk/tls/public/article731185.ece
Brass, Ken. Interview with Manning Clark. *Weekend Australian Magazine*. 2 Mar. 1985. Print.
Campion, Edmund. Rev. of *A History of Australia*. Scripsi, 5:2 (1989): 183–7. Print.
Clark, Manning. Papers. MS 7550, Series 25, Box 173, 'Correspondence and drafts relating to Quest for Grace'. National Lib. of Australia, Canberra.
Clark, Manning. Diary. 11 Mar. 1988. MS 7550, Series 2. National Lib. of Australia, Canberra.

Clark, Manning. Papers. MS 7550, Series 25, Box 175, 'Illustrations for Quest for Grace'. National Lib. of Australia, Canberra.
Clark, Manning. *The Puzzles of Childhood*. Ringwood: Penguin, 1989. Print.
Clark, Manning. *The Quest for Grace*. Ringwood: Penguin, 1990. Print.
Clark, Manning. *Speaking Out of Turn: Lectures and Speeches, 1940–1991*. Melbourne: Melbourne UP, 1997. Print.
Craven, Peter. Interview with Manning Clark. Sunday Herald 8 Oct. 1989: 42. Print.
Hancock, Ian. Interviewed by Mark McKenna. Mar. 2007.
Holt, Stephen. *Manning Clark and Australian History, 1915–1963*. Brisbane: U of Queensland P, 1982. Print.
Holt, Stephen. *A Short History of Manning Clark*. Sydney: Allen, 1999. Print.
Inglis, Ken. "Notes after the death of Manning Clark 1991." Personal correspondence, May 2007.
Jones, Barry. *A Thinking Reed*. Sydney: Allen, 2006. Print.
Lane, Terry. "Terry Lane Talks with Manning Clark." ABC Spoken Word Cassette, 1990. (copy held at Manning Clark House, Canberra).
Lee, Hermione, ed. *Moments of Being: Autobiographical Writings*. By Virginia Woolf. 1976. London: Pimlico, 2002. Print.
Malcolm, Janet. "Thoughts on Autobiography from an Abandoned Autobiography." *Forty-one False Starts: Essays on Artists and Writers*. Melbourne: Text, 2013. 297–8. Print.
"Manning Clark's History of Australia: the Musical." Programme, Melbourne: 1988. Print.
Matthews, Brian. *Manning Clark: A Life*. Sydney: Allen, 2008. Print.
McKenna, Mark. *An Eye for Eternity: The Life of Manning Clark*. Melbourne: Miegunyah, 2011. Print.
McLachlan, Noel. Rev. of *The Quest for Grace*. Weekend Australian 20–1 Oct. 1990. Print.
McQueen, Humphrey. Papers. MS 4809, Folder Addition 31.5.1990, 'Correspondence with Manning Clark, 1988–1990.' National Lib. of Australia, Canberra.
Mitchell, Glen. "Interview with Professor Manning Clark." *University of Wollongong Historical Journal* 1:1 (1975): 65–75. Print.
Riemer, Andrew. Rev. of *The Quest for Grace*. Sydney Morning Herald 13 Oct. 1990. Print.
Rickard, John. Rev. of *A History of Australia, vol. 6*. Times on Sunday 23 Aug. 1987. Print.
Rutherford, Andrew. Interview with Manning Clark. Sunday Age 14 Oct. 1990: 11. Print.
Salter, James. *Burning the Days*. New York: Vintage, 1997. Print.
Tate, Alan. Interview with Manning Clark. *The Virgin Press* Oct.–Nov. 1981: 20. Print.
White, Richard. Rev of *The Quest for Grace*. Australian Society Nov. 1990: 39–40. Print.

# The Relational Imaginary of M. G. Vassanji's *A Place Within*

Vera Alexander

Department of European Languages and Cultures, University of Groningen, Groningen, Netherlands

**ABSTRACT**
Currently life writing criticism shows a growing interest in relationality. In the context of lives written after empire, relational dimensions are often fragmented, misremembered and semi-imaginary. This essay explores life writing in a diasporic context, focusing on M. G. Vassanji's travel-self narrative *A Place Within: Rediscovering India* (2008). Relational dimensions do not solely encompass human subjects. Selves and subjectivities are formed and transformed by objects and environments. I argue for extending the category of relational life writing beyond the human sphere to include two significant non-human others: books and places and analyse their role in the fraught project of constituting a life in writing.

## Introduction

Life writing criticism has been occupied with two major problems for the past decades. The first of these revolves around the question of how to distinguish life writing from fiction. The second might be termed a relational turn: tergiversating from viewing human subjects as autonomous entities, life writing analyses now increasingly regard selfhood as constituted by and responsive to significant others. A general outline of the state of the art suggests that critics currently worry much less about the former and more about the latter. But if formalist and structuralist preoccupations with genre divides have become unfashionable in criticism, this does not necessarily mean that writers of personal narratives have come to terms with blurry boundaries between history, memory and the imagination, nor the partial recognition, misremembrances and paradoxes experienced when trying to fabricate a text based on their own lives. This challenge is arguably exacerbated in the case of lives fractured and multiplied by long-term effects of Empire, such as migration, diaspora and transcultural unbelonging.

In this essay, I reposition the overlapping critical enquiries into the nature, use and potential of life writing in a diasporic context in a travel-self narrative, M. G. Vassanji's *A Place Within: Rediscovering India* (2008). As Vassanji's narrative combines a reflection of the nature of life writing with an investigation into a relationship with the author's largely imagined ancestral homeland, it is relational in the open dimensions outlined by sociologists (Gergen *Relational Being*; Donati). I use this text to make a case for extending the category of relational life writing beyond the human sphere. I do this by factoring two significant non-human others into relationality: books and places. Lives are not just constituted by relations to a formative 'key other person' (Eakin 86), such as a parent or sibling, or other mentor and tempter figures that make up the typical *dramatis personae* of a biography, *bildungsroman* or memoir, or even collective entities such as a family or peer-group. While such inter-human and intersubjective relationships naturally dominate discussions of human selfhood, relationships do not exist solely between human subjects. Selves and subjectivities are formed and transformed by objects and environments. The concept of relationality ought therefore to be opened to include encounters with texts, mediated voices, films, artworks on the one hand, and spaces and places on the other. Uneven and unequal in that these relations rest on one-sided projection and the imagination of just a single human partner, such patterns challenge the notion of the relational as it has become established, in a comfortable dialectical contrast to earlier assumptions about the self as autonomous or monolithic. Relationality conceived beyond the human sphere moreover resituates the narrated self as a confection which is always partly mediated, invented and imagined.

## M. G. Vassanji's stories within stories

Although mainly known as a writer of fiction, being the author of two short story collections and seven novels, M. G. Vassanji lends himself to an investigation of life writing After Empire. For one thing, his life links several Anglophone locations marked by colonialism and decolonisation. Born in Kenya in 1950, he grew up in Tanzania and trained as a nuclear physicist in the USA. He became a resident of Canada in 1978. Struggles with transcultural identity formation, mobility and migration are among the key themes that constitute a family resemblance between Vassanji's writings. His transcultural narratives explore hyphenated diasporic life-worlds that span a variety of chronotopes and connect East Africa, India, the USA and Canada. They tend to occupy a border zone linking history, storytelling, metafiction and self-constitution. Through his fictional works, Vassanji has drawn the attention of an international reading public to the lives of Indian minorities in Kenya and Tanzania, and their complex histories of multiple migrations. His recreations of East Africa during its independence struggles and the personal crises of young migrants of colour in the USA are based on personal memory and have received critical accolades for their detailed realism.

Vassanji's novels depend on a *mise en abyme* of interconnected stories. Fragmentary stories are found in unexpected places: a gunny sack full of mementos that are extracted, one story at a time (*The Gunny Sack*), a diary falling into the hands of a retired teacher triggers research (*The Book of Secrets*), and the feverish memories of a traumatised traveller (*A Magic of Saida*). Books, texts and stories form a connective tissue between characters from different times and places. Reality and story-telling form an interdependent and dynamic web where individual truth is imagined into being with the help of stories. Books are metafictional time-travelling vehicles that carry a sense of belonging across divides of time and place and generate empathy. Meta-texts convey a sense of the transient status of identity or closure. Often, texts stand in for missing parent figures, allowing characters to conduct one-sided dialogues across time and place that help them come to terms with the challenge of inventing coherence in diasporic conditions.

In Vassanji's writing, these transactions operate across the divides between fiction and non-fiction. Many of his novels and short stories make metafictional use of the presence of journals, diaries, letters and other life writing 'foundlings', some fictional, others historical, to introduce layers of meaning, and to trigger plots and journeys. By understanding the motivations of unknown storytellers, the lost and forgotten writers of diaries and letters, Vassanji's protagonists are led to examine and comprehend their own motivations. To learn about the past and to own its murky aspects are strategies that help define the relations with the here and now. Life writing is a metatextual representative of a diasporic subject: scattered across the pages, dissected and removed from their context or 'home', Vassanji's migrant characters connect implications of different texts while being set off from the main body of the text, signalling unbelonging, or plural belongings. Pieces of life writing function as a recurring trope that invites readers of Vassanji's novels to question the veracity and authenticity of any document.

And yet, his disjointed plots almost always converge on the monologic presence of a central protagonist figure, often an individual in search of himself or a missing lover or ancestor. Even in their articulations of dislocation, his frame narrators constitute hierarchical presences who make the many anecdotes assembled in Vassanji's novels as ancillary to a large-scale plot of finding, or constructing, a sense of truth, learning by telling. Vassanji's polyphonic technique allows a deceptive authority of a dominant voice as even the most assertive of his narrator protagonists find themselves displaced and alienated by relentless historical developments and hegemonic structures. The multitude of stories serves as a window-dressing for an endeavour which is ultimately monologic.

A case in point is Vassanji's most recent novel: *The Magic of Saida* (2013) unravels the memories of an East African physician resident in Canada who travels to Tanzania in the attempt to reconnect with his childhood sweetheart. Although the protagonist Kamal's quest is broken by numerous flashbacks that bring the eponymous heroine's story to life, it is *his* image of Saida which is related and refracted through a transmogrified image of a Mother Tanzania. Readers witness a male protagonist's search for closure. They never hear Saida's voice. Although an encounter between the former lovers seems to take place, the scene is delivered in the form of a feverish passage with overtones of both *Heart of Darkness* and *Frankenstein*, in which an uncanny witch-creature poisons Dr. Kamal: the creation renders her own narrator unreliable.

## Self-Encounters in *A Place Within*

Whereas Vassanji's fictional works are relatively unapologetic about plying the plots with all-encompassing protagonist figures, his travel narrative dissects such a presence. The multitude of contradictory impressions presented by India leads Vassanji to question his right to impose the subjective views of someone whose relationship with India is tenuous:

> on one hand I receive the confidences and treatments due to an insider, one of them; then I become the outsider, someone who doesn't know and has to be protected, someone who hasn't lived close to the fire and felt the heat. (Vassanji 10)

Such considerations are not prompted by postcolonial theorisations of subjectivity, the abject and even diasporic hyphenation.[1] Such discourses are in fact met with distrust by an author who is so suspicious of labels as to go by his initials in order to escape being assigned to a particular religious group. Vassanji hails from the Ismaili Khoja community of diasporic Indians whose traditions bridge Muslim and Hindu customs, a syncretism that potentially elicits confusion and controversy. Vassanji explains his origins somewhat wearily in his award-winning travel memoir, only to immediately write himself into a genealogy of storytellers:

> To tell people that politically and culturally you don't subscribe to this gulf among the same people, and that in matters of faith you were brought up in a very local Indian tradition that was a blend of the two faiths, is to appear naïve or quixotic. It is to meet a blank stare, it is to end a conversation.
> I come from a simple Indian village and town folk who happened to follow a line of Muslim mystical singer-preachers, the first of whom, per legend, arrived from the Near East nine hundred years ago and was welcomed in the capital, Patan, of the Gujarat kingdom. (Vassanji 84)

The phrase 'come from' in this passage needs to be taken with a pinch of salt. Vassanji comes to the country he 'comes from' in his early 40s. *A Place Within: Rediscovering India* is based on 10 visits between 1993 and the early 2000s. His personal experience is interspersed with processed images as the author's relationship with India has been prepared by way of family narratives, films and history books. His conflicting impressions of a land which he finds both familiar and alien include topical events such as the aftermath of the 1992 demolition of the Babri Mosque and subsequent riots in Mumbai, as well as subjective meditations on communal violence. Other passages reach back to the Middle Ages to explain the significance of sites and shrines the author finds particularly poignant. Both in Vassanji's fictional works and in his memoir, story-telling, stories and history function both as tools and as subjects of a metatextual enquiry.

In *A Place Within*, Vassanji engages in an autobiographical quest of the sort he has dispatched many of his protagonists on: he is on a journey supposed to enable him to exteriorise something that he knows to be a part of himself, Indianness. To be able to see and touch, smell and imbibe things Indian are acts designed to help him understand the elusive presence of diasporic Indian culture he has grown up with in East Africa. To visit India is to come to terms with relationality itself, with what it means to be connected. These connections are both real and imaginary, historical and emotional.

Many of them are established and sustained through acts of reading. *A Place Within* explores the power of writing to make sense of the random, multifarious and overwhelming experience of life in transit. Just as there are several selves to be choreographed, the book balances multiple images of India. While heterogeneity is to be expected from any portrait of India, Vassanji's episodic narrative is interpenetrated with self-referential reflections on the relationship between that which is experienced and that which is written, and the seductive yet unreliable role of memory as a chaordic force that factors loss of authorial control into an aesthetic principle of life as a quest.

Travelling on a Canadian passport gives him privileges, but it also gives rise to anxieties. Faced with the diversity presented by India, his narrative is acutely mindful of the limitations of a single perspective, and he piles his authorial self-doubts before his readers: 'Do I simply yearn for the exotic, for its shock, to tell myself I have now *been* in India, *really* seen it?', he muses at the outset (Vassanji 6), eliciting nods, perchance a shrug. Awareness of clichés does not preclude them as he demonstrates repeatedly, for instance when reproducing stereotypes of India as a timeless (read: backward) repository of a particular sensibility: 'Such poetry, such yearning, lives on in the romantic heart of the nation, even as the airwaves and newsprint dazzle and bewitch with the transitory magic of the material' (Vassanji 78). Worse yet:

> This is still a land of romance, I tell myself, of song and love. Hearts are still given and taken away. It's a place of signals, with looks, and handkerchiefs and small gestures. A place of laughter. How well do I recognize these, how utterly have I lost them. The cynicism is reserved for politicians, among this middle-class crowd, the irony for foreign consumption. (Vassanji 14–5)

Vassanji self-consciously locates himself on an 'after Empire' stage. As a life writer, he finds himself caught in a double role, as performing actor of his narrative and as its director, facing questions to which only temporary and subjective answers can apply: Is writing, establishing coherence and control, somehow inherently a colonising act? Is essentialism inevitable on a quest for belonging? Being both a representative of Western culture and a diasporic individual, Vassanji experiences ongoing and dislocating shifts of perspective. The visual dimensions of the observer and the seeker on a personal quest are addressed in various places:

> On one hand I stood at an objective distance, watching and observing; and yet everything I saw I took personally, conscious all the time. This is India, this is the homeland, to which I am returning on behalf of my family after seventy, eighty, a hundred years. (Vassanji 3)

The encounter with India forces Vassanji to shift between being an authority and a witness, western representative and fellow-postcolonised for the many locals he speaks with. Headless and bereft of the fixed point of a master-narrator, he ponders the question of whether his intense engagement with writing and history ought to be pathologised: 'History is addictive, is an obsession' (Vassanji 53). Being the narrator-protagonist leaves him without a vantage point from which to lay a trail of narrative scraps for the plot to come together.

Vassanji prefaces his portrait of India with an apology reminiscent of a classical chorus sent in before the act, to introduce the plot and beg the reader's indulgence: 'Ever since my first visit, there has been the irrepressible urge to describe my experience of India; yet in spite of copious notes this was not easy, because that experience was deeply subjective, my India was essentially my own creation' (Vassanji ix). Vassanji's modern-day *captatio benevolentiae* immediately launches him into the chief drama of his narrative, the struggle to balance rational and sentimental motivations for writing which he grounds in his diasporic origins.

His imagined homeland is a confection which collapses upon exposure to the real India. Mirroring the literary and autobiographical endeavours of several predecessors and book-shape mentors, notably Nehru and Gandhi, Vassanji uneasily 'locates' his India in the processual vocabulary of quest and discovery, even as he identifies the repetitive circularity of this approach as specious. India challenges his attempts to formulate responses to the people and places he comes across. Subsequent to almost every episode, he is forced to concede that reality outstrips his expectations. His wearied résumé after a particularly humbling encounter is symptomatic: 'this truism keeps playing on my mind, as it has many times before: This country that I've come so brazenly to rediscover goes as deep as it is vast and diverse. It's only oneself one ever discovers' (Vassanji 321–2). And why would that be worth narrating, unless one wanted to affirm the unique value of that self occupying its particular spot within its specific time and place?

As with inter-human relationships, the questions that arise out of Vassanji's relations with India and his process of coming face to face with his multiple roles suggest a complex relational panorama: often violent feelings of love, fear, curiosity, disgust, shame, exhilaration, surprise, shock, embarrassment, pride, and familiarity accompany his portrait of India and often come into conflict with his ambition to deliver a rational, coherent and persuasive account. Before outlining how these contradictions play out in Vassanji's depiction of place and his writing back to the various works which inspired his imagined India, I would like to pause for a brief consideration of how his struggles with his experiences fit into the paradigm of relationality.

## Relationality beyond the human sphere

Or: paradigms. The concept of relationality seems to lead several separate lives in different disciplines. Derived from sociology, the term has conquered life writing criticism, mostly thanks to Paul John Eakin. Édouard Glissant has developed relationality into a poetological concept to capture the fragmented histories of the Caribbean.[2] The term's potential as an analytic tool for an enquiry into life writing after Empire has only received scant attention.[3] In a context at least adjacent to the postcolonial, relationality is a key principle of knowledge organisation in several indigenous cultures of North America, as emphasised by the title of Thomas King's anthology *All My Relations* and theorised, among others, by writers such as Jeannette Armstrong, Richard Atleo/Umeek and Margaret Kovach (King). Peripheral to the advent of relationality in literary criticism is the concept of relational art as developed by Nicolas Bourriaud.

The sociologist Kenneth Gergen investigates the 'generative process of relating' (Gergen *Relational Being* xv) with a view towards promoting an interdependent approach to the self as something connected rather than separate, so as to contribute to a transformation of the competitive workplace and other institutions into more mutually supportive structures.[4] A transfer of ideas about actual society to literary works is aided by the fact that Gergen's book draws on literary works, 'textual companions' (*Relational Being* xvii), and investigates the construction of relationships via chains of emotions (*Realities* 35) and the behaviours through which they are displayed. Texts, narrative scenarios and even fiction constitute common grounds between his work in sociology and the literary analyses of Eakin, and those attempted in this essay.

Both Gergen and Eakin frame relationality as inter-human relations, initially conceived as a binarism of self and other which gradually becomes dissected. For Gergen, relationships are fundamentally tied to language and perception: 'our mental vocabulary is essentially a vocabulary of relationship' (*Relational Being* 69–70). Gergen ties this thought to an impulse to punctuate the fundamental otherness and unknowability of other persons: 'How can we know what is in the mind of another? We are presented with their words [ … ] Yet, we have no access to another's mind save through what we take to be its expressions' (*Relational Being* 118). The plurality inherent in relational perspectives entails an acceptance that part of the world will always remain unknowable.

This also happens to be a cornerstone in Glissant's relational poetics which portrays relationality as a mode of adjusting to unknowability. In Isabell Hoving's paraphrase, 'Glissant's poetics [ … ] argues that the interrelated world can never be completely known' (Hoving 165–6). His meditations are useful in accommodating other uncertainties, such as those about place relations. The interplay of knowledge and emotion generates tension, as life writers become involved in a dynamic of constituting and letting go of a sense of control. Place and travel thus epitomise the constant human struggle to accommodate change, both within and without.

All relationality is a matter of approximation through interpretation of signs. Intentions themselves remain invisible, and Gergen's book illustrates powerfully how little is known of the workings even of human consciousness. A spatial Other such as India with its multitudes of inscrutable inhabitants, invisible signs, inaudible sounds, and only partially decoded messages, presents an even more unknowable otherness than the social others Gergen focuses on. Such a relationship is rendered elusive not only because of the inability of the writer to speak to every single inhabitant but also because of the unfathomable powers of places with their sounds, smells, flavours, colours and temperatures to affect feelings of subjecthood.

Sporadic observations on the relational nature of autobiographical writings have been made from the mid-1970s onwards: Karl Weintraub argues that the meaning of autobiography unfolds in an interaction between individuals and their surroundings, describing autobiography as 'a weave in which self-consciousness is delicately threaded throughout interrelated experience. It may have such varied functions as self-explication, self-discovery, self-clarification, self-formation, self-presentation, self-justification. All these functions inter-penetrate easily, but all are centred upon a self aware of its relation to its experiences' (Weintraub 824). But for the most part, relationality has been conceptualised in accordance with Paul John Eakin's chapter on 'Relational Selves, Relational Lives: The Story of the Story' which directs critical attention to the importance of formative relationships, with reference to family members that shaped the lives of writers of autobiographies. Eakin credits relational appreciation mainly to feminist criticism and women's autobiographies. It is through others that the self is realised, comes into being and is constructed as individual. It is through reconstructive narratives of their own and other people's lives that writers contextualise their own stories.

One of the side effects of a relational enquiry is that it interrogates the binary assumptions of self and other or centre and periphery that have come to underpin relational debates. While deconstructing dichotomies can be seen as a kneejerk reaction triggered by the powerful stimulus of investigating life writing 'After Empire', this kind of enquiry is not restricted to the postcolonial arena. Leigh Gilmore suggests a comparable widening of the relational sphere in an analysis of 'posthuman' writing that depicts life with chronic pain and which 'locates the self/life/writing weave of self-representation in relations of dependence and interdependence across living and non-living matter' (83).

Gilmore's focus on dependency draws attention to a workshop aspect of relational criticism whose terminologies are still in a process of being shaped. In many discussions of life writing, the relational is rather problematically conflated with intersubjectivity, often in an attempt to juxtapose the relational mode with notions of an autonomous self, as Katja Sarkowsky explains (628–9). Relationality encompasses more than mere connection or dependence. These technical-sounding terms insufficiently capture a linkage invested with emotions and personal history. Relationality involves thinking about contact, not merely experiencing it. For the purposes of this essay, relationality is used to capture a connection endowed with meaning and invested with emotion and responsibility. Relationality emphasises that a connection has been enriched by thought, feeling and the imagination.

## Relationality of place: feeling India

Vassanji's travel narrative attempts to disentangle these factors in his relationship with India while reflecting on life in transit on several levels. Concrete travel is only one typical manifestation. He gives the occasional itinerary and evaluation of the relative merits of different sites and monuments, some of which he prefaces by historical introductions. But the crucial journey for Vassanji is a personal one that takes him back into his family's past and into his own reading history. He is aware of the fact that mobility is part of epistemological growth. To think about travel, transit, and passages, to perform the acts involved in motion and to reflect them in his writing practice help him understand and define his place within life. In a modernised vignette of the topos of *navigatio vitae*, life as a journey, Vassanji links his special relationship with motion and in-betweenness to his diasporic experience:

> I remember musing, many years ago when I was a student and would often find myself between cities on a train in North America, that it could go on forever, this journey, for all I cared, I could give my life to this long moment of rolling and roaring, of endless rhythm. I was a displaced person, like Zeno's arrow going someplace else even as I was stationary in another, and a train ride vivified the feeling of constant motion, going somewhere endlessly. (18)

The evocation of a staple experience in fictions about protagonists in their formative years makes for a frustrating memory in the musings of a middle-aged traveller expected to approach India in expert mode. The above train of thought comes to a mundane halt:

> Trains here in India are the next best thing to endless constant motion. [ ... ] What better way than to sit in a train responding to the ancestral homeland, every scene and every moment full of meaning and possibility, blooming epiphany? The only torment: the wet washrooms. (Vassanji 19)

He quails before the prospect of visiting the region his forebears have come from: 'They tell me, please come to Gujarat, but not on kite day, a Gujarati festival; it might provide just the opportunity for a riot. - Am I not supposed to be afraid?' (Vassanji 10). Apart from problems of hygiene and communal terror, there is a constant familiar struggle with writing, history, memory—the ever receding frontier of textualising experience: 'the urge persists, and grows, to step into the past, look behind the ruin, the beauty, the enigma—and find coherence, impute meaning and relevance. It's risky, I know, like walking into a dream. (Vassanji 53). Busy enacting his old dream of finally being in India, Vassanji knows that he cannot do that, he can only feel overwhelmed by the thought. In Vassanji's piece of travel-life writing, two unfinishable projects interpellate one another: from the first sentence onwards, India is depicted as being beyond grasp: 'It would take many lifetimes, it was said to me during my first visit, to see of all India. It was January. The desperation must have shown on my face to take in all I possibly could' (Vassanji ix). And this only concerns the unknown country he visits, the India 'without'.

Space and place are categories which narratology struggles to accommodate, as Mieke Bal confirms: 'few concepts deriving from the theory of narrative texts are as self-evident and have yet remained so vague, as the concept of *space*' (93). Bal defines narrative space as '*location* or *place* as an element of the fabula' (93), and as 'the topological position in which the actors were situated and the events took place' (93). She clarifies the narrative functions of spaces in binary terms:

> Spaces function in a story in two ways. On the one hand, they are only a frame, a place of action. In this capacity a more or less detailed presentation will lead to a more or less concrete picture of that space. The space can also remain entirely in the background. In many cases, however, space is 'schematized': it becomes an object of presentation itself, for its own sake. Space thus becomes an 'acting place' rather than the place of action. It influences the fabula, and the fabula becomes subordinate to the presentation of space. (Bal 95–6)

For Vassanji, the Indian subcontinent is more than a tourist trap. Even to describe it as a key space to help him unlock a better understanding of family identity does not do the book justice. To activate the imagined place of his ancestral past is both nostalgic and fraught with pain, as he wryly observes in several passages: 'My older son has taken to cricket, and hunting for a lost ball in the bushes with him has brought back memories of my own childhood; it's also given us rashes from poison ivy' (Vassanji 167). In other passages, mundane streets and corners engender flashes of emotional memory which elude communication, even geographical coherence, as Vassanji's conflation of India and Tanzania in the following vignette demonstrates:

> I recall a scene in suburban Delhi [ … ] during a family visit to India. We had taken a bus from our guest house in South Delhi to go to Connaught Circus, the heart of New Delhi. On the way we passed certain residential areas of the city, and glancing at my wife I saw a sudden emotion come over her face. She, who had not been back to Dar es Salaam in over twenty years, was reminded of it by the neighbourhoods we passed through. Such is the meaning of home. How could I possibly explain this to Krishan Chander, whose one ambition seems to be to send at least one of his children 'there'? (Vassanji 50)

'There' is indicative of an otherness of longing, it gestures towards the great wide world abroad. Vassanji's idealisation of India is matched by an idealisation of the West in most of his middle-class interlocutors whose children either already live abroad or hope to go soon. Their relationship with the West is invested with as much emotion as Vassanji's own. Being motivated by his dreams of making an imaginary place relation into a real life experience, he elicits and collects other people's declarations of *fernweh*, the longing to be elsewhere. The emotions engendered by places are something of a *leitmotif* throughout his memoir: 'I am going to the state of my ancestors, Gujarat, where people speak a language I speak. How do I feel?' (Vassanji 36). Feelings are both a challenge to language, and part of the language of place. In this sense his book is less a portrait of India than a personal rumination about limitations to the language of memory as provoked by a place experience. For Vassanji, place is where human relationships become tangible. He elevates setting to a creative force. His is essentially a romanticising view of place, motivated by a conventional sense of materialist presence. This is epitomised by the satisfaction the narrator expresses when receiving an edible gift:

It is an emotional send-off. So much had been expected of this visit, but it's too short. This has been a meeting of minds, but even more a meeting of hearts. This was India's embrace, its kiss, to an Indian however many times removed.
And yes, somebody gave me a box of mithai to take back with me. (Vassanji 39)

Postcolonial writings have long been preoccupied with rectifying false assumptions about the 'within' and the 'without' which Vassanji's title alludes to. From Frantz Fanon's analytic rage at racist interpretations of black skin colour to Ashis Nandy, Ganesh Devy and Gauri Viswanathan's deconstructions of the indirect invasion of the mind via English literary education, a mismatch of that which is visible to the world 'without' and that which is felt 'within' is central to the postcolonial experience, and, by corollary, theory. Trying to come to terms with this mismatch, however broadly conceived and intensely felt constitutes one of the motivations that have drawn writers and critics to their desks.

Vassanji's interiorisation of India as a 'place within' gives rise to the question in how far the term relationship is applicable to places. The connection between individuals and places is uneven. The difference between a human being and a place is clear; while one is clearly bounded and contained, at least physically, the other is a vague collective term which cannot reciprocate any of the emotional energy invested in it. Place relations can be broken down into memories, often of other people associated with a place, reducing the actual place to a mere conductor of emotional energy. For Vassanji, internalisation of place is prompted and mediated by stories and books. It is the narrated, 'worded', processed experience which he can own. The 'India without' he traverses—unwieldy, chaotic and cacophonous—and the 'India within' which he recounts to his readers reflect different ways of knowing. What he sees 'without' still lacks meaning, explanation, and most importantly of all, emotional presence.

## Text relationality: writing struggles

Through reading, travelling and writing, Vassanji relates past and present in his imagination. His traveller persona during his Indian trips is clearly defined as a writer, and quite a renowned and prominent one at that. Similar to Naipaul, he travels 'for a book' as much as he travels for himself. He is invited to give talks, introduced to literati, treated to poetry jams, is moved to the front of queues (Vassanji 18).

In writing about visiting his ancestral homeland, Vassanji follows a long line of forebears in Anglophone and diasporic literatures. His passage to India echoes E. M. Forster's novel as much as the section of Walt Whitman's *Leaves of Grass* which inspired its title. V. S. Naipaul's *India: A Million Mutinies Now* (1990) charts the author's 1962 visit to confront what he terms his Indian 'nerves' (8, 516), 'the darkness that separated me from my ancestral past' (516), reluctantly approaching a country framed by the 'abjectness and defeat and shame' (517) of his family's indentured past. Such raw postcolonial discourse is predictably absent from Vassanji's book. Though deeply concerned with East African decolonisation, he keeps a distance from the postcolonial lexicon. In its place, he employs a vocabulary of self-fashioning, identification and personal growth that links the experience of his nation's independence with his own adolescence and growing awareness:

# LIFE WRITING AFTER EMPIRE

> My first serious engagement with India began when as a student strolling along the aisles of a university book sale one spring in Cambridge Massachusetts, I happened upon a remaindered copy of Jawaharlal Nehru's autobiography and quickly—though I cannot say with what expectation—picked it up. Something of the liberal expansiveness of the author, educated in Harrow and that other Cambridge, in England, and his generosity of spirit, appealed to this expatriate student barely out of his teens and foundering upon questions of identity on alien shores. I was of Indian descent, born in East Africa, had recently seen the independence of my country, amidst great euphoria and hope for Africa. Nehru wrote his autobiography (as he did his *Discovery*) during one of his several terms in jail during India's own struggle for independence. Reading him I became aware of India as a real, modern country—as opposed to a mythical one—a recent phenomenon [ … ] I was reading, for the first time after a colonial education, words written by an Indian, and I felt a swell of pride in that. [ … ] Gandhi brought India even closer: he had lived many years in South Africa, and he had given an opinion regarding the so-called Indian Question in East Africa (Vassanji xii–xiii).

Travel and books, spatial and metaphoric mobility, come together in forging the self-image of the writer as explorer that Vassanji makes for and about himself. In this process books not only help structure the experience of place. They are instrumental in managing a place change central to Vassanji's narrative logic, both here and in his fictional works: narrated places, story places and individuals in and from stories are perceived and depicted as more real than the ones encountered 'without'.

In defining relationality, one runs the risk of producing a concept which is so general as to become meaningless. Even the most personal confessions and revelations entail collateral narratives locating the narrator within social parameters and implicating other individuals, places, and monuments. With this in mind, 'relational writing' is almost tautological, since 'relate' etymologically covers a dimension of telling. Can any text be 'unrelational'? Kenneth Gergen explicitly addresses the process of writing as a means of illustrating the polyphony of the self. Writing is exposed as a relational tool. It only makes sense to write in order to reach a reading and potentially writing Other, real or imagined, and in producing a piece of writing, an author makes the offering of a relationship, and possibly enacts both parts of Self and Other. However, the act of writing to the unknown has its ambiguities. Language is felt to be a set of confining conventions; writing is 'layered'. As Gergen has argued, all writing has a communal dimension: 'writing is fundamentally an action within a relationship; it is within relationship that writing gains its meaning and significance, and our manner of writing simultaneously invites certain forms of relationship while discouraging or suppressing others' ("Writing as Relationship").

For Vassanji, India, the place where he finds himself both recognised and completely lost, or scattered, becomes a heterotopian mirror where he confronts, not so much his genealogical past, but his professional one, as a storyteller. If India is a place 'within', this title exposes the unknown status of the writer's own psyche, the black box of memory from which Vassanji produces disjointed and uncontrollable stories which he struggles to string into a narrative that can withstand the clear light of day. Encountering the real India without is an uncanny process of doubling, and his textual forebears are a part of this. Ensconced in one of Shimla's landmark colonial relics, the Indian Institute for Advanced Study, formerly the Viceregal Lodge, a building as British-looking as J. K. Rowling's Hogwarts castle, he fantasises about being haunted not only by the poltergeist of Lady Curzon ('England still haunts the place, from a distance' [Vassanji 169]), but also by fictional ghosts:

> During the rains a thick swirling fog may overhang the area, its effects enhanced by the white and yellow lamps on posts; and with the grey gothic building in the background the entire place acquires a certain macabreness. If one lingered a little in this night, did not turn away quickly into the embrace of a hearth, then that shadow figure in the near distance who is barely visible might just respond to the call: 'Heathcliff!' (Vassanji 168)

The filmic language in which this fantasy is rendered, under the telling chapter heading of 'A Spell in the Mountains', creates ironic distance to match the irony of the experience itself, of a migrant visitor viewing the Lodge through a Victorian lens. While English books are used to evoke atmosphere, the importance of family as a constituent of identity cannot be recruited from the West. Although his portrayal of Delhi is put under the heading of 'The City of Poets', Vassanji inserts references to the nineteenth century Urdu-Persian poet Ghalib, Ahmed Ali's *Twilight in Delhi* (1940), Attia Hosain's novel *Sunlight on a Broken Column* (1961) and others chiefly to introduce the authority of family and the significance of individual rebellions against patriarchy.

The imagination enables a self-relationality where the different roles and practices an individual assumes are put in relief. A relational mode of enquiry that compares his situation, his meandering, with the local intelligentsia and the numerous academics who act as his guides on his travels yields lists of similarities between Vassanji's life-world and theirs. All of them have the world of books to dip into as an escapist exercise of hide-and-seek or as a source of inspiration. Books and stories constitute shared ground even as they cancel out actual place and location. As a writer he feels less in control than a storyteller, more like a scribe who transcribes or translates stories he is surrounded by:

> Monuments tell a story, reflect a mindset; Aibak's tower of victory and his great mosque built over a Hindu temple; Alauddin's vain attempt at a bigger tower; his more practical Hauz Khas water reservoir for the people of Delhi; his fair-trade regulations; Akbar's new capital Fatehpur Sikri for his ideal of a unified India; Shah Jahan's incomparable Taj Mahal for his beloved dead queen, and his new city, Shahjahanabad. Each visitor must surely have a favourite among the monuments that transport him or her to a mood, a vision. (Vassanji 94)

India becomes a master-narrator who casts the former creator and lord of all he surveys as a character in a narrative which constantly eludes comprehension. His journeys frame a variety of selves and roles which are often in conflict: the renowned Canadian academic and writer is expected to attend a symposium in one location while the private individual M. G. Vassanji would prefer his itinerary to continue elsewhere:

> At this point I would have preferred to make Calcutta my next stop. [ ... ] But Trivandrum, Kerala, needs me; there are two emissaries from the south to tell me that, to beseech me to come; there is a workshop there they would like me to attend. (Vassanji 18)

Thrown into the map of India, Vassanji loses the constructed control granted by his status as the inventor of stories.

There is a moment where Vassanji's monologic stance breaks down in a moment of striking clarity, if not quite self-recognition. This occurs in a chapter which recounts his meeting with the novelist Mulk Raj Anand, one of the first Indian authors writing in English to gain international renown, notably with *Untouchable* (1935) and *Coolie* (1936). This passage, marking the centre-point of the book, could have been used to signal an epiphany, a home-coming, the culmination of Vassanji's Indian quest: to meet an Alter Ego, a living monument, a fellow novelist who not only precedes him in the field of 'the Indo English novel' (Vassanji 222), but an Ishmaili like him; a relative to boot, who inscribes a gift with an affectionate greeting from 'Uncle Mulk' (Vassanji 222). Instead of witnessing a writerly apotheosis, readers are confronted with an anticlimactic tussle between two alpha males who purport to know little about one another, and to care even less:

> I am a little wary about meeting a writer with such a reputation. He knows nothing about me, and my knowledge of him is superficial. My only interest at this point is to take a look at him and to confirm the family connection, hopefully find out more about that. [ ... ]
> He takes up an aggressive posture at the start. (Vassanji 219)

Anand is not the only one to take up such a posture, and it is stubbornly maintained by both combatants from start to finish. Vassanji's somewhat petulant account of his tête-à-tête with Anand is ripe with rivalry. The age gap becomes a peg for a patronising portrayal of Anand's shorter stature, his deafness, his 'memories of relevance and glory' (Vassanji 222). These passages evince a violence Vassanji might just as well have explicitly directed at himself. Instead, it is Anand's self-centredness which is exposed: 'What can this old man tell me? But Mulk, my witness, is deaf, and his interest is focused on something else, his own life, about which he goes relentlessly on' (Vassanji 221). In a similar vein, he lampoons Anand's penchant for name-dropping: 'He talks about Nehru, Muhammad Iqbal, Gandhi. But his life in London, where he fraternised with the literati of the time, including the Bloomsbury group, he remembers with pride, speaks of with confidence. It's the favourite soundtrack' (Vassanji 219). Vassanji's sarcasm is as jarring as his indictment of inauthenticity. Having severally professed his own inability to fathom the thoughts of the Indians he meets, he now surmises that Anand's writings about the lower castes 'don't have the immediacy of caste experience that a native Indian reader might demand' (Vassanji 221). The insider-outsider who worries about opportunistically exchanging one diasporic hat for another implies that Anand's expressions of Anglophilia make him less Indian than he ought to be, and so does the time he spent abroad: 'What's so special about returning to India? He should know, he returned having missed a crucial part of its history, but I keep quiet' (Vassanji 219).

Quiet, except for four strikingly venomous pages. In them, a volcano of anger erupts, aimed at least partially at the project of speaking about the self: the writerly ancestor Anand whom Vassanji meets, but to whom he cannot get through, due to what David Lodge wryly calls a 'deaf sentence' and to a loss of focus which Vassanji attributes to age. 'This is not a discussion but a one-way discourse' (Vassanji 221). In other words, it is a synopsis of the writing process as it is felt by the writing subject, the nightmare scenario of trying to formulate one's own history and confronting one's fear of falling short. In meeting a writer who lives in the past, Vassanji shifts to an evasive third person narrative that masks a fear of aging, of looking into the distorted mirror of a future he dreads: 'What does a writer do at this stage of life, his energies spent, his vogue diminished?' (Vassanji 219). No writer is more equal than the other; there is no revelation to be found here, only the unnerving prospect of a potentially monologic stance in telling about one's life —'It's only oneself one ever discovers'. The relationship between life and text remains as elusive as ever, or even more than ever in Vassanji's encounter with his personal ghost of Christmas to Come. It is in the passages portraying his failed encounter with the figure of a writer that Vassanji's struggle with India morphs into an agnate battle, the enactment of an inner joust with the compulsion to write, to live writing.[5]

## Conclusion

Life writing has become one of the most vibrant workshops within literary criticism, and beyond. One of the reasons for the rise in interest in life writing is its meta-fictional potential to enable inter- and trans-disciplinary contact and collaboration, for instance between literary studies, history and psychology. Key to the self-image of an age obsessed with individual self-documentation and open access on the one hand and anxieties about post-privacy exposure on the other, life writing has grown from a collective genre term into a phenomenon, and it is being described as something processual: 'a mode of phenomenological and cognitive self-experience' (Eakin 100) and as 'an ongoing and often contentious engagement with humanistic discourses of identity and truth' (Gilmore 83). The elusiveness of the self-writing process which used to be a valid reason to dismiss its literary quality, now contributes to making it the most appropriate and trustworthy response to a stream of self-perceptions in overwhelming and fragmented life-worlds. For individuals such as Vassanji, whose histories are marked by post-Empire displacement and diasporic hyphenation, life writing has been an especially exhilarating instrument for filling gaps in official history, unearthing silenced voices, and writing belonging into being.

Writing establishes patterns and Vassanji approaches this normalising activity with a degree of weary, self-critical mistrust. His authoritative stance periodically collapses as Vassanji alternates between his western visitor status and his membership in a minority. In some places, it is the Gujarati he speaks which becomes his admission ticket to a community, in another anecdote he is thrilled to spot his uncommon family name on a placard. The act of writing forces him to make an *essai* of experience: his travels become a chain of introductions, tableaux and brief, subjective attempts at closure. Books, films and well-known anecdotes are recruited to support his narrative, not as evidence or truth claims but as a way of breaking the relative monotony of his reminiscences: he searches for a way of building coherence as much as any truths about India that have not already been published. In referring to his journeys as a pilgrimage (in his final sentence he refers to the book as 'a token of pilgrimage' [Vassanji 423]), he accommodates the (for him) most uncomfortable aspects of his Indian encounter, the confrontation with communal violence and the religious sources to which he attributes these. Instead of revelation or redemption, he ends on observations about circularity, the future next visit, the inconclusiveness of his project, which he renders in the shape of a dialogue with one of his many hosts. Travel and narrative still form the core of his belief system of how to align life and the imagination, but how and why they matter and are made to matter has acquired a new interrogative potential.

The Indian scholar, musician and novelist Amit Chaudhuri has produced a poignant reflection on the relationship between life and writing, collective events and individual interpretations. He pins down the relationship between the global scope, the 'big picture' of Empire and the personal sphere of experience and meditates on the nature of that word 'After' which connects them as follows:

> It might be said that freedom and Partition, which would affect my parents' lives profoundly, were met by them with a certain degree of incomprehension and even indifference; for key moments, unlike their representation later in texts, do not really have clear outlines, and might not even be perceived as having really happened [ … ] The human reaction to change, whether personal or in the form of historical events, is extremely complex, a

hiatus of the mystery or incomprehension of a response, not allowed for in official versions of history. (Chaudhuri)

It seems to me that the time lag Chaudhuri pinpoints here is key to understanding the challenge of trying to understand the relationship between life and writing, and even in making sense of memory, traumatic or otherwise. What a writer can achieve is an attempt to pave a path between experience and text and to explore the myriad of relations and encounters 'within' and the formative role of writing, reading and books in general that have led to the journey 'without' and its visible product, the book.

## Notes

1. Vassanji has tended to be dismissive of these and other critical labels. He has contributed to the material postcolonial scholars work with. He is the co-founder (with his wife, Nurjehan Aziz) of *The Toronto South Asian Review* (now *The Toronto Review of Contemporary Writing Abroad*) and edited an essay collection titled *A Meeting of Streams: South Asian Canadian Literature* (1985). However, he likes to distance himself from discussions of diasporic literature. During a conference on his oeuvre held in London in 2013, he opined that the complicated terminologies stand in the way of readers' just enjoying the stories.
2. The term is moreover used in other disciplines, notably theology and pedagogy, exemplified in George Allan and Malcolm D. Evans, eds., *A Different Three Rs for Education: Reason, Relationality, Rhythm* (2006).
3. A laudable exception would be the late Bart Moore-Gilbert's chapter on 'Relational Selves' in *Postcolonial Life-Writing, Culture, Politics, and Self-Representation* (2009).
4. Relational sociology is succinctly characterised in Pierpaolo Donati, *Relational Sociology, a New Paradigm for the Social Sciences* (2012). Donati addresses the danger of making the concept of relationality, which he sees as '"the unknown object", virtually the *terra incognita* of social relations' too unwieldy, as well as distinguishing it from relativism (3–7). Glissant, too, operates with ideas of interdependency as a characteristic of a decolonised state of being: 'Gradually, premonitions of the interdependence at work in the world today have replaced the ideologies of national independence that drove the struggles for decolonization' (143).
5. In a recent chapter, Hermione Lee offers a poignant synopsis of similar moments of encounter between notable literati and their textual records. She highlights shared patterns across different generations of writers. Her critical focus on techniques of remembering indicates a suggestive route relational life writing criticism might fruitfully expand on.

## Disclosure statement

No potential conflict of interest was reported by the author.

## References

Allan, George, and Malcolm D. Evans, eds. *A Different Three Rs for Education: Reason, Relationality, Rhythm*. Amsterdam: Rodopi, 2006. Print.

Bal, Mieke. *Narratology. Introduction to the Theory of Narrative.* Trans. Christine van Boheemen. Toronto: U of Toronto P, 1985. Print

Chaudhuri, Amit. *Partition of India. Partition as Exile.* 2 July 2000. Web. 4 May 2015.

Donati, Pierpaolo. *Relational Sociology, a New Paradigm for the Social Sciences.* London: Routledge, 2012. Print.

Eakin, Paul John. *How Our Lives Become Stories: Making Selves.* Ithaca: Cornell UP, 1999. Print.

Gergen, Kenneth J. *Realities and Relationships. Soundings in Social Construction.* Ed. Kenneth J. Gergen. Cambridge: Harvard UP, 1994. Print.

Gergen, Kenneth J. *Relational Being. Beyond Self and Community.* New York: Oxford UP, 2009. Print.

Gergen, Kenneth J. *Writing as Relationship.* 2000. Web. 4 May 2015.

Gilmore, Leigh. "Agency without Mastery: Chronic Pain and Posthuman Life Writing." *Biography* 35.1 (2012): 83–98. Print.

Glissant, Édouard. *Poetics of Relation.* Ann Arbor: U of Michigan P, 1997. Print.

Hoving, Isabel. "Moving the Caribbean Landscape: Cereus Blooms at Night as Re-Imagination of the Caribbean Environment." *Caribbean Literature and the Environment. Between Nature and Culture.* Eds. Elizabeth DeLoughrey, Renée K. Gosson and George B. Handley. Charlottesville: U of Virginia P, 2005. 154–68. Print.

King, Thomas, ed. *All My Relations. An Anthology of Contemporary Canadian Native Fiction.* Norman: U of Oklahoma P, 1992. Print.

Lee, Hermione. "Literary Encounters and Life-Writing." *On Life-Writing.* Ed. Zachary Leader. Oxford: Oxford UP, 2015. 124–41. Print.

Moore-Gilbert, Bart. *Postcolonial Life-Writing, Culture, Politics, and Self-Representation.* London: Taylor, 2009. Print.

Naipaul, V. S. *India: A Million Mutinies Now.* London: Minerva, 1991. Print.

Sarkowsky, Katja. "Transcultural Autobiography and the Staging of (Mis)Recognition." *Amerikastudien* 57.4 (2012): 627–42. Print.

Vassanji, M. G. *A Place Within: Rediscovering India.* Toronto: Anchor, 2008. Print.

Vassanji, M. G. *The Magic of Saida.* Toronto: Doubleday, 2013.

Weintraub, Karl. "Autobiography and the Historical Consciousness." *Critical Inquiry* 1.4 (1975): 821–41. Print.

# 'A Nation on the Move': The Indian Constitution, Life Writing and Cosmopolitanism

Javed Majeed

English and Comparative Literature, King's College London, London, UK

**ABSTRACT**
The Indian Constitution (IC) has been considered in terms of its intertextuality with preceding colonial documents such as the Government of India Act 1935. This essay relocates the IC in intertextual relationships with anti-colonial autobiographies and texts such as Gandhi's *Hind Swaraj*, showing the parallels between the way they dramatise self-rule and mix global, Indian and regional levels of identity. Both the IC and these texts are marked by processes of transnational and internal dialogue, and reflect transnational aspects of Indian print culture and the subject positions it gave rise to. Widening the discursive sites of the IC to include anti-colonial autobiographies raises questions about the IC as a species of autobiography itself, and it also gives us another perspective on the tensions within the IC, showing how the conflict between liberty and power is manifested in its linguistic cosmopolitanism and its approach to translation. Constitutions embody the aspirations of a nation's citizens, and the IC's verbal skills grade and structure these aspirations, plotting them along a spectrum of possible futures and grounding them in a variety of pasts. This concern with temporality has a parallel in some anti-colonial autobiographies where the consciousness of time is particularly acute. Finally, both the IC and Indian anti-colonial life writing can be seen as instances of South Asian literary modernity in terms of the style of their creative choices.

## Introduction

The Indian Constitution (IC) has been considered in terms of its intertextual relationships with preceding colonial and other political documents, such as the Government of India Act 1935. This essay relocates the IC in intertextual relationships with anti-colonial autobiographies from the same period. James Tully argues that a post-imperial language of constitutionalism has to recognise and accommodate appropriate forms and degrees of self-rule in accordance with diverse customs and ways (4–6, 55). Amongst other things, anti-colonial Indian autobiographies and texts such as Gandhi's *Hind Swaraj* (1909) are textual experiments dramatising different modes of self-rule, mixing global, Indian and regional levels of identity in doing so. So, too, the IC combines its cosmopolitan inception with a rootedness in India as it defines self-rule. Widening the discursive sites of the IC to include anti-colonial autobiographies raises questions about the IC as a species of autobiography itself, but it also points to tensions between the two and it can give us another perspective on the tensions within the IC itself. Both the IC and anti-colonial autobiographies are marked by processes of dialogue, and this essay begins with the cosmopolitan nature of these in the former.

My essay also explores the IC's cosmopolitanism in terms of its linguistic texture. Constitutions are not just legal documents; they also create appropriate salutary effects through a mixture of tones. I explore aspects of this, as well as the IC's verbal orientation towards temporality which has a parallel in autobiography as a genre of writing, especially in its anti-colonial manifestations. Constitutions embody the aspirations of a nation's citizens, and the IC's verbal skills grade and structure these aspirations, plotting them along a spectrum of possible futures.

## 'A nation on the move'

James Tully argues that constitutions are not fixed and unchangeable agreements made at foundational moments, instead we ought to see them as a form of activity. They are intercultural dialogues in which the culturally diverse citizenry of contemporary societies negotiate agreements on their forms of association according to the three conventions of mutual recognition, consent, and cultural continuity (Tully 30). The Indian Constitution, enacted on 26 November 1949, can be seen in these terms. The sense of it being an activity rather than a fixed and unchangeable agreement was captured in Nehru's remark that the Constituent Assembly was a dynamic body representing 'a nation on the move' (qtd. in Tiwary 43). Tully envisages this intercultural dialogue taking place amongst the members of a culturally diverse population within an already established nation-state. The nation-state is a stable background category in his argument. The inception of the IC occurs against a different background—here the nation-state cannot be taken for granted, its contours and the scope of its sovereignty are unclear, and the content of its nationality is open. Its dialogue takes place in the traumatic context of Partition violence, the influx of refugees and their resettlement, conflict over Kashmir, and an economic crisis (Austin 44–5). The Preamble to the Indian Constitution originally referred to securing 'FRATERNITY assuring the dignity of the individual and the SOVEREIGN DEMOCRATIC REPUBLIC' (India *Constitution* Preamble; capitals original). The Objectives Resolution, moved by Nehru on 13 December 1946, was the basis for the Preamble, but the Resolution did not provide for fraternity. This was added by the Drafting Committee because after Partition the need for fraternity was greater than ever (Tiwary 52, 74–7, 83–4). The IC's dialogical processes therefore had to induce and secure fraternity, but it was also marked and constrained by the traumatic counter-currents resulting from Partition.

The IC was the outcome of dialogue and debate amongst the members of the Indian Constituent Assembly which met in 66 sessions from December 1946 over three years. While the framers of the US constitution began *ab initio*, the Constituent Assembly accepted the framework of the Government of India Act of 1935, incorporating its language and embodying its substance in specific ways (Tiwary 327; for the influence of the Act see Tiwary 8–10, 90, Ch. 5). While there are many continuities between the IC and the 1935 Act, it also marked a transformative break as it was not legitimated by an Act of the British Parliament. Instead of being written in the Colonial Office of the imperial power and passed by the British Parliament, the Constitution could be described as 'home-made' (Austin 2 f.n.; Elangovan 3). The IC is the Constitution of an independent state, whereas the 1935 Act laid down the administrative structure of a colony. Furthermore, the IC's chapter on fundamental rights is unprecedented in the Indian context (Tiwary 111, 327). The Constitution was not imposed by a foreign power, in the way that the Japanese and the West German constitutions were, and some would argue, as the Iraqi constitution is being imposed today (I owe this point to E. Sridharan, University of Pennsylvania Institute for the Advanced Study of India, New Delhi). Some 250 members spoke in the Indian Constituent Assembly, and although it was not a popularly elected body and was dominated by the Indian National Congress, its membership reflected a wide range of ideological and political positions (Austin 10–3). While the INC's dominance created some irregularities in practice, it also gave a measure of cohesiveness to the proceedings (Tiwary 64–6, 324–5). These were open to the public, and some 53,000 visitors were admitted to the gallery when the draft constitution was considered (Tiwary 66). This process of consensus building included the Assembly's committee system, the dialogue between provincial and Union government leaders in the Assembly, inter-governmental communications, and off-the-record discussions between the Assembly leaders and dissidents among its members. Public bodies (such as chambers of commerce and industry, private companies, bar associations, linguistic associations, and minority groups) and private individuals in substantial numbers also made their views known to the Assembly. The Assembly Secretariat acknowledged nearly all these communications and frequently summarised them for the Drafting Committee or Assembly leaders (Austin 9–10, 312–4, 316, 324). The Constituent Assembly's need for representativeness and its concern to combine cohesiveness with flexibility were reflected in the Rules of Procedure Committee's first report. When submitting this on 21 December 1947 to the Constituent Assembly, K. M. Munshi observed

> These are the rules of the Assembly. They can be altered or added to when we next meet. We can always add new points of view if some are omitted. But it is highly essential that we should adopt the Rules and appoint one or two committees which keep the organisation of the Constituent Assembly going. (qtd. in Tiwary 53)

This aspect of the IC as being rooted in a culture of debate, consensus building and interaction with a range of public associations, resonates with an important feature of Indian intellectual and political life in British India which saw a growth in societies and associations, new cultures of public association, debating clubs, and a wide array of rhetorical models and modes of address in the public sphere (Bayly; Samaddar). This is also reflected in Indian anti-colonial life writing during this period, in which speaking and debating in public are referred to as formative personal and political events. In articulating nationalism as akin to a religious faith, Surendranath Banerjea's autobiography focuses on a quasi-mystical union between himself and the audiences he addresses in his public speeches (Banerjea 129–34). When Nehru speaks to crowds of peasants, his addresses turn into question and answer sessions on how to define being Indian. These sessions also point to Nehru's own anxieties about the gap between his class position and the 'masses', and therefore his claim to represent India (Nehru *Discovery* 59–61). For Gandhi, on the other hand, the experience of stage fright when speaking in public is key to individual and collective self-empowerment (Majeed *Autobiography* 226–31). In different ways, then, anti-colonial life writing explores modes of address in the public sphere in terms of the relationships between subjectivity and the political realm.

While we can view the IC as the product of a 'home-made' dialogue, that was enacted and was rooted in the 'rich heritage of our composite culture' (India *Constitution* Art. 51 A), this dialogue also took place as an intercultural, transnational one between the Indian constituent assembly and the constitutions of other nation-states. This was part of the same process of the Indian nation on the move, so that the IC emerged from within both Indian and global fields of meaning.

The Indian Constituent Assembly, as has been noted by others, drew on the constitutional traditions of the US, Canada, Switzerland, Australia and Ireland. Nehru referred to the Philadelphia convention, the French experiment, and the Russian revolution as sources of inspiration for the Constituent Assembly. The formulation of the Objectives Resolution and subsequent Preamble was influenced by the American Declaration of Independence, the French Declaration of the Rights of Man, and the Preamble to the Constitution of Eire (Tiwary 42, 67). The Assembly modified established ideas about the construction of federal governments and their relations with constituent units in order to define a new kind of federalism to meet India's needs (Austin 186). One of its members, B. N. Rau, visited Europe and the US gathering information and insights into how constitutions work. This affected the general tenor of the Indian Constitution and some of its specific provisions. For example, it was after his trip to Ireland where he understood that functional representation was not working effectively there, that the provision for functional representation in the Draft Constitution was done away with (Austin 152). During the same trip he concluded the 'general welfare should prevail over the individual right' (Austin 202), and that federalism with its independent spheres of legislative power could be a hindrance in this respect. The members of the drafting committee agreed with him, supporting their belief with reference to an opinion handed down in a Canadian case, that matters affecting peace, order, and good government were the responsibility of Parliament even if they touched on matters reserved for provincial legislatures (Austin 202). Of the three provisions which enhanced the wide range of authority given to the Union government, one was adapted from the Australian constitution (Austin 201). It was after Rau's visit to the US and talks there that the IC's framers dropped the clause 'due process' in favour of the clause 'procedure established by law' in relation to personal liberty in Pt III of the IC. The influence of US constitutional practice is also evident when dealing with 'Police Power' of the state and the theory of 'eminent domain' in respect to the right to property and the position in the IC of the Indian judiciary (Tiwary 327–8). The inclusion of a variety of detail in the Constitution by the Assembly from the 1935 Government of India Act and from other constitutions meant that the existing case law concerning the interpretation of these provisions would be available in interpreting the Constitution. In interpreting the Constitution, case law from the US and other countries, as well as Indian precedent, have frequently been drawn on by the Supreme Court (Austin 327). The influence of other Constitutions on the IC is also evident in the drafting of the directive principles of State policy and Fundamental Rights. Other twentieth century constitutions, reflecting the rise of the idea of the welfare state, stated such directives (Tiwary 153). In making these non-justiciable, the IC's framers were influenced by the Irish Constitution, but the principles were also influenced by the

International Bill of Rights drafted by Sir Hersch Lauterpacht in 1945, and the international context of debates about human rights following the experience of the Second World War, the Holocaust and post-war economic devastation (Jayal 145). By the late 1940s, the drafting of a Universal Declaration of Human Rights was underway, and in 1947 a committee was established by UNESCO to inquire into the philosophical underpinnings of human rights. This committee sought responses from Indians including Gandhi (Jayal 145).

Thus the IC draws upon the globally available language of Constitutions while inflecting and territorialising that language. The Directives of State Policy reflect this; while they were influenced by other constitutions, they are also underpinned by an internal Indian narrative. The Nehru Committee Report of 1928 recommended amongst other things free elementary education, the maintenance and improvement of labour and economic conditions, and health provisions (Tiwary 153–4). Situating this report in the context of international rights discourse in the late 1920s suggests that this was 'a rather exceptional document in its early envisioning of social and economic rights' (Jayal 139), so that in part the foundations for these rights were autochthonous. The 1931 Karachi Resolution of the Indian National Congress (INC) on Fundamental Rights referred to economic justice, while Gandhian philosophy also had an influence in the shaping of these Directives (Tiwary 154).

The IC therefore emerged as a dialogue within as well as across national boundaries. This reflects the nature of India as a civilisation and not just a nation-state. As Dhavan has argued, scripting a Constitution for India is like scripting one for the world (320). The transnational dimensions of the IC reflect India's character as a complex civilisation with a global reach, containing strands drawn from many world religions. These global and cosmopolitan aspects of the IC are rooted in an important feature of Indian intellectual life in the colonial period. In some ways, the IC is the culmination of an aspirational anti-colonial cosmopolitanism in India in the nineteenth and twentieth centuries. Indian thinkers, writers and intellectuals participated in what Kris Manjapra and Sugata Bose have called cosmopolitan thought zones, debating, translating and interpreting key texts and ideas in transnational public spheres which, while they were structured by asymmetrical power relations, were also marked by a degree of shared dwelling (Manjapra 1–2). Chris Bayly has examined how Indian writers and thinkers cannibalised, hybridised, and localised liberal ideas and concepts, re-authoring them as they participated in transnational public spheres in this period (Bayly). As he reminds us, neither an area studies approach nor a simple model of transnational exchange are adequate for Indian intellectual history of the nineteenth and twentieth centuries (Bayly 95), and this applies to the IC as well.

Re-framing the Indian Constitution as a cosmopolitan and transnational dialogue therefore helps us to avoid the dangers of what Goswami has called 'methodological nationalism' (4, 7,19). It moves us away from the language of originality and imitation as a framework for understanding the inception of the IC. The latter was criticised by some as 'a slavish imitation' of and a 'slavish surrender to the West' (Austin 325). Austin has argued that what matters is the skilfulness of the Constituent Assembly's borrowing and the quality of its modifications (Austin 321). However, the paradigm of originality and imitation with its assumptions of original sources and derivative texts, is problematic in the field of constitutionalism because of the latter's multiple origins and sources of inspiration, which cannot be neatly sequenced in a linear history or a clear-cut chronology of source and influence. If we think of constitutionalism in terms of a cosmopolitan and transnational dialogue, then clarifying different kinds of cosmopolitanisms can be productive (Breckenridge et al.). For example, in outlining the general principles of a Gandhian constitution, Shriman Narayan Agarwal used the language of originality to criticise the idiom of Indian constitutionalism current at the time. Referring to India as 'an ancient laboratory of constitutional development', he argued that a mixture of western constitutions should not be 'manufactured' for her and that 'a system of administration foreign to its own genius' should not be foisted on India (Agarwal 11). However, in one of its key chapters (Ch. 4) entitled 'The Gandhian Way' (Agarwal), the author refers to Joad, the Greek city states, Huxley, syndicalists, anarchists, Mannheim, Kropotkin, Sir Henry Sumner Maine, Baden-Powell, Marx and even Henry Ford as representing different positions analogous to a Gandhian one. So the text subscribes to an Indian essence or 'genius', and is critical of borrowing, but has a cosmopolitan range of reference which helps it to secure and define a Gandhian position in dialogue with, rather than in opposition to, other political traditions. Here, then, we have an unconscious and disavowed cosmopolitanism. In the Constituent Assembly and its leaders, on the other hand, we have a critically self-reflexive cosmopolitanism which avows cosmopolitan dialogue in the process of inflecting it for its own purposes. The IC might be seen as articulating a critical and dialogical cosmopolitanism from the perspective of a bundle of local histories that had to deal with the global project of 'modernity/coloniality'. To adopt some terms from Pheng Cheah, we might consider the language of Indian constitutionalism in its period of formation as a 'nationalistic awareness of the cosmopolitical', a 'risky agency of the national-in-the-cosmopolitical' (Cheah 'Given' 316), where cosmopolitical refers to a global political field imbued with a sense of new cosmopolitanisms as alternatives to colonially imposed ones (Cheah 'Cosmopolitical' 31–2). Indian citizenship and its language of constitutionalism were not defined against cosmopolitanism. They were mutually constitutive. In the Indian context at least, the choice between rootless cosmopolitanism and territorial nationalism is a false one, and cosmopolitanism and territorial nationalism were imbricated from the start.

Thus, the IC was both home- and globally-made; the Constituent Assembly took a genre of writing that had circulated globally since the eighteenth century and inflected and territorialised it locally. This process has a parallel in the autobiographies of such figures as Gandhi and Nehru, who rework the globally circulating genre of autobiography and root it in their experiences of colonial modernity and a struggling Indian selfhood. Both also articulate their selfhood through varied representations and concepts of travel in order to negotiate global, regional, and national strands in their identity (Majeed *Autobiography* Ch. 3), and a mixture of the global and the Indian inform their autobiographies of self-rule just as it informs the IC.

Nehru's reflections on his identity in various forms of life writing, from his autobiographies and letters to essays and public addresses, explore how his personal identity, India, and an emerging modern world order are interconnected. He tries to bring himself and others together in the autobiographical act of becoming Indian through the method of collage, and here his views on the nature of a letter, themselves expressed in a letter, are instructive:

> What indeed are letters? Not surely just budgets of news, although they contain news ... They are something far more; they are, or ought to be, bits of the personality of the writer, quivering shadows of the real self. They are also, or they at least endeavour to represent and to

mirror, something of the personality of the person written to, for the writer is full of the person he is writing to. Thus a real letter is a strange and revealing amalgam of the two—the one who writes and the one who receives. If it is such a letter, it has considerable value for both the persons concerned. (Nehru 'To Indira' 393)

His autobiographies evoke 'quivering' bits of himself in an amalgam of his own and readers' selves within the greater amalgamation which is India. In one letter, he mentions how he tries to 'weave together' the 'numerous strains' of his identity into one pattern 'for my country and for the world', a pattern which is related to the 'emergence of a world order' (Nehru 'To Eleanor' 621) and in other letters he argues that the problems defining the nationalist struggle in India are global (Nehru 'To Mahatma' 528; Nehru 'To Rajendra' 39). Becoming an Indian national, then, is necessarily imbricated with becoming a world citizen. This is apparent in his autobiographical texts. In *Discovery* Nehru envisages a defining feature of post-colonial India as being a 'multinational' state, which would be a development of its own past history (Nehru *Discovery* 392). This is in keeping with a modern tendency in which the 'idea of the national state itself [is] giving way to the multi-national state' (Nehru *Discovery* 456). In this sense, then, the quasi-national differences between the different regions of India which Nehru points to in some of his essays and speeches ('Presidential' 189; 'On the Selection' 198) make India a microcosm of the modern world. Moreover, the 'world-wide' development of a global culture connecting a variety of cultures with 'common links' is manifested in India itself (Nehru 'To Syed' 392), where a new world civilisation combining 'East' and 'West' is being prefigured (Nehru 'The Eastern' 192). This is captured in Nehru's own sense of himself in his *An Autobiography* (Nehru 596, 28). The mixed formal elements and styles of Nehru's autobiographies evoke this self-conception and the conception of India as amalgams, and the two work together as a flexible coalescence of the global, regional and national. (Majeed *Autobiography* 161–3).

Describing the IC as 'home-made' (see above) begs the question as to what 'home' means in the context when so many have been uprooted from their homes and are creating new ones during Partition. Here we might again have recourse to Nehru's life writing. Even before Partition, for Nehru there is no simple home-coming to India. In the epilogue to *An Autobiography*, Nehru writes of how he has become 'out of place everywhere, at home nowhere', of how he is 'a stranger and alien in the West' and yet also experiences 'an exile's feeling' in 'my own country' (596). It would be too strong to apply this exact sense of belonging to the collectivity of the Constituent Assembly itself, nonetheless its notion of 'home' was similarly complex, partly because what constituted 'home' was in question following Partition.

The form of Gandhi's *Hind Swaraj* also has cosmopolitan implications. The text is cast in a dialogue between an editor and a reader and arises out of an actual dialogue between friends (Gandhi 6). While there are differences between the dialogue in *Hind Swaraj* and the dialogues of the *Gita* and Plato (not least in the absence of Socratic irony), nonetheless it does suggest that dialogue is a cross-cultural mode of investigation into the nature of 'Truth'. The editor and reader might also represent different internal aspects to Gandhi's own self, on the one hand an angry, violently inclined self, and on the other the more restrained, self-controlled self that seeks to edit the nation and to control and sublimate its violent impulses. This dialectical interplay between violent and anti-violent impulses also marks Gandhi's *Autobiography*. In other words, the dialogue in

*Hind Swaraj* is a form of self-interrogation and internal searching, an interaction between different parts of the same self. This internal questioning is a feature of the experiments in his *Autobiography*, in which *satyagraha* is grounded in deep introspection and an inner struggle with one's self alongside a struggle in the political realm. Nehru's autobiographies too were interrogative and self-questioning, openly acknowledging the author's doubts and confusions, but these questions led him to different answers from Gandhi (Majeed *Autobiography* 30–1, 154–5). We could also say that self-interrogation marks the Constituent Assembly; it is a site of debate and discussion looking outwards to the world, and it is the space for collective introspection and an inward search for the meaning of the term 'Indian' in the aftermath of Partition.

There is another dimension to the cosmopolitan dimensions of the IC. It is important to foreground the fact that the IC is a written text. This seems obvious until we remind ourselves that Britain does not have a written constitution in the conventional sense. India as a postcolonial successor state to British India incorporates parts of British colonial legislation in its Constitution, but the very existence of the IC as a written document marks a transformative break from empire. One of the common characterisations of postcolonial literature is that it writes back to empire and its metropolitan texts (Ashcroft, Griffiths and Tiffen); here there is no writing back as such because there is no text to write back to. Rather the existence of the IC as a written text calls attention to the absence and lack of an imperial metropolitan text. The colonial symbolic order is inverted; from the perspective of colonial modernity India was constructed as lacking in many respects, but here it is the erstwhile metropolis that is lacking. Moreover, the authority of colonial rule in India was often associated with the weight of the printed word, hence Orientalists such as H. H. Wilson were anxious to rectify any 'grave blemishes in documents emanating from authority' (iii). The IC is one of the longest constitutions in the world; its printed text serves as a weighty and material visual icon of a nation whose internality is in motion but whose exterior is like the discrete object that is a bounded book. Through the weightiness of its own print, the IC subsumes part of the colonial printed archive and displaces and marginalises it. As a printed document, the IC also emerges from the distinctive history of print cultures in India, which since the end of the eighteenth century was multilingual, cross-cultural and transnational. These print cultures created a range of discourses which sustained various subject positions including those of 'constructive hybridity' and 'cultural ambidexterity' (Dharwadker). The IC's own transnational and cross-cultural elements as a printed document resonate with these aspects of the evolution of print cultures in India; the imbrication of global and local influences in the IC exemplifies 'constructive hybridity' and 'cultural ambidexterity'. Some of Gandhi's and Nehru's key texts also reflect this transnationalism of Indian print cultures. *Hind Swaraj*, for example, was published by Gandhi's appropriately named International Printing Press in the *Indian Opinion* in South Africa, a press that was staffed by a multilingual, multi-religious and multi-ethnic work force (Hofmeyr 2013). The Gujarati and English versions of his *Autobiography* were also first published in serial instalments in journals, this time in India itself. Taken together, the location of these publications illustrates how Gandhi's textual enactments of self-rule were imbricated with a print culture that was at once transnationally diasporic and Indian. Nehru's *An Autobiography* was published by John Lane in London in 1936, by John Day in New York in 1941, and by the Bodley Head in London in 1942, while *The Discovery of India* was first published in

1946 by the Signet Press in Calcutta and Meridian Books in London. Nehru's textual enactments of self-rule are similarly entangled with a print culture that is both Indian and global in scope.

Thus, anti-colonial Indian autobiographies and other texts such as *Hind Swaraj* test out different forms of self-rule and styles of dialogue, mixing global, Indian and regional contexts and levels of identity in doing so. They appropriate a global textual genre to express different versions of Indian selfhood and explore the question of the relationship between individual and group identity. As such, they are also part of an Indian print culture that was multilingual and transnational from the eighteenth century onwards. They can therefore be seen as a parallel discursive site to the IC and its notions of self-rule. There are of course a number of other autobiographies that can be re-read in this framework, such as those by Lajpat Rai, Surendranath Banerjeea, and M. R. Jayakar, but being Indian is an emergent process and a quest rather than a given in Nehru's and Gandhi's texts. In some ways, the Indian Constitution can also be seen as a quest for citizenship (Jayal 11). Just as the IC has become an icon of the Indian State, the autobiographies of such canonical figures as Nehru and Gandhi have also acquired an iconic quality, and like the IC, this iconicity is rooted in the structured open-endedness of their texts. The Preamble to the Indian Constitution exemplifies this. As it now stands, it contains an amendment of the original 'sovereign democratic republic' to 'sovereign socialist secular democratic republic'. The entire text of the IC with subsequent amendments inserted into it (for the powers of amendment see IC part XX) and the original clauses being footnoted (for some good examples see Art. 341 and Art. 342), means that the IC reads as a text in process and not as a finished artefact. Its fabric evokes a text that is always in the making, and therefore a nation that is also always in the making, just as Nehru and Gandhi's life writing evokes a sense of Indianness in the making.

I have argued elsewhere that anti-colonial autobiographies in British India explore the relationships between notions of interiority and the public realm of politics in South Asia, and between the individual and community or group identity (Majeed *Autobiography*). For the IC the relationship and balance between individual and community rights is a crucial concern (Tiwary Ch. 5; Jayal Ch. 7; Bachpai). One defining feature of the autobiography as a genre is that the narrator and the protagonist are formally the same, formally because in practice it is not self-evident that the narrator and his or her past selves are necessarily or logically the same person. In the case of the IC, both the narrator and the protagonist are formally identical (although problematically so), and in this sense the Indian Constitution could be seen as the Indian State's autobiography. It is a text of self-authoring as well as a text of self-authorisation, and one that, like many autobiographies, selectively appropriates its past as it comes into autonomous being.

## Linguistic cosmopolitanism

The cosmopolitanism of the IC is also evident in its linguistic texture, which is noteworthy in a number of respects. It contains administrative and other terms transliterated from Indian languages such as *panchayat, gram sabha, begar, jagir inam, muafi, janmam, ryotwari, raiyat,* and *devaswom* (Art. 31A; Art. 40; Part IX; Part IXA; Art. 290A). It also uses Latin terms, like *habeas corpus, mandamus, quo warranto,* and *certiorari* (Art. 32 clause 2; Art. 139). The IC is written in English as a world and imperial language, incorporating lexical items from earlier imperial languages such as Latin and Persian, as well as terms from Indian languages. It is thus linguistically multi-layered, reflecting its global reach and cosmopolitan inception combined with a rootedness in India. Moreover, these Indian terms are transliterated but not translated. Transliteration is part of the linguistic and aesthetic creativity of the Indian novel in English in this period, for example, in G. V. Desani's *All about H. Hatterr* (1948). However, unlike Kipling's *Kim* (1901) with its self-consciously laboured transliterations, the IC is linguistically at ease with itself. It is self-reflexively eclectic in its cosmopolitanism but it is not burdened by an embarrassed self-consciousness when it comes to its own language. Its linguistic ease grounds its cosmopolitanism as well as its air of authority.

To a certain extent, the IC's linguistic cosmopolitanism emerges from the texture of British colonial English in India. The jargon of the administrative English of the East India Company in the late eighteenth and early nineteenth centuries reflected the continuing powerful influence of Persian as the Mughal language of administration. This language began to change in important respects by the 1830s, especially after the supplanting of Persian by English as the language of the courts in 1837 (Majeed 'The Jargon' 183–8). It remained the case, however, that the official documents of the colonial state in India were 'thickly studded with terms adopted from the vernacular languages of the country, often inserted without any explanation of their purport' (Wilson i). The IC's language partly reflects this history of Indian English. As we have seen, it drew on the 1935 Government of India Act, while also departing from it in important ways. This Act contained terms (to adopt Wilson's words) 'inserted without any explanation of their purport' from Indian languages and Persian. Like the IC, it has *ryot, ryotwari* and *jagir*, but it also includes terms that are not to be found in the text of the IC, such as *kist, inamdar, fasli, khot, khoti village, bhagdari, chaukidari tax, jhankar, ganda, kotwar, jagalia, mahar, watander patel* and *watander patwari, thekadar, deshmukh* or *deshpandia, lambardar, mahal, malik makbuza, kamil jama, sir land, khudkasht, haisiyat, kamil jama, malik makbuza, zaildar, sufedposh,* and *lambardar* (United Kingdom 26 Geo.5. Ch. 2). These terms occur in the Sixth Schedule dealing with the income and property qualifications defining the limited franchise of Indians, and refer to property ownership and land revenue, as well as local positions of power based on ownership of property. In contrast, the IC granted Indian citizens universal suffrage (Art. 326) and therefore its lexicon does not have such an extensive range of terms drawn from land revenue systems and property ownership that dominate the Sixth Schedule of the 1935 Act. Moreover, the right to property (Art. 31) was not taken as self-evident and the article which dealt with this was one of the most intensely debated in the Constituent Assembly (Tiwary 143–9). As is to expected, the legal Latin terms in the IC referred to above have no place in the Government of India Act, which seeks to clarify the administrative framework of India and limited mechanisms of political representation within that framework, rather than to grapple with issues of liberty, legal and prerogative writs, judicial remedies, and the powers of review. Thus, while the IC emerges from the history of colonial Indian English, its own lexicon of Indian and Latin terms marks a departure from the 1935 Act, as it is orientated towards the creation of a Constitution for a democratic republic.

From the perspective of this paper, locating the IC in a different set of intertextual relations suggests overlaps between modes and processes of self-rule in anti-colonial life writing and the IC. But re-framing the IC and anti-colonial life writing as parallel discursive sites also calls attention to the tensions between the two. As I have argued elsewhere, in the field of life writing Nehruvian secularism enabled and dramatised strategies for an interplay between a secularised constitutionalism and individual selfhood. Nehru's dramatisation of a self in global disarray grounded his sense of Indian nationalism (Majeed *Autobiography* 150–1, 172). However, there is an obvious conflict between the experimentation of self in life writing and the political exigencies of cohering the nation-state as a mode of governance and political agent in the aftermath of Partition. One key feature of the Indian Constitution is notable here. During the drafting process of the Constitution, the authority of courts in cases of personal liberty was lessened and the individual lost the remaining vestiges of protection of due process. The provisional Parliament passed the first preventive detention act in February 1950. In the Act, courts were forbidden from questioning the necessity for any detention order issued by the Government. The subjective satisfaction of the authorities was to be the determining factor in every case. The courts could not enquire into the truth of the facts put forward by the Executive as grounds for detaining an individual. In short, 'the authority given to the Government in India is a potential danger to liberty' (Austin 102, 112–3). Moreover, preventive detention came to India with the Bengal State Prisoners Regulation III of 1818, and was extended to Madras and Bombay 1819 and 1827. Here, then, the Indian Constitution was extending the more repressive aspects of its colonial legacy. British colonial legislation ensured the supremacy of the central government in the executive and legislative spheres and this remained the case under the IC, which in some respects went further in the vestment of residuary powers than the 1935 Government of India Act did (Tiwary 2, 329). The extension of aspects of the colonial legacy calls attention to how the conflicts within the postcolonial Indian polity also need to be understood in terms of its critical dialogue with the colonial past. Indian constitutionalism was simultaneously constrained and enabled by that past, as well as by the events of Partition. As the expression of a cosmopolitan dialogue which sought to give shape to cultural and linguistic diversity, it was able to decolonise elements of the imperial language of modern constitutionalism and its 'empire of uniformity' (Tully Ch. 3), while remaining trapped in some of its other terms and strategies.

The cohering but overweening executive power of the State is manifested in the field of language. On the one hand, there are striking illustrations of the porous boundaries around the IC's text. For example, originally the IC referred to a Governor or 'Rajpramukh' when dealing with provincial governments but the latter term was omitted by the Seventh Amendment Act 1956. The current text of the IC therefore refers to the 'Governor *** of the State', with the footnote 'The words "or Rajpramukh" omitted by the Constitution (Seventh Amendment Act, 1956, s. 29 and Sch ... ' (see parts XII and parts XXII). The asterisks mark the absence of a text which is re-incorporated as an excised portion in footnotes; lacunae are marked but are also filled at the same time. It would be interesting to know if other Constitutions have asterisks dotted through their texts in this manner. This suggests something of the creative messiness around the edges of the IC's text and its sophisticated sense of the boundaries between inclusion, exclusion and amendment. In contrast to this, the executive power in the IC is quixotic when it comes to the question of translating the IC into Hindi as the national language. Here the IC circumvents the problems surrounding the slipperiness of translation and the fragility of meanings across languages by sheer fiat, that is by deeming a translation to be 'the authoritative text thereof in the Hindi language' (Art. 394A). The combination of open-endedness and flexibility of provision and dialogue with executive coherence and fiat is also manifested in the way the IC approaches the field of language in general (see Arts. 120, 210, 343–51). One might contrast here Gandhi's conception of authorship as being closely allied to translation: his reinforcement of the secondary nature of translation is key to his experimental engagements with the tree-like structure of 'Truth' in his *Autobiography*. His framing of 'Truth' through translatability is evocative of this text and *Hind Swaraj*. When in the preface to the latter, Gandhi stresses he is not being original (Gandhi 10), he is also stressing that because of the translation-like character of 'Truth', there are no original texts, only texts in translation (for a fuller discussion, see Majeed *Autobiography* 270–9). The IC, by contrast, seeks not to work with the fragility of translation, but to secure a final authoritativeness which cannot, because of the very nature of language, be obtained in the field of translation.

## Temporalities

As representing a nation in the making, the IC is a historically layered text, a palimpsest with tracked changes that calls attention to its own evolution and the craft of its own production. It draws upon the colonial past, and beyond that on earlier world languages and their lexicons. On the other hand, through the Directive Principles of Part IV it is a future-orientated text, designed, in Ambedkar's words, to give 'certain directions to the future legislatures and the future executives to show in what manner they are to exercise the power which they will have' (Tiwary 158). The debates on some of the IC's articles mixed time frames, drawing on different epochs simultaneously. With regard to the right to property (Art. 31), the framers drew on the theory enunciated by American jurists of 'eminent domain', but the article was also discussed with reference to notions of property in ancient India (Tiwary 147). The IC therefore draws on an Indian and world historical past, a global present, and looks to the future, and at times its clauses are framed in different time zones. As a future-oriented text, it evokes a layered sense of futurity through the use of different verb forms, thereby plotting a spectrum of futures as graded possibilities. In Part 1 on the Union and its Territory, the first article states 'India ... shall be a Union of States', and articles 2 and 3 begin with 'Parliament may by law'. This combination of 'shall' and 'may' expresses a mixture of definiteness and possibility with regard to the future. With regard to the Directive Principles, Articles 38 to 48A begin variously with 'The State shall strive', 'The State shall [ ... ] direct', 'The State shall take steps', 'The State shall endeavour to secure', 'The State shall make provision', 'The State shall endeavour to provide', 'The State shall endeavour to organize', 'The State shall endeavour to protect and improve', 'The State shall endeavour to promote [ ... ] maintain [ ... ] foster [ ... ] encourage', 'The State shall promote with special care', and 'The State shall regard'. In these articles, the IC expresses a complex sense of the future, which is broken down into possibilities, expressed by 'shall' to suggest an imperative, then further modified by infinitive forms of verbs ('to endeavour', 'to promote', 'to secure' and so on). The result is a graded verbal orientation towards the future, an imperative qualified by other imperatives to suggest a grammatical and emotional mood grounded in a firm but open-ended determination. As Tiwary reminds us, a Constitution also embodies the aspirations of its inhabitants (333–34). The verbal skills of the IC grade and structure these aspirations through forms of command, prescription, and orientation, pointing to different degrees of futurity.

In some ways, the IC's sense of temporality is also precise. It refers to 'the Indian people's' adoption, enactment and giving to themselves of the Constitution 'this twenty-sixth day of November 1949'. It is useful to contrast here Habermas' view that with German reunification, East Germany should have a founding constitutional moment to compensate for West Germany's lack of one. This would help to constitute a future collective memory for all Germans (Specter 107–8). In contrast, as noted above, Tully argues that we should move away from seeing constitutions as fixed agreements made at foundational moments. It is not clear that there could be, or that it would be desirable to have, a clear-cut founding moment in India. Behind any such moment would be other moments and historical conceptions that have made the IC possible, stretching from the Government of India Act 1935 back to the Bengal State Prisoners Regulation III of 1818, and beyond to conceptions of rule and representation in medieval and ancient India (Bayly 13–15, 20, 50–60, 164–5, 279, 281, 293). A focus on a singular founding event would keep in check the political imagination that is in play in the IC, an imagination that is also evident in its complex orientation towards, and articulation of, temporality.

Despite the attempt by many autobiographers to follow a chronological sequence in their plotting of events, a mixing of time frames necessarily characterises autobiography as a genre of writing because autobiographical retrospection changes the status and significance of past events and deeds. Events are given significance in relation to events which at the time had yet to occur. In contrast to other Indian anti-colonial autobiographies which try to follow a chronological narrative but fail to do so, Nehru's life writings deliberately disrupt the conventions of chronology. In doing so, he articulates a distinctive view of India and Indians as temporal entities; for him the eschewal of a linear chronology strengthens the tie between individual subjectivity and India's mixed temporality (Majeed *Autobiography* Ch. 5). The question of what constitutes historiography, linearity, and even the nature of time itself were issues that Indian thinkers, poets, and writers grappled with in colonial India. The existence of multiple calendars, the inception of geological time alongside Indian Standard Time, the onslaught on Indian notions of historicity, all contributed to a productive crisis in notions of temporality. In a 'proto-modern' Indian text of the late eighteenth century, we already see a mixing of formal paradigms of life writing that creates a structure of many-layered temporalities and interwoven time frames (Shulman). The IC's sense of temporality, then, and its mixing of time frames, parallels the complex sense of temporality in autobiography as a genre of writing that is brought to an acute state of awareness in the conditions of colonialism in India.

## Conclusion

Placing the IC in the same field as anti-colonial autobiography raises a number of issues. These range from the difficulties of identifying authorship, to the tensions of making the State, the democratic republic, and the Indian people align with each other as the positions of author and protagonist slide and slip. Subaltern life writing also needs to be brought into dialogue with the IC; here gender and caste become important, given the unconscious gender bias in the term 'fraternity' in the Preamble, and the question of how to bring dalits into this 'fraternity'. Constitutions are not just legal documents but also have to create the appropriate salutary effect through a mixture of tones. Here we might think of the Preamble with its carefully weighed punctuation of commas and semi-colons and its capitalisation of key terms, suggesting the momentous and stately nature of the event taking place. It reads like an invocation to the dramatic performance of the coming into being of a democratic republic, with the dramatis personae being the people of India. Were the Constituent Assembly and the production of the IC to be examined in terms of dramatisation and theatricality, the term 'dialogue' would take on added meanings. Finally, an inquiry into how the Constitution resonates with Indian epics might also be fruitful as the latter deal with questions of power, duties, obligations, rights, caste, peace and war, the crises of kingdoms, and individual dilemmas. Lukács famously wrote that the novel 'is the epic of an age in which the extensive totality of life is no longer directly given, in which the immanence of meaning in life has become a problem, yet which still thinks in terms of totality' (Lukács 56). This could also be applied to Constitutions in the modern age; for the IC, the totality of life is not given (especially after Partition) and yet it has to think in terms of totality. In some ways it is an epic quest for the meaning of citizenship in the context of multiple crises, with a range of dramatis personae and intertwined narratives about power, authority, rights, duties, and obligations. Here the caste politics embedded in canonical Sanskrit versions of the epics and alternative renditions of them would be germane to such a discussion (Richman).

For the moment, though, we can suggest that both the IC and nationalist Indian autobiographies might be seen as instances of South Asian literary modernity, whose creativity is characterised by a cosmopolitan moving across literary traditions and languages while being rooted in India. The technical problem Indian authors encountered was that of negotiating an expansive range of material and literary traditions made available to them through colonialism (Majeed 'Literary'). Anti-colonial Indian autobiographies also manage expansiveness on multiple levels, in terms of intercontinental geographical scope combined with local and regional rootedness, and a cast of characters that is necessarily multi-ethnic and multi-religious. These autobiographies can also be read against the background of Indian life writing, ranging from the telling of exemplary lives to collectively authored life writing, conversion narratives, and autobiographies that inaugurated privacy as a new institution in Indian social life (Arnold and Blackburn; Kaviraj; Orsini; Metcalf). Nehru and Gandhi also experiment with the dominant textual conventions of Western autobiographies in their texts in order to define themselves (Majeed *Autobiography* Ch. 4 and Ch. 6). Their creative choices reflected the cosmopolitan nature of modern South Asian literatures, which in their genesis and development are indicative of the freedom of Indian authors to move across and appropriate the resources and conventions of a variety of traditions (Majeed 'Literary'). It is the anxious but hopeful nature of this burdensome choice in cosmopolitan and Indian fields of meaning that animates both the IC and anti-colonial Indian autobiographies.

## Acknowledgments

Earlier versions of this essay, focussing on the nature of Indian secularism, were presented at the Annual South Asia Conference in Madison, the University of Witwatersrand, the Open University and the University of Sunderland. The version of the essay published here was presented at a supportive workshop in Copenhagen University in May 2015. I am grateful to the participants and the organisers Astrid Rasch and Stuart Ward for their helpful comments at the time, and especially to Astrid Rasch for her subsequent comments on the paper. I also presented versions of this paper at the invitation of the South Asia Centre, LSE, to students and officers from India visiting LSE as part of the 125th birth anniversary celebrations of Dr. B. R. Ambedkar, at the High Commission of India in London in October and November 2015. Thanks to Mukulika Bannerjee, Nilanjan Sarkar, and the First Secretary (Protocol) M. P. Singh for organising the lectures, and the audience for their insightful questions and comments. I have not been able to address all the issues that were raised by them because of the constraints of space.

## Disclosure statement

No potential conflict of interest was reported by the author.

## References

Agarwal, Shriman Narayan. *Gandhian Constitution for Free India*. Allahabad: Kitabistan, 1946. Print.
Arnold, David and Stuart Blackburn. "Introduction." *Telling Lives in India. Biography, Autobiography, and Life History*. Eds. David Arnold and Stuart Blackburn. Delhi: Permanent Black, 2014. 1–28. Print.
Ashcroft, Bill, Gareth Griffiths and Helen Tiffin. *The Empire Writes Back: Theory and Practice in Post-Colonial Literatures*. 1989. London: Routledge, 2002. Print.
Austin, Granville. *The Indian Constitution. Cornerstone of a Nation*. 1966. New Delhi: Oxford UP, 2004. Print.
Bachpai, Rochana. *Debating Difference: Group Rights and Liberal Democracy in India*. New Delhi: Oxford UP, 2011. Print.
Banerjea, Surendranath. *A Nation in the Making. Being the Reminiscences of Fifty Years of Public Life*. 1925. Bombay: Oxford UP, 1963. Print.
Bayly, C. A. *Recovering Liberties: Indian Thought in the Age of Liberalism and Empire*. Cambridge: Cambridge UP, 2011. Print.
Breckenridge, Carol A., Homi K. Bhabha, Sheldon Pollock, and Dipesh Chakrabarty, eds. *Cosmopolitanism*. Durham: Duke UP, 2002. Print.
Cheah, Pheng. "Given culture: Rethinking cosmopolitical freedom in transnationalism." *Cosmopolitics. Thinking and Feeling beyond the Nation*. Eds. Pheng Cheah and Bruce Robbins. Minneapolis: Minnesota UP, 1998. 290–328. Print.
Cheah, Pheng. "The Cosmopolitical Today." *Cosmopolitics. Thinking and Feeling beyond the Nation*. Eds. Pheng Cheah and Bruce Robbins. Minneapolis: Minnesota UP, 1998. 20–41. Print.
Dharwadker, Vinay. "Print cultures and literary markets in colonial India." *Language Machines. Technologies of Literary and Cultural Production*. Eds. Jeffrey Masten, Peter Stallybrass, and Nancy J. Vickers. New York: Routledge, 1997. 108–33. Print.

Dhavan, Rajeev. "The Road to Xanadu: India's Quest for Secularism." *Religion and Personal Law in Secular India. A Call to Judgement.* Ed. Gerald James Larson. Bloomington: Indiana UP, 2001. 301–29. Print.

Elangovan, Arvind. "The Making of the Indian Constitution: A Case for a Non-nationalist Approach." *History Compass* 12.1 (2014): 1–10. Print.

Gandhi, M. K. *Hind Swaraj and Other Writings*. Ed. Anthony J. Parel. 1909. Cambridge: Cambridge UP, 2009. Print.

Goswami, Manu. *Producing India. From Colonial Economy to National Space*. Chicago: Chicago UP, 2004. Print.

Hofmeyr, Isabel. *Gandhi's Printing Press. Experiments in Slow Reading*. Cambridge, MA: Harvard UP, 2013. Print.

India. *Constitution of India*. National Portal of India. Web. 11 Nov. 2015. <http://india.gov.in>.

Kaviraj, Sudipta. "The Invention of Private Life. A Reading of Sibnath Sastri's Autobiography." *Telling Lives in India. Biography, Autobiography, and Life History*. Eds. David Arnold and Stuart Blackburn. Delhi: Permanent Black, 2014. 83–115. Print.

Jayal, Niraja Gopal. *Citizenship and its Discontents. An Indian History*. Ranikhet: Permanent Black, 2013. Print.

Lukács, Georg. *The Theory of the Novel. A historico-philosophical essay on the forms of great epic literature*. Transl. Anna Bostock. 1920. London: Merlin, 1971. Print.

Majeed, Javed. "'The jargon of Indostan': an exploration of jargon in Urdu and East India Company English." *Languages and Jargons. Towards a Social History of Language*. Eds. Peter Burke and Roy Porter. Oxford: Polity, 1995. 182–205. Print.

Majeed, Javed. *Autobiography, Travel and Postnational Identity. Gandhi, Nehru and Iqbal*. 2007. Delhi: Primus, 2015. Print.

Majeed, Javed. "Literary modernity in South Asia." *India and the British Empire. Oxford History of the British Empire companion series*. Eds. Douglas M. Peers and Nandini Gooptu. Oxford: Oxford UP, 2012. Print.

Manjapra, Kris. "Introduction." *Cosmopolitan Thought Zones. South Asia and the Global Circulation of Ideas*. Eds. K. Manjapra and S. Bose. Basingstoke: Palgrave, 2010. Print.

Metcalf, Barbara D. "The Past in the Present. Instruction, pleasure, and blessing in Maulana Muhammad Zakariyya's Aap Bittii." *Telling Lives in India. Biography, Autobiography, and Life History*. Eds. David Arnold and Stuart Blackburn. Delhi: Permanent Black, 2014. 116–43. Print.

Nehru, Jawaharlal. "Presidential address at the All-Bengal students conference." *Selected Works of Jawaharlal Nehru*. Vol. 3. Ed. S. Gopal. New Delhi: Orient Longman, 1972–78. 188–96. Print.

Nehru, Jawaharlal. "To Mahatma Gandhi." *Selected Works of Jawaharlal Nehru*. Vol. 5. Ed. S. Gopal. New Delhi: Orient Longman, 1972–78. 526–30. Print.

Nehru, Jawaharlal. "To Indira Nehru." *Selected Works of Jawaharlal Nehru*. Vol. 6. Ed. S. Gopal. New Delhi: Orient Longman, 1972–78. 393–8. Print.

Nehru, Jawaharlal. "To Rajendra Prasad." *Selected Works of Jawaharlal Nehru*. Vol. 7. Ed. S. Gopal. New Delhi: Orient Longman, 1972–78. 38–44. Print.

Nehru, Jawaharlal. *An Autobiography*. 1936. New Delhi: Jawaharlal Nehru Memorial Fund, 1982. Print.

Nehru, Jawaharlal. "On the selection of the new working committee." *Selected Works of Jawaharlal Nehru*. Vol. 7. Ed. S. Gopal. New Delhi: Orient Longman, 1972–78. 197–9. Print.

Nehru, Jawaharlal. "To Syed Mahmud." *Selected Works of Jawaharlal Nehru*. Vol. 7. Ed. S. Gopal. New Delhi: Orient Longman, 1972–78. 385–93. Print.

Nehru, Jawaharlal, "The Eastern federation." *Selected Works of Jawaharlal Nehru*. Vol. 11. Ed. S. Gopal. New Delhi: Orient Longman, 1972–78. 191–2. Print.

Nehru, Jawaharlal. "To Eleanor F. Rathbone." *Selected Works of Jawaharlal Nehru*. Vol. 11. Ed. S. Gopal. New Delhi: Orient Longman, 1972–78. 619–36. Print.

Nehru, Jawaharlal. *The Discovery of India*. 1946. Delhi: Oxford UP, 1989. Print.

Orsini, Francesca. "The Reticent Autobiographer. Mahadevi Varma's Writings." *Telling Lives in India. Biography, Autobiography, and Life History*. Eds. David Arnold and Stuart Blackburn. Delhi: Permanent Black, 2014. 54–82. Print.

Richman, Paula, ed. *Many Ramayanas: the diversity of a narrative tradition in South Asia.* Berkeley: California UP, 1992. Print.

Samaddar, Ranabir. *Emergence of the Political Subject.* New Delhi: Sage, 2010. Print.

Shulman, David. "Cowherd or King? The Sanskrit Biography of Ananda Ranga Pillai." *Telling Lives in India. Biography, Autobiography, and Life History.* Eds. David Arnold and Stuart Blackburn. Delhi: Permanent Black, 2014. 175–202. Print.

Specter, Matthew. "Habermas's Political Thought 1984–1996: A historical interpretation." *Modern Intellectual History* 6.1 (2009): 91–119. Print.

Tiwary, Uma Kant. *The Making of the Indian Constitution.* Allahabad: Central Book Depot, 1967. Print.

Tully, James. *Strange Multiplicity. Constitutionalism in an Age of Diversity.* Cambridge: Cambridge UP, 1995. Print.

United Kingdom. "Government of India Act 1935." 1935. Web. 11 Nov. 2015. <http://Legislation.gov.uk>.

Wilson, H. H. *A Glossary of Judicial and Revenue Terms, and of Useful Words Occurring in Official Documents relating to the Administration of the Government of British India, from the Arabic, Persian, Hindustani, Sanskrit, Hindi, Bengali, Uriya, Marathi, Guzarathi, Telegu, Karnata, Tamil, Malayalam, and other languages. Compiled and Published under the Authority of the Honorable Court of Directors of the East India Company.* London: Allen, 1855.

# 'This Union-Jacked Time': Memories of Education as Post-Imperial Positioning

Astrid Rasch

Department of English, Germanic and Romance Studies, University of Copenhagen, Copenhagen, Denmark

**ABSTRACT**
The end of the British Empire saw profound changes to collective narratives of identity in former colonies—changes which did not leave individuals untouched. This essay examines how individuals use their autobiographical memories of education to position themselves within the new discursive and aesthetic frameworks of their postcolonial societies. Australian historian Russel Ward and Canada-based Barbadian novelist Austin Clarke both wrote their autobiographies in the 1980s and their texts reflect the after empire context in strikingly similar ways. As they recall their education, they link a curriculum focused on Britain to alienation from their local surroundings and associate their adoption of English speech patterns with snobbery. Clarke and Ward employ different positioning strategies in terms of their former selves, suggesting either their complete immersion in an imperial world view or their budding criticism of the curriculum. However, both authors signal to their postcolonial audiences that they now reject the politics of their schooling and by extension the imperial system which it is retrospectively made to represent.

As he sets the scene for a description of his school years, Edward Said opens the third chapter of his memoir with a comment on the Englishness of his education: 'Schoolteachers were supposed to be English, I thought. Students, if they were fortunate, might also be English or, as in my case, if they were not, not' (Said 36). Here, he reflects upon the role of his English education in Cairo in making him feel, as the title has it, *Out of Place*. It is an axiom of postcolonial studies that education was one means by which the imperial administration sought to cement its position of power in colonies across the world, to the detriment of local peoples' relationship to their own cultures (Mangan; Tiffin "Institution"; Viswanathan). So much so that several of the most famous postcolonial critics, like Said, have written autobiographically about that moment by way of signalling their own experience with the 'colonisation of the mind' (Bhabha x; Ngũgĩ 9–16). When these authors recall their education, they reveal not only the colonial past but how they feel about it in the present—and how they want their readers to think they feel about it. Said leaves us in no doubt about the foreignness of his education and his adult scepticism towards it:

> Our lessons and books were mystifyingly English: we read about meadows, castles, and Kings John, Alfred, and Canute with the reverence that our teachers kept reminding us they deserved. Their world made little sense to me, except that I admired their creation of the language they used, which I, a little Arab boy, was learning something about. (39)

The emphasis on the foreignness of curricula and language reappears in many accounts of colonial education. And the effects that Said describes, the teacher-instilled reverence and admiration as well as the distance between the curriculum and the students' lived experience, are also central features in the representations of such education in end of empire autobiographies from across the world (Chung; Conway; Gladwell; Horne; James; Mittelhölzer). Whether from informal colonies like Said's Egypt, from plantation colonies like Barbados, or from settler societies like Australia, autobiographers writing after empire respond to the same global phenomenon of decolonisation, and they seize upon their memories of education as a useful vehicle for positioning themselves in relation to the colonial society that came before decolonisation. As we will see, while using different narrative strategies, autobiographers use the stories of their school years to present their child or adult selves as critics of the imperial system, here represented by their schooling.

I will examine two such autobiographical narratives of education by Barbadian novelist Austin Clarke (1934–) and Australian historian Russel Ward (1914–1995). Clarke and Ward have both made their name as compelling writers who combine a critical stance on Empire with examinations of identity: Clarke's novels and short stories deal with 'cultural exclusion' and 'the twin evils of colonial self-hatred and Caribbean poverty' (Brown and Harris). And Ward's historical work is focused on the Australian national character, notably his 1958 *The Australian Legend* which outlines a radical, egalitarian and anti-authoritarian 'bush ethos' and creates a dichotomy between the English and the 'real Australian' (Bridge). While Clarke and Ward come from widely different types of imperial experience, the remarkable similarities in their representations of their school years make for valuable comparison. Clarke's memoir *Growing Up Stupid Under the Union Jack* (1980) and Ward's autobiography *A Radical Life* (1988) were both written after the break-up of the British Empire, and both authors reflect in copious detail on the colonial nature of their schooling.

Education can be read as an interface between the individual and society. Through participation in rituals of loyalty such as Empire Days, war parades and commemorations, colonial children became quite explicitly part of the imperial project and it was school which was the most prominent organiser of such professions of loyalty (Clarke 15; Gladwell 58; Horne 61–3). For authors of end of empire autobiographies such as Clarke and Ward, the world views and power structures which underpinned their education had changed dramatically by the time they came to write their stories. Because of the importance of education to the bygone imperial world order, many autobiographers use their school experience to remark more generally upon the imperial social conditioning of the societies of their past. Descriptions of education are tools for positioning: they allow the autobiographers to signal their concurrence with anti-colonial discourses and to distance themselves from past imperialism, including their own 'complicity' with the snobbery and exclusionary behaviour they now associate with colonial schooling. Rather than examine parades and public rituals, my focus is on the more private performances of the pupils' place in the Empire which are nevertheless remembered as distinctly imperial. As we will see, the authors recall the literary and historical curricula as well as the spoken language of their schools as having been geared towards making school children into imperial subjects. The autobiographers argue that schools promoted Britishness from early on through a sustained programme of readings, rituals and rhetoric. Here, I study how the writers recall their own personal experiences of this and to what purpose they put those memories. I argue that autobiographers use their school memories to position themselves in relation to past and present societal discourses as well as to their past and present selves.

To understand their autobiographical positionings, we need to situate Clarke and Ward in their contexts, both in terms of their individual careers and the societies in which they have grown up and in terms of how decolonisation has changed the discursive frameworks within which they write. Historian Anne Spry Rush refers to Clarke when she claims that Caribbean school children were encouraged to consider themselves 'also as the conquerors, Britons in their own right'. She suggests that this mitigated against a sense of alienation and uses Clarke's memoir to support her case (40). However, Clarke's irony may have been lost on Rush, for this certainly does not seem to be his message. The Barbados of Clarke's childhood was known as 'Little England', and Clarke repeatedly invokes this phrase to illustrate the parochial atmosphere in which the 'Mother Country' was held up as the ideal for Barbadians to mimic (Clarke 41, 52, 71, 183). An émigré to Canada, Clarke's oeuvre deals with the Caribbean diaspora in Canada, but he also returns to Barbadian themes, writing with fondness about vernacular culture and with scathing criticism of colonialism and racism. Thus, the legacy of Empire remains an abiding concern for Clarke, a fact which comes out not only in his memoir but in his other writings as well as in interviews. He insists that this legacy is so strong as to make the term 'post-colonial' a misnomer (Hewson).

In Ward's earlier work, too, issues of identity and the relationship to Britain have been important. The central project of Ward's classic *The Australian Legend* was to uncover the Australian national character, but this also implied, for him, demonstrating its distinctness from British identity. While historian Carl Bridge points to the British origins of a number of the traits which Ward identified as peculiarly Australian, Ward did not emphasise that likeness but rather portrayed 'all middle and upper-class Englishmen [as] incompetents' (195–9). The Australia in which Ward grew up prided itself on its Britishness; something Ward also observes in his later autobiography. This leads historian John Hirst to suggest that Ward was arguing 'against his experience' when he insisted that the distinctly Australian bush ethos had always had a strong hold on even respectable Australians (90). Instead, Hirst argues that the popularity of Australian folklore as well as of Ward's own work were the result of a change in national sentiment: 'the respectable, or more precisely, their children were becoming less British and more Australian in outlook' (91). This was even more clearly the case 30 years later when Ward was writing his autobiography. Indeed, by that time Australians had entirely ceased to self-identify as British.

Writing in the 1980s, Clarke and Ward thus had decades of empire-critical work behind them. In addition, they were now living, working and writing in societies with a dimmer view of the British Empire than was the case when they went to school in the 1920s–1940s.

# LIFE WRITING AFTER EMPIRE

In the years leading up to and following global decolonisation, a critical apparatus was developed among colonial and metropolitan nationalists and intellectuals which fundamentally challenged the imperial world view and demanded respect for local cultures. The decolonising process looked different depending on the setting. Barbadian independence involved a clear-cut moment of transition of power in 1966, while Australia as a self-governing dominion since 1901 saw a more gradual loosening of the imperial ties and an increasing degree of independence and self-confidence over the course of the twentieth century. But there are also striking similarities. In Australia, as in Barbados, the idea of belonging to an imperial family came under increasing pressure, and by the 1960s it was replaced by strengthened nationalisms which sought to define a distinct national identity. In the cultural sphere, historians and artists were providing ways of understanding the local which did not depend on the relationship to Britain (Curran and Ward; Hall "Negotiating"; Higman). By the 1980s, imperialism had been firmly relegated to the past, and postcolonial critics across the globe, like Said, were beginning to expose the cultural implications of Empire. Within the emerging field of postcolonial studies, there was particular attention to the role of discourse and cultural products in the constitution of the subjectivities of colonised and colonisers alike (Moore-Gilbert, Stanton, and Maley). In their autobiographical texts, these personal and societal agendas combine to make Ward and Clarke's representations of their school years vehicles for a grander interrogation of imperialism and its ramifications.

I want to suggest that these depictions of colonial education are used by the authors to position themselves in relation to discourses on imperialism, past and present. In psychology, the idea of 'narrative positioning' has been developed to account for the way in which 'in conversation [ ... ] people position themselves in relation to one another' (Bamberg 336). One of the proponents of positioning analysis, Michael Bamberg, suggests that we should study the phenomenon on three levels: '*How are characters positioned in relation to one another within the reported events?*', '*How does the speaker position him- or herself to the audience?*' and '*How do narrators position themselves to themselves?*' (Bamberg 337, italics in original). While the framework has been developed to study identity construction in spoken conversation, I believe it can be usefully applied to autobiographical texts as well. As the study of life writing has moved beyond reading autobiography as a transparent account of 'what actually happened', the construction of self and of the past has come to the fore (Saunders). Fundamental to this is the way in which individuals position themselves in relation to others, in relation to an imagined audience and in relation their own past and present selves. Intrinsic to all these questions is the relation to societal discourses past and present. Narrators may signal, through strategies of distancing or rapprochement, that they buy into certain discourses and not others and that they feel in a particular way about past discourses and about their former attitude to those discourses. The positioning that takes place is thus multidirectional in terms of its temporal and social parameters.

Specifically, as we will see in the two autobiographies studied here, authors may fashion a younger self who was critical of or compliant with imperial discourses and they may use either trope as a means of critiquing the past while aligning their narrating self with a contemporary, anti-colonial discourse. While we can use their autobiographies as witness accounts of the destructive effects of colonialism, we can also take the analysis one step further and use them to examine how people retrospectively make sense of their first-hand contact with imperial propaganda. This is by no means an attempt to discredit their value as testimony, but to suggest that the texts may also teach us about the authors' postcolonial present as they reveal how people position themselves to show that they no longer align themselves ideologically with the aesthetics of colonialism.

In the following, I want to consider firstly some of the recurring tropes and techniques which the authors use to illustrate the damaging effects of their colonial education, before I move on to discuss how they refer to their own role as critical or compliant school children. One trope which reappears in many end of empire autobiographies is a sense of alienation brought about by a foreign curriculum and speech. This is related to another trope, namely that colonial education was premised on a sense of British superiority and that the private schools they attended invited elitism and snobbery, adding to their alienation from their own environment. Here, I will look first at how imperial curricula are linked to alienation before turning to the retrospective association of the English accent with snobbery. As they couch their school memories in these terms, the authors more or less explicitly communicate their adult criticism of colonial education and by extension of imperialism.

## Alienating curricula

Historians and literary scholars writing around the same time as Ward and Clarke pointed to the use of metropolitan defined curricula to instil certain values in colonial children in order to enforce a subtle but pervasive control (Mangan; Nandy; Ngũgĩ; Viswanathan). These and later critics have linked this to a sense of alienation from local surroundings. Ian Smith describes the discrepancy between the world of colonial children and the literature they were made to read in school. These 'decontextualized signs', as he terms them, 'cut off from observable reality' have profound emotional effects as they 'foster a pernicious aestheticism that not only favors cultural selfdevaluation but promotes a looking away from one's own history' (816). As we will see in the autobiographies, Clarke and Ward are keen to emphasise precisely the distance between the curriculum and their lived experience and the lamentable consequences of that distance. This includes attempts to imitate the metropolitan ideal and a neglect of one's own history and culture. Whether by stressing their childhood questioning of the imperial curriculum or by implying their later rejection of it, the authors are generally concerned to voice their criticism of the teaching and its consequences, thus using descriptions of imperial curricula to distance themselves from imperialism more broadly.

Clarke describes a school curriculum which did not invite the students to connect their school learning with their real life experience. Echoing Said, Clarke comments how 'I was under a chloroform of learning things which made no immediate sense' (48). Helen Tiffin has termed this 'the daffodil gap', a syndrome referring to the oft-invoked daffodils of Wordsworth's poem 'I wandered lonely as a cloud' which were wholly unfamiliar to many colonial children. Tiffin calls rote learning 'an effective mode of moral, spiritual and political inculcation' in which children, by learning to recite poems by heart, 'absorbed into their bodies ("*hearts*") the "tongue" of the coloniser' in 'a ritual act of obedience' (Tiffin "Cold" 913). Similarly, Clarke suggests that the syllabus entered his body. Associated with anaesthetic, the chloroform learning can be seen to have rendered Clarke's body and mind vulnerable and passive to other people's impositions. While the texts 'made no immediate sense', he represents his childhood self as though in a daze of school learning.

When Clarke, too, mentions daffodils (although referring not to Wordsworth but to a poem by Robert Herrick), we see how his childhood self was not easily shaken from school teachings. Clarke reports a conversation between himself and a pupil of his former school, St Matthias, which illustrates different kinds of imperial education. At St Matthias, the public school, there were overt rites of loyalty where they sang *God Save the King* and paid respect to British war dead; at the private school Combermere, the loyalty was of the more subtle kind which Tiffin describes:

> 'All we got to do at Cawmere is learn a few lines of Latin from Vergil, recite a poem like *Fair Daffodil we hate to see thee haste away so soon ...* '
> 'What's a daffodil, though? They have daffodils at Cawmere?'
> 'A daffodil? A daffodil is only the name of a flower, man!'
> 'But we got flowers growing all over the place, wild flowers and good flowers. In the school garden and *out the front road*. And why we never call them a daffodil?'
> 'A daffodil is a English flower!'
> 'We is English too, man.'
> 'One of these days I am going up in the Mother Country to further my studies.' (Clarke 56, italics in original)

While the conversation seems a little too neat in its exposition of the problem of 'the daffodil gap' to be convincing as simply a memory, there is no doubt that it is precisely a critique similar to Tiffin's that Clarke wants to articulate in memory form. While his friend challenges what constitutes Englishness, the young Clarke remains defensive of the connection to 'the Mother Country'. The very adult phrase, 'further my studies' in a child's mouth suggests the internalisation of the language of an English school system, providing the vocabulary through which the children can conceive of their own future despite its inability to account for their present, like the flowers they have 'all over the place'.

Just as literary models were drawn from England, so, Clarke says, his history teaching caused him to live mentally in an England of his dreams. He presents a childhood self who began to see the world through the stories he learned at school and who fitted the Barbadian reality around him into this framework. He lists people and events in English history, saying how he learned 'about Kings who lost their heads; about Kings who kept their heads; and about Kings whose wives lost theirs' (72). The summary of English history through an inordinate amount of beheadings illustrates the brutality of the English past, ironically undercutting the image of England as the source and pinnacle of civilisation. In contrast, 'nothing was taught about Barbados' (72). The effect, he argues, was to alienate him from that island. Thus, he would walk 'past the church which resembled castles in the *History of England* book, and sit at the table with my mother, under the weak kerosene lamp, and hope to live in a castle some day' (72). There is a stark contrast between his mother's humble house and his hopes which go beyond a good job in Barbados to becoming part of the castle-dwelling English aristocracy of his history books. 'I was', he says, 'more at ease in England, the Mother Country, than in Barbados' (72). The history books and the world around him became confused as he fell in love with the English queens. In order to relate to the women of the books, 'I painted their faces black', but conversely, Barbadian girls were also mentally adapted to his new ideal, the English queens, as he 'put their huge crinolined dresses on the girls I saw around me' (Clarke 73). Looking back, Clarke uses these stories of his absorption in another world to show how pervasively his everyday life in Barbados was affected by the metropolitan models taught in school. His daydreaming, he says, was pieced together by 'English history and culture and English civilization which were my daily intellectual fare at Combermere—all this stuck in my mind and I lived in this Union-Jacked time as if I were in an English countryside' (137). He represents his life and time as metaphorically enveloped in the flag of the ruler, so that he was unable to see the world around him as other than a scene on which to re-enact English history, as when he played out the Battle of Hastings on the Barbadian Hastings Rocks (77).

The upshot of the metropolitan curriculum, Clarke demonstrates, was both disappointment that his own reality failed to live up to the ideals set by metropolitan texts and that he began to see Barbados in a way which emphasised similarities to the natural imagery of British literature and ignored anything which did not fit that mould. His childhood daydreaming of England, he says, influenced even the way he was able to express himself artistically: 'my dreams found me writing poetry. They were copies of English poetry. What other poetry would I know? Milton and Keats' (137). He suggests that the literary fare of his education not only made him idealise British culture but also affected the very tools with which he was able to understand and express his own experience. He had, in Tiffin's words, 'absorbed' the text. As Tiffin notes elsewhere, imperial educational principles 'affected not just the place of literature within the West Indian curriculum but also the specific literary models available to West Indians' (Tiffin "Institution" 44). But when Clarke wrote his memoir, he had certainly stopped to imitate Milton and Keats and written himself into the emerging tradition of Caribbean writers who blend English and Creole modes of expression. This creates a marked difference between the narrating self and the protagonist, the former trapped in the Anglophile world created by his education, the latter able to expose the ideology behind his education.

The neglect of local history in favour of imperial or English history is a recurring trope which we also find in Ward's *A Radical Life*. He, too, reports his younger self to have accepted and internalised the imperial version of events. It is a recurring theme in Ward's autobiography that the history curriculum he met during his schooling focused on British history, to the complete exclusion of the Australian past. He recounts how he became sick as a teacher was dissecting a frog:

> Everyone laughed heartily when, quite unexpectedly, I vomited all over the history textbook open before me—a British history book, naturally. Nothing else was taught in most Australian schools fifty or sixty years ago. At Wesley we had a six-part history of Britain from the Roman conquest till World War I, one volume for each of the six years of the English secondary school course. I loved them all, though I do remember asking why we didn't learn any Australian history. The simple answer was that, because British people had arrived in Australia such a short time ago, there was no Australian history. The reply satisfied me then and for long afterwards. (Ward *Radical* 31)

Why Ward would have had his history book open during a Science lesson is not addressed, but his bodily response to the dissection of the frog serves perhaps to illustrate his adult revulsion at an approach to history which he now condemns. Ward's childhood self is torn between a love for his history books and a child's naïve questioning of the status quo, the authenticity of the memory of this critical stance insisted upon in the phrase 'I do remember'. The answer he received, that the British peopling of Australia had happened so recently that there was no history yet, comes from the anonymous reported voice of not one teacher but the educational establishment in general. The passage suggests the absurdity of claiming that Australia should not have a history. It is difficult to tell whether Ward here is also critical of the fact that history is equated with British settlement, ignoring millennia of Aboriginal history, or if his purpose is to stress that white Australians did have a history of their own by the 1920s. The idea of Australia's history stemming from and overlapping with the time since Anglo-Celtic settlement permeates his own rendition of the past in *The Australian Legend* where 'The Founding Fathers' refer to convicts and 'early demographic changes' to the influx of convicts and free settlers, ignoring the indigenous founders of the country and their place in its demography (Ward *Australian* 15–6). However, writing his autobiography at a time when the 1988 Bicentennial and new histories of frontier violence were bringing Aboriginal rights to the fore, Ward is (perhaps deliberately) vague about what kind of 'Australian history' he was requesting as a child. His autobiography contains a couple of nods to this emerging critique of settler violations against the country's original inhabitants, but overall, he does not link this oppression to imperialism which is instead associated with the kind of loyalty he was asked to perform in school (Ward *Radical* 27, 52, 114–20).

His questioning of the curriculum makes his childhood self appear sceptical, a case of what Leigh Dale describes as 'disruptive' moments when a student 'asks the "wrong" question', 'intrinsically unsettling' because 'drawing attention to the making of authority' (20). Yet despite this briefly unsettling moment, Ward says he was satisfied by the answer given by the teacher. This illustrates the difference between Ward's youthful acceptance of the imperial interpretation of history which was presented to him and his adult independent and untiring 'radical' pursuit of another version of history, thus pointing ahead to a time when he has ceased to be satisfied with the teacher's answer. As we will see below, it is characteristic of Ward's autobiography that he makes this double move in which he positions himself at once as both critical and compliant.

## Speech and snobbery

It is not only the curriculum but also the language taught in schools which is recalled as having set apart the students from their local culture. Language use is a social marker which makes the speaker identifiable to others as belonging to a certain group (Eckert). When Ward and Clarke recall their school years, they remember teachers for their way of speaking, recall lessons in correct spelling and pronunciation and how speech was defining for their identities and group affiliations. Thus, memories about speech are at once deeply personal and inextricable from their social context.

The fact that educational standards in colonial schools derived ultimately from the metropole meant that the sanctioned language use was that approved by educators in Britain. Thus, the weeding out of what was considered to be 'crude' or 'vulgar' language can be read as an attack on local culture (Ashcroft 1, 46). According to Norrel London, scholar of education policy, English teaching in the West Indies was an attempt to eradicate vernaculars and to establish the imperial metropolitan form as the only correct mode of communication (55). Historian Joy Damousi describes how speech was seen in Australia as 'reflective of character and culture' (9–10). Elocution instructions

> encouraged a generic sound that had an *Englishness* in character and tone. In the effort to improve Australian speech and pronunciation, it was the middle to upper-class English accent, the voice of empire, that was, in some quarters, still favoured over all other sounds. (Damousi 166)

In spite of the different linguistic situations in Australia and Barbados, including the influence of African languages on Caribbean Creole, Ward and Clarke describe their experiences of adopting the Received Pronunciation of Britain in remarkably similar terms.

Both authors employ memories of speech and language instruction to illustrate precisely the tension between imperial and national identities and to position the individual protagonist and narrator within that debate. For both Ward and Clarke, the memories of taking up Standard English are tinged with guilt at what is seen retrospectively as their betrayal of vernacular culture. Because Standard English did not arise effortlessly from their local surroundings, but had to be consciously adopted or even imposed upon the children, the language of school is portrayed as unnatural and as creating a division between the protagonists and their societies. The autobiographers often mock the snobbery towards foreign standards of their former selves, but ultimately the image is of the innocence and impotence of children in the face of colonial power embodied in a figure of authority—the teacher.

Ward directly links the speech of his former self and his teachers to the imperial mind set of his education. When introducing his time at university, he cites a poem about the varsity and notes that

> it was very important to pronounce the words in the clipped, affected Oxbridge way so that the final 'ty' came out, not as in 'teee' as in Australia but as a very short 'teh' as in England: and of course to make the end words rhyme by saying 'scahsity' for 'scaircity'. (Ward *Radical* 65)

In referring to the affectation of un-Australian pronunciation, Ward creates an image of young students quite out of touch with the country around them:

> Thus we emphasised that we studied, not at a university like other Australians, but at a very superior and exclusive facsimile of the very grandest institution on this planet, 'The Varsity'—of Oxford or Cambridge. In short, we loved England and ruling British institutions very much and those of our own country not at all except in so far as the latter were faithful replicas of the former. Nowhere, we passionately believed, not even in New Zealand, could there be a better, because more loyally British, varsity than ours. (Ward *Radical* 65)

In retrospect, Ward is quite explicit that something was lost in this admiration for Britain, namely love for one's own country, valued only insofar as it resembled Britain. This accusation of the derivativeness and cultural cringing instilled by the educational culture of Australia pervades his autobiography. In *A Radical Life*, Ward uses his own experiences to illustrate what Australia was like before radicals like him brought to the attention of his fellow nationals their own culture rather than the one derived from Britain. But in this passage, Ward aligns his past self with the imperial sentiments of Australian society in his youth.

What is evident in Ward's account is not only the sense of being set apart from the rest of Australian society but of being superior to it. This trope of colonial education as fostering elitism and snobbery recurs in many accounts of schooling in end of empire autobiographies (Chung; Conway; Gladwell; Horne; Said). Ward consistently associates his education with snobbery, as he suggests that he was encouraged to think more highly of himself than of his fellow-countrymen. Thus, he describes his school as a 'great pillar of snobbery and imperialist loyalty' and says of himself that he 'took readily enough to elitist snobbery' (Ward *Radical* 50, 60).

In *Growing Up Stupid Under the Union Jack*, Clarke, like Ward, describes the equation of the English accent with high status and education, and he, too, describes both the teachers' English pronunciation and the pupils' imitation of it: 'Our masters at Combermere spoke with the accents of the gentlemen of England.' Because 'we too wanted to be educated, we spoke like little black Englishmen' (Clarke 52). The assumption, Clarke suggests, was that education could only be attained through imitation of the metropolitan accent.

Retrospectively, the youthful attempts to speak like the English are used to illustrate and mock the snobbery Clarke was taught at school as well as how he himself became a snob through colonial schooling. He describes his mother making him hot chocolate and how he would try out his new word for that quintessentially imperial drink, tea, on her: 'I preferred a cuppa toy, for I was a Combermere boy, trained to be a snob, coached to be discriminating. A cuppa toy was better than a cup of rich chocolate. England drank toy, and Little England should too' (Clarke 53). Because of the symbolic import with which Clarke invests his adopted speech, we may interpret his dismissal of the hot chocolate as a rejection of local culture and a letting down of his mother, here a stand-in for all of Barbados. His mother's response, 'Boy, you gone mad?' may be read as his own adult response to his youthful adoption of a language and set of cultural standards far removed from those represented by his mother's Creole. While he describes his own compliance with the attitudes taught at school, he also emphasises that he was 'trained' and 'coached' to adopt these attitudes, implying that his snobbery did not emerge from within but was coaxed out of him by external agents in the shape of colonial educators.

Clearly these authors interpret their memories as being of profound importance for their sense of identity as well as being closely related to the imperial context of their childhood—a way of reading these memories spurred on by their post-colonial situation of recall. Both authors invest their descriptions of the inculcation of imperial curricula and language with symbolic import as they use them to demonstrate the influences of imperial standards on something as personal as their speech and everyday outlook. By so doing, they gesture both to the pervasiveness of those standards and to their critical adult stance on them. Interestingly, while they are at pains to expose the way the norms of the past shaped their judgement, Clarke and Ward betray little awareness of how the agendas of their present might itself be shaping their current judgement.

## Attitudes to empire

While Clarke and Ward both distance themselves from the imperialism taught at school and from their youthful acceptance of it, they do so differently. That is, they use different strategies to position their past and present selves in relation to the changing imperial and anti-colonial discourses of their end of empire lives. By distancing their present from their former imperial selves and through retrospective projection of current attitudes back in time, the authors signal to their audiences that they now dissociate themselves from their former lives in ways which reveal the influence of the present on the narration of the past.

I have already alluded to Ward's double move: while he often refers to his own past imperial sentiments, at other points, he locates such sentiment elsewhere and presents his youthful demands for a more local focus in his education. He describes his enjoyment of the literature he was taught in university and then adds 'And yet something, I knew not quite what, was lacking' (Ward *Radical* 69). As he will later describe his own role in recovering Australia's folk traditions, this remark points ahead to that concerted effort to fill the perceived gap in his own cultural upbringing—a gap he says was only vaguely felt when he was younger. He recalls asking his English professor about when they would be reading Australian literature: 'Leaning back in his chair and pronouncing the words in the manner later natural to Queen Elizabeth II in her Christmas broadcasts, he replied crushingly, "Orstralian literature! What Orstralian literature?"' (Ward *Radical* 69). Ward represents his English professor at university as embodying metropolitan arrogance: in him, Britishness in speech and curricula are combined when he pronounces his lack of appreciation of colonial culture in the Queen's English. While the word 'crushingly' suggests the effect on the aspiring young intellectual who had dared ask a question so roundly rejected, Ward gets his revenge by showing who is truly the ignorant party.

Thus, Ward manages to represent his undergraduate self as participating in the Varsity cult of imitating English speech and mores and yet simultaneously as sceptical of the notion that Australia had no culture of its own, an uncanny sense that 'something [ … ] was lacking'. This double move enables him to create a conversion story out of his life in which youthful imperialism impressed on him by his surroundings is discarded in favour of a radical nationalism while at the same time tracing the origins of that nationalism back in time to his school years, suggesting that he was always critical at the core.

Ward explains how having a father who was also the school principal added to his personal sense of imperial loyalty encouraged by the school. As his school received the complete backing of his home, he did not have to negotiate or question different worldviews but was, so we gather, exposed to an unremitting campaign of imperial conservatism, which he accepted at least superficially. However, he suggests, perhaps this was not the case for his unconscious self:

> Naturally, if not quite inevitably, school and home influences reinforced each other in my mind, combining to make me as arrant a conservative, as loyal a Briton and as nasty a snob as ever left any great public school in Australia; and yet, though I never dreamed it then, Princes sowed a rebel seed in me too. (Ward *Radical* 60)

Here, he prepares the ground for a narrative of before-and-after with this 'nasty snob' to be supplanted by the 'rebel' that the reader knows will be the end product for the author of *A Radical Life*. Yet while setting up this past self who is at first glance a completely and thoroughly 'loyal [ … ] Briton', he indicates that already in this apparently 'conservative' self, a 'rebel seed' was contained. So what, then, was this rebel seed? Ward explains that since he knew his school was only considered second best, outdone by the private school St Peter's, he had a natural sympathy for the underdog which remained with him. He suggests that '[t]his knowledge was an influence, all the more powerful because quite unconscious until later' which came to determine his adult strivings for social justice (Ward *Radical* 61). The pseudo-Freudian interpretation that unconscious knowledge should be more powerful works to liberate his inner true self from his outward, superficial, expressions of imperial snobbery. Thus, Ward achieves both a narrative of conversion from 'nasty [ … ] snob' to radical as well as an idea that underlying this conversion was a natural and gradual evolution of an inherent resistance to the conservative order. The youthful loyal Briton who is mocked by the author is presented as the product of external stimuli—'school and home influences'—and thus beyond his control, whereas the 'rebel seed' was so deeply personal as to be hidden even from himself.

Upon finishing undergraduate studies, Ward concludes that:

> It is quite clear now that I was becoming a pacifist, a radical and an Australian nationalist. At the time it was clear only that all I had learnt at the University had very little indeed to do with understanding the world, my own country and my function in both. (*Radical* 84)

In retrospection, then, he translates what he remembers as an unfocused dissatisfaction with the tools provided by his education into the more clear-cut political attitudes he knows he would subsequently adopt. With the benefit of hindsight, he can trace a teleological path towards the radical that he would become.

While Ward makes an effort to point to his early tentative criticism of the lack of local curricula, Clarke emphasises his wholehearted childhood internalisation of the standards he was taught in school to the detriment of even his personal relationship with his mother. Many other end of empire autobiographers describe a personal critique of imperialism as emerging in their school years, but Clarke implicitly locates the turning point in his attitude to Empire outside the narrated time of the autobiography (Chung; Conway; Gladwell; Horne; Kayira). Thus, as readers we have no doubt that such a point must have occurred between the time of his education and that of his writing, even if left unaccounted for. The effect is to make his schooling appear to have influenced his childhood self all the more profoundly, as he was never stirred from his Anglophilia nor provoked into anti-colonialism while at school. As a narrative strategy, this differs from that of Ward, who at least occasionally projects his anti-colonialism back in time while Clarke simply demonstrates through the representation of his Anglophile self that he dissociates himself in retrospect.

Literary scholar James Phelan has demonstrated how focalisation can be used for ethical positioning in narratives. He suggests that in the case of Nabokov's *Lolita*, the narrator, Humbert, variously identifies with and challenges the actions of his former self. This is conveyed, he argues, through dual focalisation in which the narrator and the protagonist perceive the same event but do so with different ethical attitudes: 'In terms of ethical positioning, then, the dual focalization indicates significant changes in the character-character relations and in the narrator's relation to the told and the audience' (120). In Phelan's reading, Humbert the protagonist had already perceived the violence of his actions when they took place but has only come to face them at a later point and in particular through the act of telling his story as narrator. In Clarke's narrative, as in Humbert's, it is only in retrospect that the alienating effects of his education are faced while his childhood self is said to have been wholly caught up in the 'chloroform of learning'. And as is often the case with Nabokov's narrator, Clarke as narrator does not explicitly condemn neither his colonial education nor his former compliance with it, but instead writes of its effects in terms which convey his adult distaste for it.

In Phelan's reading of *Lolita*, the story is focalised through both narrator and protagonist at once, but in Clarke, it is sometimes unclear where focalisation lies. Take for example a moment during the Second World War, when the school children are commemorating the British casualties:

> The headmaster brought the sad proceedings to a close by leading us into the singing of *Rule Britannia, Britannia Rule the Waves*. And in all the singing, nobody remembered to pray for the families of the Barbadian seamen lost or dead at sea. (Clarke 16)

Here, we do not know if it is the perspective of Clarke the student or Clarke the narrator through which the neglect of Barbadian seamen fighting for the British Empire is observed. Thus, it tends to be difficult to pin down the focalisation of the empire-critical remarks in the narrative, in terms of whether they belong to the child or the adult Clarke. But in terms of overt criticism, this is never articulated by Clarke the child, but always by his friends and family. Rather than saying explicitly that his idea of the world had been corrupted by his schooling, he lets his mother and his friends voice the challenge to his youthful acceptance of the standards taught in school. This is contrary to Ward whose narrating self supplies a critical interrogation of his schooling and who lets his younger self take on a sceptical attitude towards the absence of Australian topics, just like he dramatizes the moment of a turning point in his attitude to Empire instead of placing it outside the narrated time.

What Phelan also reminds us of is the narrator's relation to the audience, a remark which, when applied to autobiographies, points helpfully of the significance of the context of writing. As I indicated at the outset, the political and cultural make-up of the world in which Ward and Clarke wrote their autobiographies was widely different from that in which they grew up. The effects of this changed world order and the new prominence of postcolonial discourses can be traced in their autobiographical representations of their schooling.

Thus we can see Clarke as taking up the emerging postcolonial critique of colonial education which supplied a new vocabulary of cultural imposition and alienation through which to understand his own experiences. Similarly, his text performs a longing for a more authentic, local aesthetic which can be read as a belated response to colonial nationalists' search for new narratives of identity not dependent upon the imperial connection. By focusing entirely on his youthful self with no intrusions of the narrating self, Clarke avoids self-reflections on how his present perspective might also be 'chloroformed' by new societal agendas.

What is astonishing when reading about Ward's changed attitude to Empire is the way in which he portrays his escape from an imperial mind set to be an internal process driven by self-reflection rather than the product of those self-same societal pressures which 'colonised' him as a child. Thus, he is positioning himself as the agent of the dynamics that led to decolonisation, a lonely and original avant-garde individually seeing the problems of colonialism: 'If my life has achieved anything', he says, 'it has helped many Australians better to understand themselves and each other, by showing them the nature of their national identity or self-image' (Ward *Radical* 242). In this grand claim there is no attention to how the very idea that there is such a thing as a national identity might in itself be historically contingent. From his 1980s point of view, the Australian identity represents an inherent essence which was just waiting for Ward to uncover it.

## Conclusion

Stuart Hall suggests that 'identities are the names we give to the different ways we are positioned by, and position ourselves within, the narratives of the past' (Hall "Cultural" 225). Hall's statement relates to the two aspects studied here. On the one hand, he describes how people are positioned by narratives. Clarke and Ward bear witness to that experience when they describe how they learnt from their teachers that they had no history or culture of any worth. On the other hand, there is the positioning that the authors carry out themselves as they present us with a certain version of the past. Both these kinds of positioning relate to authorial identities, past and present.

Clarke and Ward argue that the focus on Britain meant that their education failed to familiarise them with their own history and culture, to the detriment of their relationship with their own countries. They pose this critique from a time when decolonisation has changed the normative parameters of what constitutes essential cultural understanding, rendering daffodils and lists of kings more useless and anachronistic than ever. The autobiographers use that critique to position themselves in a post-colonial age in order to stress how they, despite having been brought up in an imperial school system, have not retained its outlook or perhaps never fully accepted it in the first place.

I argued at the beginning that the school can be read as an interface between the individual and society. This is where societies have the opportunity to try to shape their citizens in a relatively consistent way. It is where individuals develop intellectually as well as personally, and they do so while being subject to a programme of instruction laid down by politicians, administrators and educationists which reflects discourses that circulate in society, informing also individual teachers' take on the curriculum. This double role as at once highly managed by society and deeply personal in its consequences means that memories of education can be employed to illustrate a person's interaction with and attitude to society. Thus, as we have seen, Clarke and Ward use their school time experiences to describe the imperial discourses prevalent in their formative years, to illustrate through their own memories how, and with what consequences, such discourses were impressed upon young people and to proclaim their adult attitude to those discourses and their dissemination.

Through his double move, Ward positions his past and present selves. On the one hand, he is able to claim first hand experience with the propaganda machine of empire and to stress its efficiency in making little imperialists out of school children. On the other, he can suggest to a post-imperial audience that he had a precocious scepticism which liberates his former self from accusations of passive compliance. Clarke, instead, stresses the pervasiveness of colonisation of the mind through stories of his wholesale adoption of the models he was presented with at school. But like Ward, the descriptions of his youthful alienation and snobbery are such that readers are left with a strong impression of the adult author's critical stance on empire.

One of the most common charges in these texts is that imperial education took the metropolis rather than local conditions as its starting point and ideal. Through the promotion of certain kinds of speech, literature and history, all to the neglect and detriment of vernacular experiences, the autobiographers argue that their education alienated them from their immediate surroundings. That experience of alienation is invested with authenticity and invites the reader's empathy as the writers draw on their personal memories. Through these memories, the authors position themselves, not only in relation to their school experience but to all that which education is retrospectively made to represent.

## Disclosure statement

No potential conflict of interest was reported by the author.

## References

Ashcroft, Bill. *Caliban's Voice: The Transformation of English in Post-Colonial Literatures*. London: Routledge, 2009. Print.
Bamberg, Michael. "Positioning Between Structure and Performance." *Journal of Narrative and Life History* 7.1–4 (1997): 335–42. Print.
Bhabha, Homi K. "Preface to the Routledge Classics Edition: Looking Back, Moving Forward: Notes on Vernacular Cosmopolitanism." *The Location of Culture*. Routledge: 2012. ix–xxv. Print.
Bridge, Carl. "Anglo-Australian Attitudes: Remembering and Re-Reading Russel Ward." *Journal of Australian Colonial History* 10.2 (2008): 187–200. Print.
Brown, Lloyd W., and Jennifer Harris. "Austin C(hesterfield) Clarke Biography —Austin C. Clarke Comments." *Brief Biographies*. Web. 14 Jan. 2016. <http://biography.jrank.org/pages/4219/Clarke-Austin-C-hesterfield.html>.
Chung, Fay King. *Re-Living the Second Chimurenga: Memories from Zimbabwe's Liberation Struggle*. Ed. Preben Kaarsholm. Stockholm: Nordic Africa Institute, 2006. Print.
Clarke, Austin. *Growing Up Stupid Under the Union Jack, a Memoir*. Toronto: McClelland, 1980. Print.
Conway, Jill K. *The Road from Coorain*. New York: Knopf, 1989. Print.
Curran, James, and Stuart Ward. *The Unknown Nation: Australia After Empire*. Carlton: Melbourne UP, 2010. Print.
Dale, Leigh. *The Enchantment of English: Professing English Literatures in Australian Universities*. Sydney UP, 2012. Print.
Damousi, Joy. *Colonial Voices, a Cultural History of English in Australia, 1840–1940*. Cambridge: Cambridge UP, 2010. Print.
Eckert, Penelope. *Linguistic Variation as Social Practice: The Linguistic Construction of Identity in Belten High*. Oxford: Blackwell, 2000. Print.
Gladwell, Joyce. *Brown Face, Big Master*. 1969. Ed. Sandra Courtman. Oxford: Macmillan Caribbean, 2003. Print.
Hall, Stuart. "Cultural Identity and Diaspora." *Identity: Community, Culture and Difference*. Ed. John Rutherford. London: Lawrence, 1990. 222–37. Web. 21 Jan. 2016.
Hall, Stuart. "Negotiating Caribbean Identities." *New Caribbean Thought: A Reader*. Ed. Brian Meeks and Folke Lindahl. Kingston: U of the West Indies P, 2001. Print.
Hewson, Kelly. "An Interview with Austin Clarke." *Postcolonial Text* 1.1 (2004): n. pag. *postcolonial.org*. Web. 14 Jan. 2016.
Higman, B. W. *A Concise History of the Caribbean*. New York: Cambridge UP, 2011. Print.
Hirst, John. *Looking for Australia*. Melbourne: Black, 2010. Print.
Horne, Donald. *The Education of Young Donald*. Sydney: Angus, 1967. Print.
James, C. L. R. *Beyond a Boundary*. New York: Pantheon, 1983. Print.
Kayira, Legson. *I Will Try (The Autobiography of a Young Malawian Who Walked 2500 Miles across Africa to Gain an Education Abroad)*. London: Longman, 1966. Print.
London, Norrel A. "Ideology and Politics in English-Language Education in Trinidad and Tobago: The Colonial Experience and a Postcolonial Critique." *Curriculum as Cultural Practice: Postcolonial Imaginations*. Ed. Yatta Kanu. Toronto: U of Toronto P, 2006. 33–70. Print.

Mangan, J. A, ed. *The Imperial Curriculum: Racial Images and Education in British Colonial Experience*. London: Routledge, 1993. Print.

Mittelhölzer, Edgar. *A Swarthy Boy*. London: Putnam, 1963. Print.

Moore-Gilbert, Bart, Gareth Stanton, and Willy Maley. Introduction. *Postcolonial Criticism*. Ed. Bart Moore-Gilbert, Gareth Stanton, and Willy Maley. London: Longman, 1997. 1–72. Print.

Nandy, Ashis. *The Intimate Enemy: Loss and Recovery of Self under Colonialism*. Delhi: Oxford, 1983. Print.

Ngũgĩ, wa Thiong'o. *Decolonising the Mind: The Politics of Language in African Literature*. London: James Currey, 1986. Print.

Phelan, James. *Living to Tell about It: A Rhetoric and Ethics of Character Narration*. Ithaca: Cornell UP, 2005. Print.

Rush, Anne Spry. *Bonds of Empire: West Indians and Britishness from Victoria to Decolonization*. Oxford: Oxford UP, 2011. Print.

Said, Edward W. *Out of Place: A Memoir*. New York: Vintage, 2000. Print.

Saunders, Max. "Life-Writing, Cultural Memory, and Literary Studies." *A Companion to Cultural Memory Studies*. Ed. Astrid Erll and Ansgar Nünning. Berlin: De Gruyter, 2010. 321–31. Print.

Smith, Ian. "Misusing Canonical Intertexts: Jamaica Kincaid, Wordsworth and Colonialism's 'Absent Things.'" *Callaloo* 25.3 (2002): 801–20. Print.

Tiffin, Helen. "Cold Hearts and (Foreign) Tongues: Recitation and the Reclamation of the Female Body in the Works of Erna Brodber and Jamaica Kincaid." *Callaloo* 16.4 (1993): 909–21. Print.

Tiffin, Helen. "The Institution of Literature." *A History of Literature in the Caribbean: English- and Dutch-Speaking Countries*. Ed. Albert James Arnold, Julio Rodríguez-Luis, and J. Michael Dash. Amsterdam: Benjamins, 2001. 41–66. Print.

Viswanathan, Gauri. "Currying Favor: The Politics of British Educational and Cultural Policy in India, 1813–1854." *Social Text* 19/20 (1988): 85–104. Print.

Ward, Russel Braddock. *A Radical Life: The Autobiography of Russel Ward*. South Melbourne: Macmillan, 1988. Print.

Ward, Russel Braddock. *The Australian Legend*. Ed. J. B. Hirst. 2nd ed. South Melbourne: Oxford UP, 2003. Print.

# REFLECTION

# Gibraltarian Oral Histories: Walking the Line Between Critical Distance and Subjectivity

Jennifer Ballantine Perera[a] and Andrew Canessa[b]

[a]Gibraltar Garrison Library and University of Gibraltar, Gibraltar; [b]University of Essex, Colchester, UK

**ABSTRACT**
This essay engages with the position of the researcher when carrying out field work on a subject close to home. If on the one hand familial relationships and intimate connections to the subject, in this case Gibraltar, are important determinants in understanding and analysing the oral histories that will be collected during the lifetime of the project, this proximity also raises questions regarding subjectivity and critical distance. This physical and emotional proximity to the subject also implies that as researcher I occupy more than one space – that of subject (as a Gibraltarian and member of the community I am studying), and that of investigator. Such a quandary has led to a reflexive process that goes well beyond questions of self-narrative and autoethnography to include theoretical thought over the wider context of Gibraltar as a British Overseas Territory and the impact of colonialism and a powerful geopolitical discourse on constructs of identity and a historical past. The oral history project we are currently embarked on offers a far more textured approach for the airing of a previously unheard perspective of history.

I press the stop button on my Fostex recorder, bringing to an end the recording of my latest interview for the project I am currently working on, a twentieth century oral history of Gibraltar. I have the signed consent form with me, which assures the anonymity of the interviewee should it be requested, and I find myself about to complete the log sheet, essential for the future cataloguing and organising of our audio files, lest we lose track of any. Still, it would be difficult for me to forget this recording, and neither will the removing of traces of the person's identity wipe away any of this information from my mind, for I have just interviewed my father. I have done so in the knowledge that much of what he has spoken about was already known to me. This, I felt, was an advantage as I could, wearing my academic hat, revisit certain key events in Gibraltar such as his experiences in London during the Blitz or the closure of the border with Spain in 1969, both key historical events, and target my questions accordingly. At the same time, I contemplate whether I have subsequently brought my research far too close to my home (both Gibraltar and into my parent's home), and feel that I may be precariously walking the line that exists between critical objectivity and subjectivity. Could the same be said for my colleague Andrew, who, although originally from Gibraltar, has lived most of his life away from the Rock? I wonder the extent to which distance, institutional and emotional, play a part in his engagement with the subject of our research project. For my part, my familial relationships and my connections to Gibraltar are important determinants in understanding and analysing the oral histories that will be collected during the lifetime of this project. As such, as a Gibraltarian and British citizen from one of the 14 remaining British Overseas Territories, and as an academic working within a postcolonial theoretical framework, my position becomes somewhat interesting as I contemplate the possibility that I may well be as much the subject of my research as my father is. In researching and writing about the history of Gibraltar, am I not also writing about myself and my family?

As the interlocutor mediating the space between my father's life story and the project outcomes, and the bridge between the Gibraltar end of the project and the UK partner institution, the University of Essex, I feel acutely aware that as a researcher, I occupy multiple spaces, some more immediate that others. My physical and emotional proximity to my research, however, makes me feel far more reflexive than ever before, and I feel compelled to ask myself questions regarding my subjectivity. My attention was especially drawn towards these reflections following the suggestion at a conference attended earlier this year that I may well be engaged in a process of autoethnography, that is, 'A form of self-narrative that places the self within a social context. It includes methods of research and writing that combine autobiography and ethnography' (Reed-Danahay 15–16). Our oral history project is clearly informed by ethnographic methodology, and whilst I have interviewed some family members for my research, I had not really considered that proximity to my subject might lead to the perception that I am, in the process, engaged in also writing about myself.

So, I read further into the subject and found myself driven towards Mary Louise Pratt's essay 'Arts of the Contact Zone', and her suggestion that a 'contact zone' is a social space 'where cultures meet, clash, and grapple with each other, often in contexts of highly asymmetrical relations of power, such as colonialism, slavery, or their aftermaths as they are lived out in many parts of the world today' (Pratt 34). In identifying a zone of contact, Pratt creates the basis for a non-hierarchical space where questions of authority and positionality can be addressed, leading to the emergence of other voices and forms of knowledge .[1] The 'contact zone', therefore, offers a very seductive space from where to launch new narratives, celebrate oral histories as opposed to canonical texts, and generally initiate a shift towards an acceptance of other forms of non-canonical knowledge. Entering the zone is also about entering the fray and about an ethnographic research methodology that understands the need for subjectivity if not connectivity. As such, I find that I may well occupy a centre position in this zone given my proximity to my area of research, and whilst I am resistant to the notion that I might be engaged in the process of autoethnography, I am interested in exploring how a reflexive approach can lead to a greater, far more textured understanding of the research subject.

The opportunity for dialogue between hierarchical constructs, such as the received version of a history of Gibraltar, and the oral histories being collected, which construct history from the bottom up, could bring about a very dynamic interaction that challenges fixed ideas about authority and history. The 'contact zone' also suggests a postcolonial positioning given the opportunities for decentring strategies and the plurality of voices.

I wonder, however, the extent to which we can refer to Gibraltar as postcolonial. It is certainly the case that references are made to Gibraltar from a postcolonial, even non-colonial perspective given constitutional development, which has brought a considerable degree of self-government. In December 2015 the Chief Minister of Gibraltar, Fabian Picardo QC, referred to constitutional progress as the key towards greater emancipation for the people of Gibraltar 'short of independence' (*Gibraltar Chronicle*). All very interesting as Gibraltar, as a British Overseas Territory, remains a colony if only by another name, yet even within this colonial context Gibraltar is moving towards a far more devolved colonial relationship without entirely leaving it behind. It seems, therefore, as though the colonial and nascent postcolonial (implied by the ascribed 'short of independence' status), find expression in the same space; one that we can perhaps describe as informed by a colonial period that has not yet entirely passed, and a postcolonialism that has not quite arrived.[2] It is not a question of suggesting that Gibraltar is neither colonial nor postcolonial but rather that Gibraltar occupies a space where both coexist.

This leads to a zone informed by a transitional dynamic that adds another layer of meaning to the 'contact zone' described by Pratt. A by-product of contact in Pratt's zone is intertextuality and opportunities for transformations. I would suggest in addition that Gibraltar occupies a space informed by a sense of incomplete (post) colonial transformations, where a somewhat devolved colonial authority resides in the light of constitutional development.

## A Gibraltarian context

The military and colonial drives in Gibraltar have had a significant impact on constructs of history and the place of Gibraltarians as actors in their history. Gibraltarians have primarily come to know of their own history through texts that focus on a past informed by military histories of sieges and of Gibraltar as a British colony. A trend that has been reinforced by a national curriculum imported directly from the UK, with the history taught in schools prioritising British and European history over and above Gibraltar's. When pupils do hear about Gibraltar, they are often directed towards accounts of military sieges with limited space being given to a social or cultural history. Although the national curriculum is slowly becoming far more inclusive of social history, education has clearly had a role to play in holding back on this subject.

Another such barrier has been the powerful geopolitical discourse generated by the border between Gibraltar and Spain. Gibraltar was captured from Spain in 1704 by Anglo Dutch forces, with the 1713 Treaty of Utrecht consolidating Gibraltar as a British territory. Spain, it must be said, has maintained her historic claim over the Rock; a claim which culminated with the closure of her border with Gibraltar in 1969. The border remained closed until 1982 (1985 when opened for full vehicular traffic) but even after being opened, the border between Gibraltar and the Spanish hinterland has continued to signify the boundaries between both territories and embody the complex relationship between both sides. The geopolitical situation informing Gibraltar's fraught relationship with Spain has also meant that all energies since the second half of the twentieth century have gone towards creating a common narrative that anchors Gibraltar within a solid British colonial context as this fact protects Gibraltar from Spain's claim. There are many other layers to this colonial relationship, and such an alignment is invariably caught up in a double bind. The border has become a monolith that has generated a very powerful discourse that serves to focus all energies down a very narrow road. This was especially true following the border closure in 1969, with feelings towards the closure finding expression in the press, in broadcasting and publications.[3] Such was the imperative that it drove forward a united front, a singular voice with the mission to defend the national imperatives within this struggle. It must be added that politics in Gibraltar have ever since become decidedly shaped by the geopolitical; Spanish foreign policy is equally driven by her claim, with a former foreign secretary, Miguel Ángel Moratinos, confirming this fact at a lecture held in San Roque in September 2015.

It is at this point that our oral history project 'Bordering on Britishness' steps in with a remit to unpack the monolithic presence of the border and to provide instead a platform on this very border for other voices that may speak of individual if not different experiences. Embarking on an oral history project that asks questions about this border and other less tangible borders within Gibraltar creates to some extent a 'contact zone' for the subjective engagement with storytelling and the interrogation of more hierarchical versions of events. The project provides strategies for people to engage with their own history as well as with Gibraltar's, thus paving the way for a history as expressed from a personal, non-canonical position (Pratt 40).

The revisiting of historical events and their documentation from this local perspective has gained considerable momentum in the last 15, even 20 years. It really does seem very late in the day for local narratives to make an appearance in the national canon of historical texts, but this has been part of the problematic. Gibraltarians have been very slow in writing about themselves. The publication in recent years of biographies and autobiographies penned by prominent public servants and former politicians have helped to re-centre life writings and historical accounts which now prioritise Gibraltarian perspectives, some of which engage with the local relationship to Britain and resistance to Spain. Others focus on social history.[4] As acts of recovery, these books help to fill the vacuum that has existed when it came to knowledge about events as experienced locally. These texts are clearly subjective, with this fact rather enriching and layering the experience.

Difference clearly exists between these autobiographical approaches and the ethnographic collecting of oral histories. I do not presume objectivity in my endeavour but I am guided by a methodology that underpins everything we do, from interviewing within all ethnic and religious sectors of the community to the languages being used and the questions we ask. Our research questions drive our project and so a high level of thought and, therefore scholarly distance, informs our interview process. At the same time, I am compelled by the fact that in the process of recording these stories, and because of my intimate connection with my subject, I can enter into a reflexive dialogue with the person being interviewed, especially if a family member or someone known to me. As suggested by Carolyn Ellis et al., whilst the focus is on the participant's story, the researcher's words, thoughts, and feelings are also considered, with these personal reflections adding context and layers to the story being told (Ellis et al.). I am also better equipped to analyse the data and to assess results. However, the question remains whether my critical objectivity becomes compromised by my subjectivity; a question which presumes that I am unable to be critical and subjective at the same time. Vinh Ngyuen has defended this corner when writing about his closeness to his research into

Vietnamese refugees. His identity as an individual and as a researcher is caught up with his own background as a refugee.

In being so intimately associated to his subject, Vinh Ngyuen proposes, after finding a photograph of his mother in a archive in Vietnam, that, 'It is impossible to posture scholarly "critical distance" when [his] past experiences *structure* everything [he does] as an academic ... ' (Nguyen 472). He argues that he cannot escape the fact that he and his family were refugees fleeing a war torn Vietnam but neither should this preclude him from being able to carry out scholarly research in this area on the grounds that his closeness to his subject undermines the rigour of his findings. Ngyuen goes on to challenge the implication that subjectivity rules out the possibility of critical engagement, opting to explore instead what it means to be both subjective and critical; to write in a critical manner that is 'attached and embodied'.

I am very taken by this argument as it offers me a considered critical position from where to engage with my positionality and from where to valorise my attachment to my family and the place I was born without writing my life story in the process.

## Oral histories and the process of recovery

Subjectivity is clearly at the root of oral histories, but this does not diminish their importance, especially in the context of Gibraltar where social history has remained largely unrecorded if not thought less important than the more official, geopolitical histories. Because the community on the Rock came together as part of a colonial society, Gibraltarians do not have a pre-colonial past that can be resurrected for the purpose of cultural recovery. Interestingly, oral histories are now facilitating points of reference for recovery; documenting these life stories is important as there are limited precursors other than the stories that are now being recorded on which to anchor a collective narrative of the (colonial) past. We are, on the whole, referring to very intimate stories about intricate details of day to day familial interactions. Family histories and memoirs are without a doubt creating bridges that connect the present to emblematic events that are now retrospectively considered as foundational moments in the making of a Gibraltarian people and a nation state. The process of recovery can prove to be, as we well know, arbitrary, especially when one considers that the full weight of history and social change often rests on selective foundational platforms.

Interestingly, the life stories now being collected are providing a much wider prism through which to engage with the past. We are finding that this is a messy process, one where stories are not in harmony and where the same event is remembered differently even by members of the same family. At the same time, diversity in how events are recollected is useful as these versions serve to fracture the official version. As a means to illustrate this phenomenon, I have selected examples of oral histories that focus on two events that have become anchors for recovery. The evacuation of the non-essential civilian population during WWII is one such point and Spain's closure of her border with Gibraltar in 1969 is another.

The evacuation which commenced in June 1940 is now referred to in terms of a diaspora because it saw the wholesale removal from Gibraltar of women, children and the elderly, with only men in essential services remaining. Evacuees were sent to London and other parts of the United Kingdom, including Northern Ireland, and to Jamaica and Madeira. When the repatriation programme commenced in 1944, this was perceived almost as a biblical return to a homeland.[5] It was also the case that educational and constitutional reform was to follow soon after, with all these advances contributing to the perception that the evacuation and subsequent repatriation were the catalyst that transformed the inhabitants of Gibraltar from a 'wandering tribe' into a people with rights, culture, and a national identity.[6]

With the closure of the border, we are dealing with an event that cemented a geopolitical discourse that shaped identity in an increasingly focussed manner.[7] To assert Britishness (as a British Gibraltarian) served to demonstrate difference and uniqueness from Spain. Configurations of a national and cultural identity were invariably shaped in response to the border. Both these historic events have become pivotal to the extent that they have come to signify foundational narratives that give birth to the modern Gibraltarian. In asking questions about these powerful narratives, we are hoping to be able to dismantle them to uncover how individuals lived through and engaged with these events.

Versions of these foundational narratives have been repeated in a number of our interviews so far, seeming almost as if there is an obligation to go through the officially accepted account of the evacuation, or the closure of the border. Some believe that this is what we want to hear, with personal experiences being channelled through the general story of how these events led to the making of a people. There is also the question of individuals believing that their life stories are unimportant; that events taking place in the intimacy of their homes are disconnected from those occurring in wider society when the opposite is in fact the case. It is also about recognising that there are many ways to talk about the border and the evacuation without having to mention these by name. I must add that it is at this stage that the researcher's stance is important as local knowledge provides an entry point through which to explore these other untold stories. Interestingly, when these emerge, we learn of the diversity of experience and memories.

When I interviewed my father, he spoke about, amongst other subjects, his experience as a child in London during the Blitz. I expected a story steeped in hardship but he instead spoke about his experience as if it had been a great adventure. My closeness to my father also helped to break down the barrier encountered in other interviews where a rehearsal of official events became a preamble to the more personal experience. My father's family evacuation experience is as follows: my grandmother was evacuated with her three boys; my father, the middle son was about 10 years old. Her youngest, Johnny, was but a toddler and her eldest son, Sergio, a young man. They were accompanied by my grandmother's elderly aunt and uncle, who were in effect her adopted parents. My grandmother was originally from Spain having been brought to Gibraltar as a child. Although having lived in Gibraltar for most of her life, she had never felt the need to learn English, as was the case with her adopted parents, as Spanish was considered as much a *lingua franca* as English. The only two English speakers in the family were my father Joe, and his eldest brother Sergio. It is within this context that my father recounts a story informed by daily searches for shrapnel and the exploration of derelict houses that lay exposed after the previous night's bombing. My father's evacuation experience opened up a whole new world for him and for many children of his age, but London also provided him with an education otherwise not available in Gibraltar schools. My father clearly felt that he had benefited from his evacuation experience, which ultimately served to widen his understanding of the world around him.

His eldest brother, on the other hand, has not wanted to speak about his experience when we broached the subject some years ago. Uncle Sergio's wartime experience was defined by his daytime job as a clerk and as a volunteer on the fire tenders at night. At the time he told me that his reluctance to talk was due to in his obligations towards the official secrets act, but I also believe that his silence could be because he witnessed things that he found painful to talk about. My role as a researcher in a privileged position has clearly helped me interpret my uncle's response, or lack of one for that matter, and whilst my interpretation is pure conjecture, I remain intrigued as to how the experience of each brother differs although Sergio was older and would have been far more aware of the dark side of the war. My youngest uncle sadly passed away two years ago and his life story has remained unrecorded, but I do know of my grandmother's experience though conversations that go back many years and through my father's present day interview, a story therefore mediated and filtered through both our subjectivities and memories.

My grandmother Anna had a hard time in London as she spoke no English. She had difficulties finding food given the language barrier, the rationing, and the cultural nuances between a Mediterranean and an English diet. In an attempt to circumvent these difficulties, she enlisted the help of her two eldest sons who acted as her interpreters, sourcing olive oil from the local pharmacist and squid from fishmongers who would sell it to them cheaply as cat food. This arrangement worked perfectly for a while, that is, until the pharmacist realised that the olive oil was not being used for medicinal purposes and the fishmonger came to learn that squid was in fact a delicacy much in demand amongst Gibraltarian families. Prices went up as a consequence. My father remembers that my grandmother never forgave the local fishmonger after that. My grandmother had said as much now over 30 years ago. Subjectivity has clearly played an important part in the recounting of these life stories, but without it, the details underpinning the subtleties of experiences would not have surfaced. At the same time, I do not feel that I am actively following an autoethnographic methodology but rather entering into the frame facilitated by my intimate and familial relationship with my research subject; an inescapable reality perhaps in this particular instance but one which serves to create layers of intertextuality and meaning that come with proximity rather than distance. These stories are demonstrating an otherwise forgotten side of the evacuation. Details surrounding diet, the procurement of food; the first experience of snow; love and marital breakups; emotions and a sense of adventure; of evacuees who did not want to return, with all these providing us with a fuller picture, one that goes well beyond the received notion of a 'wandering people' anxious to return home. Many did wish to return home, but not all; a younger generation wanted to pursue education, careers and other opportunities. Others simply sought a higher standard of living.

Oral histories that refer to the border also demonstrate a complex process of engagement with understandings of how the border with Spain relates to Gibraltar. Mainstream discourse perceives this border as a barrier, especially during the closed frontier years between 1969 and 1982, but this border also functions, for some, as a bridge.

When interviewing my mother-in-law, Francisca, who is 93, she spoke of how she met her husband during WWII in the bordering town of La Línea, in the immediate Spanish hinterland. She had just moved there to be close to her sister and in the hope that she could find work. Life was hard in the years following the Spanish Civil War, and like her sister, she was seeking a way out of her circumstances and crossing the border was a way to achieve this. What struck me during my interview/conversation with Francisca was that, as she recounted her story, she started to doubt herself because she felt that no one would be interested in her domestically informed life. She had not come to realise that her story added to those of other Spanish women like her who came to La Línea to escape the dreadful situation in a post-civil war Spain. Gibraltar was, for many of these women, a way out and the border provided a bridge to a freer country (Sawchuck 82). Her story also challenges the idea of the border as an impenetrable monolith. Although a very personal story, Francisca's occupies a wider context. This interview also offered an insight into my mother-in-law's complex attachment to Spain. As a naturalised Gibraltarian she considers herself to be British and not Spanish; in fact, she holds a UK passport and is a British citizen. Her legal and national identity very clearly locates her as British, but her cultural identity, which is what the project is interested in exploring, is codified and signified by many other variables such as culture, language and values. Francisca also manages to draw a line between the Spain she knew when growing up and the Spain under the Franco dictatorship, perceiving Franco to be the cause of all ills and subsequent policies towards Gibraltar. Her memory therefore accommodates two versions of Spain and interestingly neither represents the present day democratic Spain.

The border as a determinant for identity comes through very clearly in a number of our interviews. In my mother-in-law's case, her identity is constructed against her memory of a post civil war Spain and in response to the decision by the Franco regime to close the border with Gibraltar. The border, whilst a bridge which facilitated her new life in Gibraltar, also functions as a fixture that reminds her that she is British and not Spanish. As such, the border is an important structure for the purpose of constructing a non-Spanish identity. At a practical level, a borderless Gibraltar would facilitate the free and unhindered passage between countries, as one finds throughout Europe where borders blur. A borderless Gibraltar however draws attention towards the function of the border as an important marker of identity, but it seems to me that the border is also perceived as a 'safety' barrier that prevents the Rock from slipping into Spain.

The life stories referred to in this article belong to an older generation, my parents' generation. The life experiences of those who experienced the evacuation and the closure of the border will differ from those born during the closed border years and an even younger generation born with an open border. Their relationship to the border and the world around them will vary from that of their parents and grandparents. Interviewing this younger demographic will no doubt lead to an increasingly textured account of how individuals view themselves in relation to this structure. These multiple versions of history and articulations of identity will invariably serve to challenge received notions of what is means to be Gibraltarian; a process that invariably continues to challenge my own thoughts on identity, including my own.

## Zones of engagement

Importantly, the oral histories sampled here tell of how a shared event can elicit different responses which can contribute to building a fuller, far more textured frame of enquiry. Pratt's concept of a 'contact zone' is very appealing as it provides an ethnographic critical framework for decentring strategies and for the valorisation of plurality and difference; yet, such a zone presumes a hierarchical structure of authority based on a metropolis/

academy versus other dialectic. The complicated colonial and geopolitical bind that has determined Gibraltar for over 300 years is only now being articulated in terms that are raising questions about definitions of colonialism in this twenty-first century. Indeed, the Gibraltar example offers an insight into the notion of an overseas territory in Europe, a geographical positioning that challenges received notions that locate colonies some distance away from Europe. As mentioned earlier, whilst Gibraltar enjoys a huge degree of self-government, independence remains elusive, but then neither is Gibraltar seeking independence, as the reversionary clause in the 1713 Treaty of Utrecht would have Gibraltar decolonised in Spain's favour. The path towards decolonisation, therefore suggests, in the eyes of Gibraltarians, a further act of colonisation rather than independence. It could be said that the subsequent geopolitical discourse informing the Rock and the border is generated as a result of this complex if not complicit colonial bind that exists between Gibraltar and Great Britain.

As a means to illustrate this dynamic further, I shall refer to Néstor García Canclini's *Hybrid Cultures: Strategies for Entering and Leaving Modernity,* in which he explores the tensions and contradictions informing the incomplete process between modernisation and democratisation in Latin American nation-states. Canclini goes on to develop a very persuasive argument based on the observation that these states are caught between traditions that have not yet gone and a modernity that has not yet arrived. Both however coexist in what can be an uneasy bind determined by unequal access to modernisation and the loss of traditional culture (Canclini 184). In engaging with the vestiges of colonialism, Canclini acknowledges the messiness of the decolonisation process, viewing the current state in Latin America as somewhat incomplete.

I find his theory very seductive in relation to a Gibraltar as being caught up in a colonial period that has not yet entirely passed (and never may), and an independence, ergo a postcolonialism, that has not quite arrived but which is finding expression through constructs of identities, culture, literature and in political posturing. This is a messy situation since the suggestion goes beyond the notion that Gibraltar is neither colonial nor postcolonial, but rather that both coexist in the same space. Canclini's theoretical base becomes very useful at this point as we are not compelled to choose between the colonial and postcolonial, but to set about understanding the tensions and contradictions of these competing positions as they find expression in Gibraltar.

Entering into a reflexive process has made me think well beyond questions of self-narrative and autoethnography to include theoretical thought over the wider context of Gibraltar as a British Overseas Territory. My research has certainly brought me closer to home and my family, but this has also implied that as researcher I occupy more than one space – that of subject and investigator. Whilst it is certainly difficult to posture 'critical distance' given these credentials, closeness to my subject has great benefits despite the precariousness of proximity. I shall therefore continue to challenge the implication that subjectivity rules out the possibility of critical engagement and embrace Vinh Nguyen's suggestion to write in a critical manner that is 'attached and embodied'.

This fuller approach brings about a far more engaged process whereby the stories collected will add a previously unheard perspective to the general history of Gibraltar. With interviews ongoing, we are coming to understand how revealing life stories can be, especially in societies like Gibraltar where history has traditionally been recounted from the top down. Oral histories help fill in the gaps and silences in traditional narratives and help us understand the complexities underpinning questions of identity as something fluid and made up of many parts. The theoretical tools discussed in the course of this essay have proved constructive in understanding how a reflexive approach can open up space for a texture and meaning that comes with proximity rather than distance. It must be added that the Gibraltar subject is so rich in its complexity, that containing it within established critical tools of postcolonial thought, as indeed traditional methodology, can serve to reduce the meanings played out in these oral histories. The project is nevertheless ongoing and so the opportunity for dialogue between hierarchical constructs and stories being collected will continue to create a dynamic space that challenges fixed ideas about authority and history.

## Notes

1. The contact zone 'is intended in part to contrast with ideas of community that underlie much of the thinking about language, communication, and culture that gets done in the academy' (Pratt 37).
2. I am compelled to make reference to Néstor García Canclini, Translators, Renato Rosaldo, Christoper L. Chiappari and Sylvia L. Lopez, *Hybrid Cultures: Strategies for Entering and Leaving Modernity*, Minneapolis: University of Minnesota Press, 2005. The strategies outlined refer to a Latin America caught between tradition and modernity and the contradictions that arise by occupying the space between both.
3. See for example broadcaster Manolo Mascarenhas' '*Palabras al viento*' aired on Radio Gibraltar during the frontier closure of 1969.
4. See for example William Jackson and Francis Cantos, *From Fortress to Democracy: The Political Biography of Sir Joshua Hassan*, Grendon, Gibraltar: Gibraltar Books, 1995; Adolfo J. Canepa, *Serving my Gibraltar*, Gibraltar: Charles G. Trico Printers, 2014; Carmen Gomez, *Memories Bound up with Life*, Gibraltar: Europa Access Media, 2015.
5. See for example, *75 Years: Gibraltar Honouring a Generation*, Gibraltar: HM Government of Gibraltar, 2015, published to commemorate the 75th anniversary of the evacuation. See also 'AACR urge return of Gib. Evacuees', *Gibraltar Chronicle*, December 7th 1944, 3, and 'A Hero is Born!', *Gibraltar Chronicle*, January 15th 1945, 2, an article in which we see a shift in nomenclature taking place with evacuees being referred to as exiles.
6. See for example William Jackson and Francis Cantos, *From Fortress to Democracy: The Political Biography of Sir Joshua Hassan*, and Stephen Constantine, *Community and Identity: The Making of Modern Gibraltar since 1704*, Manchester: Manchester University Press, 2009.
7. *Documentos sobre Gibraltar Presentados en las Cortes Españolas por el Ministerio de Asuntos Exteriores*, Madrid: Imprenta del Ministerio de Asuntos Exteriores, 1965; *The Spanish Red Book on Gibraltar: Gibraltar in the Spanish Courts*, Madrid, 1965. The Spanish government issued a Red Book on Gibraltar in reply to the points raised in the White Book on Gibraltar published by the UK Government in April 1965.

## Disclosure statement

No potential conflict of interest was reported by the authors.

## Funding

This research was supported by the Economic and Science Research Council (ESRC) through a research grant awarded in 2012 for the project Bordering on Britishness: A 20th Century Oral History of Gibraltar.

## References

Canclini, Nestor Garcia. *Hybrid Cultures: Strategies for Entering and Leaving Modernity.* Trans. Christoper L. Chiappari and Sylvia L. Lopez. Minneapolis: U of Minnesota P, 2005. Print.

Canepa, Adolfo J. *Serving my Gibraltar.* Gibraltar: Charles G. Trico Printers, 2014.

Constantine, Stephen. *Community and Identity: The Making of Modern Gibraltar since 1704.* Manchester: Manchester UP, 2009. Print.

*Documentos sobre Gibraltar Presentados en las Cortes Españolas por el Ministerio de Asuntos Exteriores.* Madrid: Imprenta del Ministerio de Asuntos Exteriores, 1965. Print.

Ellis, Carolyn, Tony E. Adams, and Arthur P. Bochner. "Autoethnography: An Overview." *Historical Social Research/Historische Sozialforschung* 36.4 (2011): 273–290 Print.

Finlayson, T. J. *The Fortress Came First.* Grendon, Gibraltar: Gibraltar, 1991. Print.

Gomez, Carmen. *Memories Bound up with Life.* Gibraltar: Europa Access Media, 2015.

Jackson, William, and Francis Cantos. *From Fortress to Democracy: The Political Biography of Sir Joshua Hassan.* Grendon, Gibraltar: Gibraltar, 1995. Print.

Nguyen, Vinh. "Me-search, Hauntings, and Critical Distance." *Life Writing* 12.4 (2015): 467–77. Print.

Pratt, Mary Louise. "Arts of the Contact Zone." *Profession* (1991): 34–40. Print.

Reed-Danahay, Deborah. "Autoethnogrpahy." *The SAGE Dictionary of Social Research Methods.* Ed. Victor Jupp, 2006. Web. <http://dx.doi.org/10.4135/9780857020116>.

Reyes, Brian. "Constitutional development is 'one way road' to greater emancipation." *Gibraltar Chronicle* 15 Dec. 2015. Print.

Sawchuck, L. A., and Walz, L. "The Gibraltarian Identity and Early 20th Century Marriage Practices." *Gibraltar Heritage Journal* 10 (2003): 81–90. Print.

*The Spanish Red Book on Gibraltar: Gibraltar in the Spanish Courts,* Madrid: The unauthorised translation to English from the Spanish, 1965. Print.

*75 Years: Gibraltar Honouring a Generation,* Gibraltar: HM Government of Gibraltar, 2015. Print.

# REVIEW

BOOK REVIEW

**How Empire Shaped Us**, edited by Antoinette Burton and Dane Kennedy, London, Bloomsbury Academic, 2016, xi + 216 pp., ISBN 9781474222983

In 1996 Cambridge University Press (CUP) published an illustrated outline history of the British Empire. The California-based Indian historian Vinay Lal didn't like it much. Indeed, 'didn't like much' is a classic English understatement: and Lal had a suitable scorn for, as well as a more questionable tendency to stereotype, such supposed English traits. More truly, he hated the book and everything he believed it stood for. It was 'conservative, cautious if not retrograde', an effort of 'dubious ... moral integrity', 'a defence of an indefensible enterprise', 'deceptive', full of 'the most ill-advised judgements' and 'recklessly bold pronouncements', but also, rather contradictorily 'a lifeless and sanitised work'. Most startlingly, for Lal, the imperial British were and apparently still are 'gentler Nazis', only 'more ominous'—whatever that means—than the architects of Auschwitz and Treblinka. The British imperial historians who contributed to Peter Marshall's volume were, therefore, mere apologists for those Nazis (Lal 91–100).

I begin with that extreme example of the uses of negative polemic in historical debate not merely because it is eye-catching, and certainly not because it is typical of the careers or even controversies discussed in Burton and Kennedy's fascinating book. It is indeed *very* unusually extreme—though Vinay Lal has elsewhere and more recently expressed himself on related themes in almost equally pungent terms, while the rhetoric of comparison between British colonial policies and the Shoah was renewed, for instance, in Caroline Elkins' 2005 book on 1950s Kenya. Rather, Lal's review essay provides a convenient jumping-off point for several major themes in British imperial historiography and thus in the book to be examined here. One, perhaps the most obvious, is comparatively trivial or superficial: the phenomenon of very learned and even distinguished scholars being extraordinarily rude about each other. But there are other themes raised or implied by Lal which are of a wider or deeper significance for the history and practice of (empire-)history-writing.

That 1996 CUP volume was the product of a multinational team of historians—mostly British, but also Indian, Nigerian, Australian and American. Lal, however, sought to place it in a tradition of 'Cambridge histories'. A supposed 'Cambridge school' headed by the hugely influential figures of Jack Gallagher and Ronald Robinson has indeed often been seen as a very major, for some formative and for others malign, presence in the historiographies of both India and the British empire. Yet in fact just *one* of the 11 contributors had held a Cambridge University post (and even he spent most of his career in Oxford!), whilst three worked in the USA, three in London, one each in Oxford, Australia, Lancaster and Edinburgh. Referring to the editor as 'Emeritus Professor of history at King's College', Lal seemed to be under the impression that this was King's, Cambridge; actually, of course, Peter Marshall's chair was at King's College *London*. Again, this is not necessarily in itself interesting or significant. It is all too easy to show that any supposed historical 'school', clique or tendency is an imaginative, in part fictitious, creation: that such a group's supposed members were actually very diverse. It is still easier to play a 'geography game' and indicate that many of those identified with a reputed Cambridge approach actually had little to do with the place itself, or at least did not spend their most formative years there. It is almost equally easy to do the opposite: to trace informal and even subterranean networks and connections of influence among scholars on the basis of shared formative experiences, shared teachers and places of education, supposedly shared ideological stances, personal tastes or even sexual orientations. An intriguing kind of trail can be followed simply by looking at the Acknowledgements pages of books—but it is far more questionable whether we learn anything really significant there. I would defy anyone to draw any sensible conclusions either from who's named in my own Acknowledgements, or conversely the places where others over-generously thank me.

Some scholarly fields were always more prone to foreground autobiographical elements than were others: unsurprisingly, literary and cultural studies, perhaps the arts and humanities generally, featured it more than did social, let alone natural, sciences. History occupied a middle ground: everyone knows E. H. Carr's injunction that in order to understand history one should first study the historian. Nonetheless, most history students and beginners were and on the whole still are taught that it is inappropriate, even vulgar, to use the pronoun 'I' much, or at all, in academic writing. 'One', 'we', even 'this author': these were and are the standard substitutes, about as close to the personal as it was permissible to get.[1] To a degree that has latterly changed, with the impact of feminist scholarship having been perhaps the single most important driver for such change. From the 1970s onwards feminist writers pushed the edges of previous orthodoxy—though often there was an intriguing oscillation between an authorial 'I' and the 'we' of asserting collective identity, experience and purpose, whether this was the 'we' of a feminist movement or of women as a whole.

By the early 1990s, what some wrote of as a full-fledged 'autobiographical turn' had emerged, again especially in literary studies but extending far more broadly. Another major influence here was surely that of psychoanalytical themes and interests in forming scholarship in many disciplines. There was also, more obviously close to home for students of imperial history and colonial studies, the language of authenticity—the assertion of, or search for, 'the real me or us' which owed much to struggles for cultural decolonisation and especially in the USA those for black and other minority rights. There was an intriguing paradox here as well: the post-1960s battles over various kinds of collective identity with their collectivist and often primordialist languages of authentic selfhood sat uneasily with a more individualist language that could also, at the risk of caricature, be seen as a 1960s legacy, but this time one of hippyish expressive personal liberation and before that of a popularised existentialism. There was also an uncomfortable liaison with notions derived initially from psychoanalytic theory, then broadcast by influential strands of poststructuralist thought, that the self could never be unitary, stable, or transparent but was always internally divided and ever-shifting. For some academics the act of writing became, or was presented as being, explicitly now what it had always been for so many creative writers in the narrower, more conventional sense of that term: that to write was necessarily to search for and perhaps to struggle with one's true self—or selves. For others, though, it became ever more prominently something which to many of us (that phrase is used here in full recognition of its slipperiness) is less attractive: self–exposure or public 'self-discovery' as self-aggrandisement, self promotion, or even a means towards 'promotion' in the career sense, including that within an academic star system, again perhaps especially in the USA.

Much of this of course impacted on empire histories only at second or third hand and diffusely. Explicitly autobiographical excursions remained there relatively rare: perhaps rarer even than in many other fields of historical writing. Certainly historians in imperial and colonial studies had seemed rather less prone than those in an adjacent postcolonial cultural studies to invoke personal identity, experience, or ancestry as claims to special knowledge, authority or priority. Inherited credentials were, most felt, no credentials at all. A while back, several historians of British empire—mostly people born between the mid-1940s and the early 1950s, including Bernard Porter, David Cannadine, and Catherine Hall—did offer reflections on how empire had shaped their childhoods and their selves. This however remained then on an essentially anecdotal level. And there lingered a broad tendency in imperial history to echo a division often noted, but almost as often questioned, in African-American history. This is one by which, it was suggested, black scholars (or, in the present context, ones from formerly colonised places) were more likely to be interested in culture, in subjective experience, in foregrounding autobiography, and in pointing political lessons, while whites and/or the British-born were more likely to be self-proclaimedly dispassionate, more likely to be engaged in quantitative or statistical analysis, simply less prone to write 'I'.

There have also been powerful voices in the field, or in closely related ones, fiercely deploring certain supposed effects of the personal-as-political-as-academic in writing about empires. Thus another of the most widely, globally influential of relevant scholars, Edward Said, argued strongly in his later work against an identitarian authorial politics (even whilst also becoming ever more plainly autobiographical in much of it). Empire itself had created a new integration, and diversity, of the world on every level, including the physical presence of large formerly-colonial populations in most European and North American societies. All these manifestations of the 'interdependence of cultural terrains' were themselves products of the imperial experience, and thus demanded to be understood historically. Separatist and chauvinist discourses, 'whether in India, Lebanon, or Yugoslavia, or in Afrocentric, Islamocentric, or Eurocentric proclamations', in academic writing as elsewhere, underlined both the ubiquity of the urge to proclaim cultural independence, and the disastrous dangers of its misappropriation:

> In our wish to make ourselves heard, we tend very often to forget that the world is a crowded place, and that if everyone were to insist on the radical purity or priority of one's own voice, all we would have would be the awful din of unending strife, and a bloody political mess, the true horror of which is beginning to be perceptible here and there in the re-emergence of racist politics in Europe, the cacophony of debates over political correctness and identity politics in the United States, and—to speak about my own part of the world—the intolerance of religious prejudice and illusionary promises of Bismarckian despotism, a la Saddam Hussein and his numerous Arab epigones and counterparts.

Such damaging insistences on 'one's own voice', Said urged, were all too common even in scholarly modes of writing about empires and their legacies (Said xii, xxii, xxiv).

Meanwhile Rosalind O'Hanlon and David Washbrook, criticising especially the work of some 'second generation' Subaltern Studies historians, asserted that too much postmodernist/postcolonial theorising enabled career moves in a North American identitarian game, by which 'self-defined minority or subaltern critics are saved from doing what they constantly demand of others, which is to historicise the conditions of their own emergence as authoritative voices' (O'Hanlon and Washbrook 165–6). This meant in turn that

> the true underclasses of the world are only permitted to present themselves as victims of the particularistic kinds of gender, racial and national oppression which they share with predominantly middle-class American scholars and critics, who would speak with or in their voices. (O'Hanlon and Washbrook 166)

As all the foregoing implies, as the editors' introduction here notes and several other chapters more obliquely suggest, as this reviewer and many others have elsewhere explored at length, and as indeed Vinay Lal's rant all too well exemplifies, British imperial history has often been a markedly contentious field. And that contention has very often come to involve, crucially, claim and counter-claim about the implications of either espousing, or (ostensibly) eschewing, an autobiographical voice, mode or register in one's writing. When is adoption of such a voice a valuable, even ethically necessary, 'historicisation of the conditions of one's (my) own emergence as authoritative voice'? And when might it be rather an 'insistence on the radical purity or priority of one's own voice', perhaps merely ostentatious or abjectly self-promoting, if not potentially contributing to an 'awful din of unending strife, and a bloody political mess'?

Both of the editors of *How Empire Shaped Us*, and some of the other contributors, have been notable and combative participants in these arguments. Antoinette Burton especially has referred sweepingly to 'the siege mentality of British history[ians?]' and to 'traditional British historians' almost pathological fear of contamination by literary studies'—the latter explicitly linked to fear of infection by dark-skinned aliens, to 'denial of black presence in Britain'. She went on: 'those in charge of safeguarding Britain's national heritage, from Whitehall to the Senior Common Room, have raised the standard in defence of the nation's impenetrability to outside forces'('Who Needs' 229–30). Burton's more recent writing has rarely argued in quite such stark terms for correspondence between scholarly and politico-ethical sins, or between certain historians' methodological conservatism and their alleged racism (though the 'Introduction' and 'Epilogue' to her 2015 book *The Trouble With Empire* in part return to this territory). Dane Kennedy's related work has never tended to paint quite so desolate a picture; nor does their jointly written 'Introduction' here do so. Yet these little personal histories help underline the extent to which this volume is not just a set of reports on an intellectual (battle)field, but an intervention in it.

Maybe, in saying all this, one is (I am) however indulging also in critique-as-disguised-autobiography—a mode which has been much explored, for instance, by another writer whose influence has been huge in some parts of colonial studies but does not (perhaps unsurprisingly) figure among any of the accounts here: Jacques Derrida. I should thus, dropping part of the disguise, note that I have had personal and/or professional relationships of various kinds with the great majority of the contributors (after all, British imperial history writing, however globally widespread, is not a very big world) and that some are close friends. Equally, I have once or twice written very critically about bits of the work of some others; while one contributor long ago once misinterpreted something I'd written in a way which, at the time, I thought quite maddeningly obtuse (Oh, alright then, that was Tony Ballantyne).

Perhaps one should not overinterpret the choice of contributors here, or the 'balance' among them in terms of national or ethnic origin, location, gender, generation, or indeed ideological disposition. The editors, indeed, themselves plainly mark some aspects of this, and also sadness at the enforced omission, for instance, of the late Jeff Guy. Of 17 contributors, including the editors who also write individual chapters, nine are women. This of course is an over-representation when set against any rough headcount of all scholars in the field across the last several decades. If that might perhaps reflect a deliberate affirmative action choice on the editors' part, that would be in some respects admirable—but if so perhaps should explicitly have been signalled as such. Birth dates range from 1934 (Thomas Metcalf) to 1984 (Jonathan Saha). It might be noted that the present reviewer falls roughly midway in the range: 10 of those featured are older than him, seven younger. As one would expect, and as indeed is a recurring theme in many contributions, several of the lives and careers concerned have been highly geographically mobile, indeed continent spanning. Seven were born and/or mainly brought up in the United Kingdom, five in North America, three Asia (India and Japan), two Australasia, none the Caribbean, Africa or Latin America. Two continents, and very large parts of Britain's imperial system, are thus effectively 'unrepresented'. At the time of publication five work in or are recently retired from British academic institutions, eight North American ones. Overall, this 'sample' might be thought rather to underweigh the UK, overstress the USA. Only one author could be called even in the broadest sense an economic historian (Shigeru Akita), while seven have been for significant parts of their careers historians of gender. Perhaps most intriguingly, if not necessarily significantly, none has been distinctively an 'Oxbridge person', with the partial exception of Roger Louis. A few were undergraduate or graduate students at Oxford or Cambridge, but none except Louis has had very much subsequent association with either place. This will naturally surprise only those familiar (or, as some might say, all too familiar) with the extent to which these two universities have bestridden British Imperial historiography, not least via the notion of an overmighty Cambridge School of empire writing.

The focus is of course the British empire; surveying its impact is after all the announced purpose and the implicit titular thrust of the volume as well as being the main lifework of almost all the contributors. Yet in light both of the 'globalising' emphasis in the editors' introduction and the general pervasive current historiographical trend to relate imperial to global histories and even sometimes substitute the latter for the former, a further near-omission is striking. Very few contributors say anything about imperial systems other than the British. Given the origins or locations of so many contributors, one might have expected ideas of American empire in particular to have featured more. France and its colonies are also notable by their near absence, whether as cases for comparison or spheres of interrelation. In other ways too some contributions—though certainly not all or even most—are disappointingly narrow. The present writer, with many others, has long noted how much doubt and dispute there has been over what should properly 'count' as imperial history; and how uneasy, sometimes distant, have been relationships between writings that engage with empire as global system or project, and those which focus on particular formerly colonised places. In that vein, some of those represented here have been thought of as at least mainly historians not of empire(s) but of, say, Australia or the Caribbean. More explicit and sustained reflection on the relationships among these things, as they have shaped individual interests and careers, would have been welcome here. For one or two, evocation of family history—especially that of migration from Britain to settlement colonies—seems to be a kind of substitute for this, but surely not a sufficient one. This again relates back to Vinay Lal's polemic: he was ostensibly reviewing a book which, whatever its faults, at least dealt with the British empire as a whole, as a truly global phenomenon. His responses and counter-examples were almost all Indian, indeed almost entirely Bengali, ones. His comments, whether on colonial cricket, education, literature, religious or racial attitudes, create an inescapable impression that for him, quite literally, India *was* the Empire. In this his has unfortunately not been an exceptional case among modern Indian historians.

Contributors vary greatly, and unsurprisingly, in how strong a personal element there is in their reminiscences. Shigeru Akita exhibits perhaps the least of this, focusing almost wholly on his academic career and strictly scholarly interests. This might seem almost to confirm certain stereotypes of Japanese people as, in North Atlantic eyes, disinclined to the confessional, emotional or overly subjective—though one well knows of other Japanese historians in related fields whose intellectual interests have quite explicitly been shaped by political or ethical engagements. Overall, although several contributors—perhaps most especially among the British born ones—mention early awareness of racial difference and controversy, one might be surprised by how few place political passions or involvements as such in any prominent place. Those who most strongly do so are the youngest contributor, Jonathan Saha, and Catherine Hall among the older ones. More surprisingly still for this reader, almost nobody gives place either to the arts, or for that matter to sex, among the legacies of empire which made them. If I were myself to write a parallel account, I do not think I could possibly leave out as shaping influences certain African and Caribbean writers and musicians, or early girlfriends from various ex-colonial places. Little is said by most about intellectual influences outside the particular historical fields with which they have mainly engaged. It seems hard to imagine that so few of these historians were moved or 'shaped' as seems evident here by, say, Freud or Marx (indeed influences from Marxism are, again surprisingly, barely mentioned anywhere—Richard Price is the main exception), Fernand Braudel or Edward Thompson, Heidegger or Habermas, Sartre or Foucault, Yeats or Tagore, Darth Vader or Bilbo Baggins...

There is also (to my eyes) surprisingly little stylistic diversity among the chapters here. Everyone writes in more or less the same way: an Anglophone-demotic 'plain style' which features little specialist vocabulary (or jargon), but also little idiosyncrasy, literary flourish, in short little that is *personal* to the writer. Writing in and about the first person involves a shift in matter but not in manner. If 'the style is the man or woman', as the Comte de Buffon (or maybe Oscar Wilde) is supposed to have established, then few of the imperial historians sampled here are really very individual (sic). If a further personal anecdote may be forgiven: I recall another of the field's great figures, Ranajit Guha, once passionately lamenting how no historian ever tries to write in the manner of Heidegger or Nietzsche.[2] I'm not sure, myself, that I'd want them to do so, especially in light of that particular pair's political views—but maybe a *bit* more experimentation would be welcome...

This has been an ungenerous appraisal of a stimulating and welcome book, in its emphasis on what isn't here rather than what is, which is a lot. There are almost inescapably numerous minor matters at which one might also quibble. Philippa Levine, who is perhaps closest among the contributors in background and upbringing to this writer's, claims (111) that in her adolescence ruins left by IRA bombings were 'a common sight'. Since she is explicitly referring to mainland Britain, not Northern Ireland, this is a very considerable exaggeration. In their 'Introduction', Burton and Kennedy surprisingly manage even to mis-cite (in almost Freudian fashion) one of their own previous works. The essay of Kennedy's which they mention appeared not in a (non-existent) *Journal of Imperial Studies* but in the *Journal of British Studies*. OK, they might well think that the *JBS* should be renamed thus, and indeed its contents have over the years sometimes edged somewhat in that very direction: but, says the irredeemable positivist, it has not yet been so.

Such trivia aside and in sum, this is a rich and rewarding collection. It would have been still more compelling if more of it had lived up more fully and directly to the title; or perhaps rather, more explicitly addressed the relationships but also the necessary distinctions among 'how Empire made *me*', 'how Empire made my career of formal employment', and 'how Empire shaped what and how I write'. In other words, taking the three words 'Empire', 'life' and 'writing', one would like to know more about the relation of the second to the third as well as the first to the others.

## Notes

1. It will already have been noted that this essay deliberately alternates between direct first-person usage and those other formulations, and will hereafter occasionally play with both.
2. The false-modest mock-apology with which that last sentence opens is another unattractive quirk of this particular scholarly demotic. The rather arch self-consciousness of this footnote is another...

**References**

Burton, Antoinette. "Who Needs the Nation? Interrogating 'British' History." *Journal of Historical Sociology* 10.3 (1997): 227–248. Print.

Burton, Antoinette. *The Trouble With Empire: Challenges to Modern British Imperialism*. Oxford: Oxford UP, 2015. Print.

Lal, Vinay. "Good Nazis and Just Scholars: Much Ado About the British Empire." *Race and Class* 38.4 (1997): 89–101. Print.

Marshall, P. J. ed. *The Cambridge Illustrated History of the British Empire*. Cambridge: Cambridge UP, 1996. Print.

O'Hanlon, Rosalind and David Washbrook. "After Orientalism: Culture, Criticism and Politics in the Third World." *Comparative Studies in Society and History* 34.1 (1992): 141–167. Print.

Said, Edward W. *Culture and Imperialism*. London: Chatto, 1993. Print.

Stephen Howe
*University of Bristol*

# Afterword: The Ends of Empire
## *In memory of Bart Moore-Gilbert, 1952–2015*

Gillian Whitlock

School of Communication and Arts, The University of Queensland, Brisbane Queensland, Australia

It is no surprise that Bart Moore-Gilbert was part of the project that has generated this special issue of *Life Writing* on 'After Empire', and this Afterword draws together his criticism on postcolonial theory and his own life writing in memoir and social media to sustain his presence here. The problem of where to begin mapping postcolonial life narrative and what coordinates are fit for the purpose preoccupied both of us, as authors of two books that survey the field, and we last discussed this when I visited Bart at Goldsmiths to draw (again) on his encouragement and advice a few years ago. We talked about the uncertain beginnings of postcolonial life narrative in the refectory at Goldsmiths campus in East London, and later in standing-room only space of a crowded train back into the city, when Bart began to talk about a new project: his quest to understand his father's role as an officer in the India Police Service at the end of the Raj, on the eve of Indian Independence in 1947. The postcolonial critic was turning to memoir, and pursuing a haunting question raised in an email from an Indian historian: what did your father do in service of empire?

Is it too much to suggest, Bart asks, that without the engagement with the non-West, autobiography might have developed very differently? This question preoccupied his critical writing, mapping the 'roots and routes of postcolonial life writing' and energising the postcolonial project of 'deprovincialising' autobiographical studies (Moore-Gilbert "Confessions" 1). Returning to a founding moment of life writing, Saint Augustine's *Confessions* (397–400 A.D.), Bart argues that the concerns conventionally associated with 'western man' and the European Enlightenment are determined significantly by engagements with non-western others. In his reading, Augustine's *Confessions* foreshadows many of the concerns of postcolonial life writing—in its conflict over cultural location and affiliation in the Roman Mediterranean world, for example, and particularly in the distinctive cultural identity of the North African province where Augustine was born and raised, and where he acquired the African regional accent that was audible in Rome, where he was 'sometimes patronized for being an alien' (Moore-Gilbert "Confessions" 158), a stranger from a southern 'colony'. The north African context of the *Confessions*, Bart argues, helps explain some of its radical novelty of form, that transforms the generic conventions of early Christian autobiography—with its extended focus on Augustine's pre-conversion African experiences, for example, and its distinctive orality and aurality. This 'founding' text of western autobiography and its sovereign subject is, then, constructed in a dialogical relation with non-Western others.

The experience of being a stranger from an African colony in the imperial metropolis that is the focus of his critical writing on Augustine's *Confessions* resonated with Bart's autobiography more than I knew. It is an insight that emerges from reading his memoir, *The Setting Sun. A Memoir of Empire and Family Secrets,* published in 2014. This book was triggered by that email from an Indian historian, Professor Bhosle, which draws on recent historical scholarship in India that alleges his father engaged in the violent repression of civilians as a member of the Indian police force in the last decade of the Raj. We now read this memoir, inevitably, alongside the blog that Bart began in April 2015, 'oftherightkidney'. This is a thanatography (an account of the experience of dying and the changes it brings) in a new mode of writing for Bart: the blog. He relished this writing of everyday life addressed to his circle of friends, recording not only the progression of his terminal illness that year but also his marriage, experiences of fatherhood, family reunion, and the birth of his son in late November. Finally, (in a post written by his wife Anna Hartnell) the blog records his death early in December. We have many ways of approaching Bart as an autobiographical 'I' now, across memoir, criticism, and blog, *The Setting Sun, Postcolonial Life-Writing*, and 'oftherightkidney'. As the title and the image of the pith-helmeted British officer on the fading red cover of the memoir suggests, Bart's childhood coincided with the demise of the British empire and decolonisation in the 1950s, and the memoir records the rise of nationalisms and militant resistance in both India and British East Africa. It is an archetypal end of empire story, written by a postcolonial critic of autobiography, and a loving son. How are these identities of son and critic articulated in memoir? In his blog, a daily writing practice that he enjoyed and sustained as long as possible (inspired by Montaigne as 'in some ways the prototype blogger ... he launches into quirky discussions of whatever interests him ... and there's a strongly engaging autobiographical streak ... ' [13–14 April]) Bart suggests that memoir opened the way to his writing in the first person, intimately. Academic writing:

> involves keeping your emotions in strict check (unlike in a blog). So perhaps I can keep up my writing but in a different form, following on from the memoir. I think it will really help me to understand my feelings, manage them, see things in perspective, acknowledge what's most important to me and remain of, or acquire, 'the right kidney.' Besides, it'll be an additional intimate narrative for Maddy to read when she's older ... (Moore-Gilbert *oftherightkidney* 4 Apr. 15)

The articulation of different modes and genres of life narrative—print and online; criticism, memoir and blog; academic and intimate—in a relatively brief span (2009–2015) is striking here. How do the cultures of colonialism, decolonisation and post-colonialism in Africa, India and the metropolis shape this medley of life writing?

The memoir is a story of father and son, and it is dedicated to Bart's infant daughter, a vibrant character in his blog postings: 'This book is for you, Madeleine. It's no substitute for your grandfather, but it will help you to know him better' (*Setting* np). In this way the memoir is both relational and generational. Recently a special issue of *Life Writing* was devoted to 'patriographies', a sub-genre focussing on autobiographical investigations of the father. In conversation with the editor, Stephen Mansfield, G. Thomas Couser speculates that the rise of patriography late last century is a generational phenomenon, associated with the ageing of the Boomers and their preoccupation with their own mortality, the death of their parents, and generational inheritance. In postcolonial life narratives, this generational frame connects patriography to the stories of the ends of empire and decolonisation in the middle of the twentieth century, the time when the sun did finally set on the British Empire. Although patriographies have been written by daughters—Kathryn Harrison's *The Kiss*, for example—and they can recall abusive relationships as well as deeply loving ones, they are most often written by sons and in memory of a father, with longing and an enduring sense of loss—most famously perhaps in Barack Obama's *Dreams from My Father. A Story of Race and Inheritance* (1995). Obama's memoir, that narrates his journey to Kenya in search of his paternal family, is one of many that suggest postcolonial criticism can have things to say about patriography and the intimate empire of life writing, and how this sub-genre engages with racialised and ethnicised discourses about men and codes of masculinity, manhood and manliness that flourished in Empire. The narrating 'I' of *The Setting Sun,* a postcolonial critic we know, recognises the associations of his memoir with *Dreams from My Father*, most particularly Obama's account of the acute disillusion he experiences when he learns what 'the Old Man' was really like in daily life in Kenya, where the singular image of the father that sustained him is questioned.

Bart's autobiographical 'I' insists that his circumstances differ from Obama's, and he has a rich collection of childhood memories of his father. But sons can be notoriously unreliable witnesses, and the narrating 'I' Bart creates in his memoir is no exception—this too is a story of race and inheritance. His quest for his father through archives and interviews in India is emotionally fraught, as Bhosle's questions about Bill Moore-Gilbert's conduct put the son's childhood hero at risk: 'The image of my father constructed in my childhood memories, such a stable emotional anchor all these years, has fractured' (*Setting* 51). This quest for the truth is also a race against time, as few eyewitnesses of decolonisation and Partition remain. This Indian quest is narrated by an academic who teaches autobiography, who knows that memories are untrustworthy, 'whatever subjective truth they embody' (*Setting* 51). As the autobiography critic turns to childhood memory, he is aware of the illusions and desires of patriography and male autobiography more generally:

> I know from talking to friends, as well as teaching male autobiography—from Edmund Gosse and Samuel Butler to Hanif Kureishi and Nick Hornby—that there comes a moment when everyone sees through the father-figures constructed in childhood. The venality or violence, the failures and disappointed hopes one day thrust like a fist through the canvases they so lovingly created. (*Setting* 66)

As a postcolonial scholar familiar with literary representations of the decline of the Indian police service at the dissolution of the Raj—in George Orwell's *Burmese Days*, for example—the son is shamed by the possibility that his father was responsible for the brutal suppression of dissent on the eve of Independence.

Two autobiographical narratives, past and present, African and Indian, structure *The Setting Sun* as intertexts. The Indian story is a travelogue, and its autobiographical 'I' is immediately recognisable: the professor of Postcolonial Studies who arrives in India for the first time in late 2008, just a few weeks after the terrorist attacks in Mumbai in November. 'No doubt you'll be wanting to write a travelogue about the mysterious East when you get home?' one of his Indian hosts suggests slyly (*Setting* 187), reminding us of the belatedness of the Indian travelogue and the fact that this memoir acknowledges that it too 'tumbles' into Kipling fantasy on occasion (*Setting* 198). The narrator confesses this is his first trip to India, despite many years of teaching and writing about Indian literature, with his first book on Kipling, the subject of his doctoral thesis: 'The subcontinent's always loomed large in my research. Why haven't I gone?' (*Setting* 25). What takes him there is the pursuit of the 'father I did not know', and a personal crisis triggered by that email from the Indian historian who is researching the nationalist movement during the 1940s in the Mumbai archive. The narrator lost his father as a boy, and these rumours of violence threaten to take him away yet again. Was his father a dutiful cog in the imperial machine? Bhosle writes that a senior police officer named Moore-Gilbert was especially brought to Satara District to deal with the powerful political agitation there prior to Independence, and he had successfully suppressed the revolt of the Hoor tribes in the Sindh province. He questions whether there are any family papers that shed light on these events? In fact, very little remains of Bill Moore-Gilbert's time in India, either in family memorabilia or childhood memory—a few Indian words, Kipling's *Jungle Books*, some photographs, Bill's medals and uniform. Furthermore, archives that chronicle the last years of the Raj are dispersed and disintegrating. Before the email from Bhosle, nothing had tarnished the memory of a man remembered as 'gallant' and benevolent, a childhood hero, whose life in India had seemed 'as remote as Mars' to his son (*Setting* 22). The travelogue records a quest for evidence of his father's unknown history in India.

There is also an African story in *The Setting Sun*, an autobiographical intertext that narrates recollections of a childhood in Tanganyika. It begins in a Prologue to the memoir that narrates the traumatic memory of the boy's 'expulsion from my childhood paradise' (11):

> '*Get up, Nigger, quick,*' Wilson's whisper rasps, '*don't wake up the others.*'
> *The boy stirs reluctantly, flinching at the icy draught from the window above his bed. Next to him, he can just make out the beached bulk of Greenwell, the largest pupil in his year, snoring softly.*
> '*The Colonel wants to see you.*'
> *The boy's instantly alert. Wilson, the head prefect, who sleeps on the floor below with the senior boys, has never acknowledged his existence before. His housemaster? Why? (Setting 1)*

'Nigger' identifies him as an African and an exile in the remote and chilly habitat of the English public school. These italicised memories of childhood recur throughout the Indian travelogue in *The Setting Sun*, in a rare turn to the third person as a narrated 'I' in autobiography, that recalls an African precursor: J. M. Coetzee's *Boyhood*. This technique creates some distance between the boy and the adult man, the historical 'I'. England is the foreign land in these fragments of childhood memory, an alien place far from the boy's home on a coffee farm on the edge of the Rift Valley, near Mbeya, in (then) Tanganyika. The traumatic memory that begins the memoir is the news of his father's death in an aircraft crash in Tanzania in February 1965. Bill Moore-Gilbert, a game warden and accomplished pilot, was killed on a UN-funded mission scouting for safe areas to settle Tutsis fleeing from Hutu terror in neighbouring Rwanda—a terror that recurs in the genocide 30 years later. These italicised fragments are 'boxes' of nostalgic memory that begin and end the memoir, recollections that surface throughout the search for records and recollections of his father's history in India. These are deeply emotional fragments of nostalgic memory, which recall a close and embodied relationship of father and son: '*It's as if his father's skin and his melt together, making them one*'

(*Setting* 15). These memories draw deeply on the conventions of the nostalgic white African childhood narrative: the boy is profoundly attached to his African minder Kimwaga, to the beloved animals he recalls by name, and memories of going on safari with his father for weeks at a time. Travelling as the 'old chap' alongside the 'childhood hero' whose influence 'still pervades so much of my life':

> Even the fact that I was writing a lecture about African autobiography when the email arrived can probably be traced back to his accident, and the consequent trauma of expulsion from my childhood paradise. It wasn't just losing my father, but Kimwaga, my beloved minder, the exotic pets and wildlife—and Tanganyika, too, its peoples and landscapes—everything that constituted Self and Home. Well into my thirties, I continued to consider myself an exile here in the UK. Those distant events—and my difficulties in coming to terms with them—underlie the unlikely transformation of a sports-mad, animal-obsessed white African kid who wanted to be a game ranger like his father into what I am today, a professor of Postcolonial Studies at London University. (*Setting* 12)

The autobiographical narrator recalls returning to Tanzania as a young adult, 'hoping to settle the ghosts of the past': 'the new African owners of the houses we'd lived in looked at me kindly but blankly, as if the times I talked about were already as remote as the Triassic era' (*Setting* 25). Despite extensive enquiries he cannot locate Kimwaga (who surfaces in the thanatography, with a photograph and news of his death in 2010). This idyllic place has disappeared entirely into history, yet remains vivid in childhood memory, in recollections of this traumatic expulsion from a lost world, and (an intriguing suggestion) in his vocation as a postcolonial literary scholar.

In his study of postcolonial nostalgias, Dennis Walder argues that nostalgia has a particular resonance at the ends of empire, with the rise of exile and dispersal associated with decolonisation, in a twilight zone created as the sun sets on empire. This is a threshold zone between history and memory that thrives as the European empires become 'memories, dreams, and nightmares' (4). Walder confesses that his own interest in these nostalgias is prompted by his family history of settler colonialism in southern Africa, and he recognises the undeniably negative 'tug' of nostalgia towards misperception and self-indulgence, a restorative desire for belonging in a lost world. Nevertheless, he argues that nostalgia can also be creative, disruptive even, and a radical and disturbing activity that raises the issue of the ethics of remembering and/or forgetting, and challenges the adequacy of recalled and reclaimed earlier times and places (12). A cluster of white memoirs recall the British enclaves in Kenya, Tanganyika and Rhodesia, the most notable by the Danish writer Karen Blixen. *Out of Africa* was first published in 1937 and it has been republished and adapted many times since. This sensual and mythic invention of the African farm is a series of autobiographical stories created for the pleasure of a specific addressee, the white hunter Denys Finch Hatton, a powerful archetype of the elite white masculinity that was celebrated in settler mythography. This tradition extends into the present, in Kuki Gallman's *I Dreamed of Africa*, for example, where the white hunter mythography is adapted to present the cause for conservation and protection of threatened species. Blixen's memoir is also an account of traumatic expulsion from the place 'where I ought to be' (14). Generations of memoirs also recall a colonial childhood in the British East African colonies with fondness, from accounts of pioneering settlement by Elspeth Huxley and Doris Lessing, to Peter Godwin and Alexandra Fuller who, like Bart, recall childhoods in eastern and southern Africa as decolonisation was under way.

These memoirs coexist with a rich and contemporaneous tradition of African patriography, by Ken Wiwa, Wole Soyinka, Aminatta Forna, and Kwame Anthony Appiah, among others.

The epigraph to *The Setting Sun*—'We have to create our lives, create memory'—is taken from Doris Lessing's autobiographical account of an African childhood in Rhodesia between the wars, *Under My Skin*. Lessing writes about her African childhood as a novelist and journalist as well as an autobiographer, returning to the enduring difficulties of narrating the colonial childhood in the enclaves of British settlement in Africa, resisting the pull of nostalgic memory in remembrances of things past, whilst negotiating the space to articulate her sense of belonging there. It is Doris Lessing, Walder reminds us, that associates nearly all white writing with nostalgia, 'a hunger, a reaching out for something lost; hard to define but instantly recognizable' (72). Her writings constantly draw attention to the unreliability of nostalgic memory, resisting its de-historicising impulses to reinstate and validate lost worlds. The multiple autobiographical forms that narrate her African experiences return repeatedly to her own complicity 'as a white writer "using" Africa' (Walder 83). In *The Setting Sun*, debates about the truth status and authenticity of autobiographical narrative are no longer theory in the classroom and the scholarly article, they have become personal, and they cause heartache and grief. The professor of Postcolonial Studies finds solace in postcolonial writers, not only Doris Lessing but also Amitav Ghosh (whose novel *The Glass Palace* is written by a son caught between loyalty to a beloved father and recognition that he fought for the indefensible imperial cause [273]), and Salman Rushdie who writes 'Memory ... selects, eliminates, alters, exaggerates, minimizes, glorifies, and vilifies also, but in the end it creates its own reality' (*The Setting Sun* qtd. in 127). Bhosle's questions risk 'tarnishing' cherished childhood memories of Bill Moore-Gilbert, and the memoir works to both question and enhance them: 'As a result of my coming to India, Bill's been resurrected, but as a much more fully human being than the outsize figure in the immobile tableaux of aberrated mourning and childhood mythology' (*Setting* 274).

Patriography presents one compelling, creative formulation for life narrative at the ends of empire. In their conversation on 'Fashioning Fathers' Tom Couser and Stephen Mansfield identify characteristics of the subgenre that feature in *The Setting Sun*: the search for an elusive or inaccessible father figure connected to a traumatic experience (the enduring memory of his father's death); a desire to renew a relationship with an absent father (that regeneration of precious memories of the African childhood); the exploration of something withheld or misrepresented in the father's life (the questions raised about his years in the Indian police force). Conventions of patriography also connect to issues of gender and writing that recur in *The Setting Sun*. Couser argues that we cannot escape the gendered nature of patriography, its 'engendered nature so to speak, in the dynamics of the patriarchal family' (16). So, for example, his father's sexuality remains a difficult issue for this memoir. Bill's sister Pat describes Bill's exploits in India 'with the starry-eyed look of someone describing a matinee idol' (*Setting* 24). 'He adored women, your father', she recalls, 'they made him thrilled skinny to be alive. It didn't matter who they were or where they came from, young or old as God [ ... ] He was always so *gallant*.' (*Setting* 17) On his travels in India, the narrator repeatedly encounters recollections and rumours of Bill as a womaniser. These rumours unsettle the son, especially as they surface in a fictional account of 'Bill', a character in an autobiographical novel written by one of his colleagues in the Indian police, interviewed for the memoir. This fictional 'Bill' is a worldly man who charms the wife of a colleague, and has affairs with several Indian women, at least one of them a servant in the household. As an autobiographical narrator, Bart dismisses some of this as 'obviously farcical' (*Setting* 121) and written to the historical Bill's disadvantage, but even so recollections of his father as a womaniser recur in Indian memories of him, and rumours of other liaisons remain. Most problematically, the narrating 'I' is drawn back to his boyhood memories of his father's sexual desires in Africa. The boy remembers peering through the window and seeing his father making love to Viva, the mother of his friend, in his parents' bedroom, whilst his own mother reads in the garden nearby. '*Can anything which makes people so happy really be wrong?*' the boy wonders, as he looks upon their postcoital pleasure (*Setting* 133). What connects the game ranger in Tanganyika with the police officer in India? Both are authoritative and privileged positions that remained available to British men in late imperialism, in the disappearing worlds that Bill Moore-Gilbert inhabited. These positions nurtured a racialised and ethnicised masculinity where benevolence, force and 'gallantry' naturalised British patriarchal authority and privilege. A code of masculine conduct that resists domestication, thrives on safari, and ends in a violent death recurs in life narratives out of Africa.

Couser and Mansfield concur that it is one of the risks of patriography that the feminine and the maternal are marginalised as the dynamics of the patriarchal family and the relationship of father to son become definitive, and the focus of attention. In *The Setting Sun* the boy's mother pales into insignificance as a remote presence in the African story, where the father is an enduring and formative presence. 'Mummy' neither sustains nor nurtures the boy:

> She steps forward quickly and hugs him. It's not something she often does, so the boy knows it must be serious. Behind his back he can hear her sniffling into the paper tissue she always carries. Despite himself, he hates the way she does that. Why can't she use a proper handkerchief like other mothers? (*Setting* 252).

The boy dimly perceives that his mother's sadness may have something to do with 'Bill' and his behaviour, and he recalls his father's whispered 'Have to try harder' in response to his wife's sadness (*Setting* 253). Tom Couser observes that it becomes a trope of patriography to apologise to the mother and pay homage to her, belatedly (qtd. in Mansfield 16). The second edition of *Dreams of my Father*, for example, includes a note where Obama is troubled by how little he wrote about his mother. In Bart's autobiographical writing we find this homage in the more emotional writing of his thanatography, which is immersed in the pleasures of shared parenthood and lives of girls and women, Madeleine and Anna. There he writes lovingly about his mother, with a deep sense of affiliation that returns to boyhood memories of Africa in a different mode. A posting in 'oftherightkidney' includes a newly acquired photograph of his mother Marise with one of her beloved creatures, a Congolese Grey parrot, and an intimate comment on 'Mum's evidently recent hair-do'. His mother becomes a living presence in the blog, and the experience of mortal illness is a reminder of their deep affiliation carried in the genes: she too endured cancer, 'She appears to look meaningfully at me, as if offering encouragement as I head down the path she's travelled before me' (17–19 Apr.). More painfully, he can now recognise her grief, belatedly, as the mourning of a woman and mother twice widowed, with insight born of his own experience as a loved father and husband who will die prematurely.

As I write this Afterword, a letter arrives from Bart's head of department at Goldsmiths, written the day after the memorial service in his honour. This slow mail announcement of his death comes a month after the news circulated in social media, via Facebook and the blog Bart began as an account of his illness. What would I like done with the copy of *Postcolonial Life Narratives* I sent to Bart, the letter asks. We decide it will be shelved in the library at Goldsmiths, adjacent to Bart's book of postcolonial criticism and memoir, for my thinking on the roots and routes of postcolonial life narrative has always been in conversation with him, and this remains so. Bart leaves a rich archive of writing on autobiography and auto-biographical writing, as a critic, a memoirist and a blogger. What would he have written about here, for this special issue on 'After Empire'? I can only make an educated guess, but he leaves an unfinished monograph on the issue that he argues must be central to post-colonial and auto/biography studies now: Palestinian lives, and the residual and emergent manifestations of settler colonialism and imperialism in the Occupied Territories that, he argues, is in direct continuity with the regime of the British Mandate in Palestine ("Baleful" 56). In 2012/13 his self-litigation of a freedom of information tribunal against the Department of Education was a passionate defence of the role of literature in human rights activism close to home, and his work on this case now stands as an integral part of his legacy (Foyle). The case of Palestine, Bart reminds us, is a graphic reminder that much of the world is not yet post-colonial, not yet decolonised, and settler colonialism endures and sustains many of the ideologies and techniques of conquest and repression that characterised earlier stages of Western imperialism: 'compare "settler" Kenya, South Africa, or Australia', he suggests (*Postcolonial* 113). Graham Huggan argues that postcolonialism does not seek a corrective to the past but it returns restlessly to its 'multiple secretions in the present', both mobilising and questioning the vocabularies it inherits' (4). For postcolonial criticism, the sun never quite sets on empire, and Bart would surely have used this special issue as an opportunity to say so.

## Disclosure statement

No potential conflict of interest was reported by the author.

## References

Appiah, Kwame Anthony. *In My Father's House: Africa in the Philosophy of Culture*. New York: Oxford University Press, 1993.
Blixen, Karen. *Out of Africa*. London: Penguin Books, 2001.
Forna, Aminatta. *The Devil that Danced on the Water: A Daughter's Memoir*. London: Flamingo, 2003.

Foyle, Naomi. "Michael Gove, the Board of Deputies of British Jews and the postcolonial professor." *Middle East Monitor* 18.2 (2016): n. pag. Web.
Huggan, Graham, ed. *The Oxford Handbook of Postcolonial Studies*. Oxford: Oxford UP, 2013. Print.
Mansfield, Stephen. "Fashioning Fathers: An Interview with G. Thomas Couser." *Life Writing* 11.1 (2014): 5–19. Print.
Moore-Gilbert, Bart. "'Baleful Postcoloniality' and Palestinian Women's Life Writing." *Biography* 36.I (2013): 51–70. Print.
Moore-Gilbert, Bart. *Postcolonial Life-Writing. Culture, Politics and Self-Representation*. London: Routledge, 2009. Print.
Moore-Gilbert, Bart. "The Confessions of Saint Augustine: Roots and Routes of Postcolonial Life-Writing." *A/B: Auto/Biography Studies* 20.2 (2005): 155–69. Print.
Moore-Gilbert, Bart. "oftherightkidney." *oftherightkidney.com*. 2015. Web. 18/03/16.
Moore-Gilbert, Bart. *The Setting Sun. A Memoir of Empire and Family Secrets*. London: Verso, 2014. Print.
Obama, Barack. *Dreams from My Father: A Story of Race and Inheritance*. New York: Broadway Books, 2004.
Soyinka, Wole. *Isara*. London: Vintage, 1991.
Walder, Dennis. *Postcolonial Nostalgias. Writing, Representation, and Memory*. New York: Routledge, 2011. Print.
Whitlock, Gillian. *Postcolonial Life Narratives: Testimonial Transactions*. Oxford: Oxford UP, 2015. Print.
Wiwa, Ken. *In the Shadow of a Saint: A Son's Journey to Understand His Father's Legacy*. London: Black Swan, 2002.

# Index

Note: **Boldface** page numbers refer to figures and tables and page number followed by 'n' denotes end notes.

act of photographing **36**, 36–8, **38**
*Akenfield* (Blythe) 15, 23n9
Alexander, Vera 2
*All My Relations* (King) 62
American literature 12–13
Anglophone periphery 10, 23n4
archives of life writing 15–19
Arts of the Contact Zone (Pratt) 110
*Australian Legend, The* (1958) (Ward) 92, 93, 98

Ball, S. J. 30–1
Bal, Mieke 65
Bamberg, Michael 94
Banerjea, Surendranath 75
Barthes, Roland, *studium* and *punctum* 37, 39
*Battle For Merger* (Lee) 32, 33
Bayly, Chris 77
Bazin, André 36–7
*Beyond a Boundary* (James) 8
Bildungsroman 9, 23
biography 7–8
Blythe, Ronald 15
*Books that Matter* (Philip) 16
Bose, Sugata 77
British Empire 3–4; and Commonwealth 17; historians of 124–5
British India: anti-colonial autobiographies in 81; intellectual and political life in 75
British literature 12–13
*Burmese Days* 10
*Burning the Days* (Salter) 50–1
Burton, Antoinette 123–8

Cambridge University Press (CUP) 123
*captatio benevolentiae* 61
Carr, E. H. 124
Chaudhuri, Amit 70–1
Cheah, Pheng 78

Clark, Manning 2; archival legacy 44, 45; Australian of the Year (1981) 44; biography 45–6; Clark's 'parochialism' 55; Dymphna's editing 51, 53; *A History of Australia* 44, 46; inner life, casting of 47; Malcolm's advice 54; in media interviews 44, 45, 50; *Meeting Soviet Man* 44; public interventions 45; *Puzzles of Childhood, The* 46, 48–9, 51; *Quest for Grace, The* 46, 49; Ryan's work for 48; Salter's memoir 50–1; task of self-examination 52
Coldstore 29–32
colonial and postcolonial life writing: American vs. British literature 12–13; archives of 15–19; *Beyond a Boundary* (James) 8; comparison of 9; Franklin's *Autobiography* 19–20; language of writing 11–12; *Our Old Home* (Hawthorne) 20–1; *Palm-Wine Drinkard, The* (Tutuola) 13–14; place of publication 10–11; and place writing 14–15; printing of literature 13; romanticism in 14; selection of readership 10–11; thematic competence 14, 15; Walcott's writing 22
colonial deficits 11–14
*Comet in Our Sky: Lim Chin Siong in History* (Wee) 33
Commonwealth Institute, The 16
Constituent Assembly, of India 74–6
cosmopolitanism: Cheah, Pheng 78; Indian Constitution's 74, 77; and territorial nationalism 78; and transnational dialogue 77–8
CUP *see* Cambridge University Press

Damousi, Joy 98
de Buffon, Comte 128
*Discovery of India, The* (Nehru) 80
Donati, Pierpaolo 71n4
Drysdale, John 30

*Education of Henry Adams, The* (Adams) 20
English, as language of writing 11–12
*Enigma of Arrival, The* (Naipaul) 14

# INDEX

fragmentary stories 58
Franklin, Benjamin 3, 19–20
fraternity 74

Gallagher, Jack 123
Gandhian constitution 77–8
*Gandhian Way, The* (Agarwal) 78
Gergen, Kenneth 62, 67
Gibraltarian oral histories 109–11; colonial context of 111–13; contact zone 116–18; and recovery process 113–16
Gilmore, Leigh 63
Glissant's poetics 63
Government of India Act 1935 73, 74, 76, 85
*Growing Up Stupid Under the Union Jack* (1980) (Clarke) 92, 100

Hall, Stuart 103
Hawthorne, Nathaniel: *Our Old Home* 20–1; *Scarlet Letter, The* 12
Head, Bessie 15
*Hind Swaraj* (Gandhi) 73, 78–81, 84
*History of Australia, A* (Clark) 44, 46
Holden, Philip 2
*How Empire Shaped Us* (Burton) 123–8
*Hybrid Cultures: Strategies for Entering and Leaving Modernity* (Canclini) 117

INC *see* Indian National Congress
India: Constituent Assembly of 74–6; Vassanji's relations with 62
*India: A Million Mutinies Now* (1990) (Naipaul) 66
Indian Constitution (IC) 73; and anti-colonial autobiographies 73–5, 82; Constituent Assembly of 74–6; and cosmopolitanism 77–8; and Government of India Act of 1935 74; individual and community rights 81; key feature of 83; language of 77; linguistic cosmopolitanism of 81–4; Objectives Resolution of 74; Preamble to 74; Rajpramukh in 83; sense of temporality 84–5; State policy and Fundamental Rights, principles of 76–7
Indian National Congress (INC) 75; Karachi Resolution of 1931 77
*In the Castle of my Skin* 11, 23n5

James, C. L. R. 8–9
James, Henry 11–12
Jones, Barry 48
Jones, Matthew 30–1
Joyce, James 18

Karachi Resolution of 1931 77
Kennedy, Dane 123–8
Kumar, Ramakrishna 32, 33, 39n1
*Künstlerroman* 9, 18

Lal, Vinay 123, 125, 127
Lamming, George 10–11, 17; *In the Castle of my Skin* 11
language of writing 11–12
Lauterpacht, Hersch 77
*Leaves of Grass* (Whitman) 66
Lee, Hermione 71n5
Lee Kok Liang 29–30
Lee Kuan Yew: *Battle For Merger* 32, 33; construction of Coldstore 29–32; memoirs 28; photograph of 37, **38**; relationship with Lim 34–5; *Singapore Story, The* 28, 34, 37
*Lee's Lieutenants: Singapore's Old Guard* (Wee) 33
Levine, Philippa 128
*Life of Johnson* (Boswell) 7
Lim Chin Siong: *Comet in Our Sky: Lim Chin Siong in History* (Wee) 33; Communist Party membership 33; *Lee's Lieutenants: Singapore's Old Guard* (Wee) 33; Lee's relationship with 33, 34; *Lim Chin Siong—A Political Life* (Tan) 33–4; photograph of **36, 38**, 38–9; Teng's poem 35
linguistic cosmopolitanism, of Indian Constitution 81–4
*Lives of the Poets* (Johnson) 7, 22n2
Lodge, David 69
London, Norrel 98
Low Thia Khiang 28

*Magic of Saida, The* (2013)
Majeed, Javed 2
Malcolm, Janet 54
Manjapra, Kris 77
McKenna, Mark 2
McLachlan, Noel 55
*Meeting Soviet Man* (Clark) 44
memoirs, Lee Kuan Yew 28
methodological nationalism 77
Moore-Gilbert, Bart 3–4
Mulk Raj Anand 68, 69
Munshi, K. M. 75

Naipaul, V.S. 14
national autobiography 28
National English Literary Museum (NELM) 16
Nehru Committee Report of 1928 77
Nehru, Jawaharlal: autobiography 74–81; in Indian Constituent Assembly 76
NELM *see* National English Literary Museum
Ngyuen, Vinh 112–13

*Our Old Home* (Hawthorne) 20–1
*Out of Place* (Cairo) 91

*Palm-Wine Drinkard, The* (Tutuola) 13–14
Phelan, James 102, 103
Philip, Marie 16

# INDEX

photographing **36**, 36–8, **38**
Picardo, Fabian 111
place of publication 10–11
*Place Within: Rediscovering India, A* (2008) (Vassanji): relationality beyond human sphere 62–4; relationship with India 64–6; self-encounters in 59–62; story collections 58–9; writing struggles 66–9
place writing 14–15
*Pleasures of Exile* (Lamming) 23n6
*Portrait of the Artist as a Young Man, A* (Joyce) 18
postcolonial studies: attitudes to empire 100–3; curriculum alienation 95–8; speech and snobbery 98–100
printing of literature 13
*Puzzles of Childhood, The* (Clark) 46, 48–9, 51

*Quest for Grace, The* (Clark) 46, 49

*Radical Life, A* (1988) (Ward) 92, 99, 101
Rajpramukh, in Indian Constitution 83
Rau, B. N. 76
readership, selection of 10–11
'Relational Selves, Relational Lives: The Story of the Story' (Eakin) 63
relational sociology 71n4
'relational writing' 66–9
Rhys, Jean 23n10
Rickard, John 47
Robinson, Ronald 123
romanticism in colonial writing 14
Ryan, Susan 48

Said, Edward 91–2, 125
Salter, James 50–1
*Scarlet Letter, The* (Hawthorne) 12
*Serowe: Village of the Rain Wind* (Head) 15
Seventh Amendment Act 1956 83
Shriman Narayan Agarwal 78
*Singapore Story, The* 28, 30, 34, 37
*Singapore: Struggle for Success* 30
Smith, Ian 95
*Straits Times* 28, 32, 38
*studium* and *punctum* 37, 39

Tan Jing Quee 33
Teng Qian Xi 35
territorial nationalism, cosmopolitanism and 78
thematic competence 14, 15
*Thinking Reed, A* (Jones) 48
Tiffin, Helen 95, 96
Treaty of Utrecht (1713) 111
Tully, James 73, 74
Tutuola, Amos 13, 15–16

Universal Declaration of Human Rights 77

Vassanji, M. G. 2, 3; *Place Within: Rediscovering India, A* (2008) 57, 59–60

Walcott, Derek 22
*Walden* (Thoreau) 14
Wee Wan-ling 33
Weintraub, Karl 63
Wilsonian moment 3